Something to Say

William Carlos Williams on Younger Poets

EDITED WITH AN INTRODUCTION

BY JAMES E. B. BRESLIN

D1310197

The William Carlos Williams Archive Series: Volume I

General Editor: Emily Mitchell Wallace

A NEW DIRECTIONS BOOK

The Introduction by James E. B. Breslin, "The Presence of Williams in Contemporary Poetry," was first published in *American Poetry Review*.

Manufactured in the United States of America
First published clothbound by New Directions Publishing Corp. in 1985
Published simultaneously in Canada by Penguin Books Canada Limited

Library of Congress Cataloging in Publication Data

Williams, William Carlos, 1883–1963.
    Something to say.
    (A New Directions Book)
    (The William Carlos Williams archive series; v. 1)
    1. American poetry—20th century—History and criticism—Collected works. I. Breslin, James E. B., 1935– . II. Title. III. Series: Williams, William Carlos, 1883–1963. William Carlos Williams archive series; v. 1.
PS324.W47 1985   811'.5'09   85–8890
ISBN 0-8112-0955-5

New Directions Books are published for James Laughlin
by New Directions Publishing Corporation,
80 Eighth Avenue, New York 10011

ACKNOWLEDGMENTS:

Grateful acknowledgment is made to the editors and publishers of the following in which versions of some of these essays first appeared: *Accent, Arizona Quarterly*, Ronald Bayes' *Dust and Desire* (A. H. Stockwell), *The Black Mountain Review*, Tram Combs' *Pilgrim's Terrace* (Editorial La Nueva Salamanca), *East and West, Fantasy*, Charles Henri Ford's *The Garden of Disorder and Other Poems* (Europa Press), *Four Pages, Furioso*, Allen Ginsberg's *Howl and Other Poems* (City Lights Pocket Bookshop), Mimi Goldberg's *The Lover and Other Poems* (Kraft Printing Co.), *The Golden Goose, Gryphon, The Harvard Advocate, Inferno, The Kenyon Review*, Irving Layton's *The Improved Binoculars* (Jonathan Williams), *The Literary Workshop*, Ron Loewinsohn's *Watermelons* (Totem Press), *MAPS*, Merrill Moore's *Case Record* (Twayne Publishers), Merrill Moore's *Sonnets from New Directions* (New Directions), *Mosaic, The Nation, New Directions Number Seven, New Masses, The New Republic, The New Quarterly of Poetry, The New York Times Book Review*, Harold Norse's translation of *The Roman Sonnets of G. G. Belli* (Jonathan Williams), *Origin, Partisan Review, Poetry, The Quarterly Review of Literature*, Sydney Salt's *Christopher Columbus and Other Poems* (Bruce Humphries, Inc.), Eli Siegel's *Hot Afternoons Have Been in Montana* (Definition Press), *Spectrum, The Symposium, Trial Balances*, ed. Ann Winslow (The Macmillan Co.), Byron Vazakas' *Transfigured Night* (The Macmillan Co.), *View, Wagner, The Western Review, The Yale Literary Magazine*, Louis Zukofsky's *"A" 1–12* (Origin Press).

Permission to quote from these copyrighted sources is also grate-
fully acknowledged: Charles Olson, *Selected Writings* (Copy-
right © 1966, 1965, 1960, 1959, 1953, 1951 by Charles Olson),
used by permission of New Directions Publishing Corp.; George
Oppen, *Collected Poems* (Copyright © 1960, 1961, 1962, 1963,
1964, 1965, 1967, 1968, 1972, 1974, 1975 by George Oppen; Copy-
right 1934 by The Objectivist Press), used by permission of New
Directions Publishing Corp.; Kenneth Rexroth, *The Collected
Shorter Poems* (Copyright © 1966, 1963, 1962, 1952, 1949, 1940
by Kenneth Rexroth), *In Defense of the Earth* (Copyright ©
1956 by New Directions), *One Hundred Poems from the Chinese*
(All Rights Reserved), *The Phoenix and the Tortoise* (Copy-
right 1944 by New Directions), all used by permission of New
Directions Publishing Corp.; Louis Zukofsky, "A" (Copyright ©
1978 by Celia Zukofsky and Louis Zukofsky), used by permis-
sion of the University of California Press.

The editor would like to thank the following for permission to
quote from previously unpublished letters in his introduction:
James Dickey, Allen Ginsburg, The Estate of Robert Lowell
(used by permission of Robert Silvers, co-executor), The Estate
of Marianne C. Moore (Copyright © 1985 by Clive E. Driver;
used with the permission of Clive E. Driver, literary executor of
the Estate of Marianne C. Moore), The Estate of Charles Olson,
The Trustees of the Ezra Pound Literary Property Trust (Copy-
right © 1985 by the Trustees of the Ezra Pound Literary Prop-
erty Trust; used by permission of New Directions Publishing
Corp., agents). The editor would also like to thank Denise Lever-
tov for permission to quote from letters by William Carlos Wil-
liams in her possession.

For permission to use manuscript materials special thanks are
due: to the Collection of American Literature, The Beinecke
Rare Book and Manuscript Library, Yale University; to the
Poetry Collection, The Poetry/Rare Books Collection of the
University Libraries, State University of New York at Buffalo;
to the Allen Ginsberg Papers, Rare Book and Manuscript
Library, Columbia University; and to the Houghton Library,
Harvard University.

Contents

PREFACE   1

INTRODUCTION: The Presence of Williams in Contemporary
    Poetry by James E. B. Breslin   5
PROLOGUE: Advice to the Young Poet   39
An "Objectivists" Anthology   42
The Element of Time: Advice to a Young Writer   47
Sequence and Change   50
The New Poetical Economy (George Oppen)   55
Notes on Norman Macleod   60
Tea Time Tales: Comment on James McQuail's "Pard and the
    Grandmother"   63
Norman Macleod's Thanksgiving Before November   65
A Twentieth-Century American (H. H. Lewis)   68
An Outcry from the Dirt (H. H. Lewis)   70
An American Poet (H. H. Lewis)   75
Introduction to Sydney Salt's Christopher Columbus and Other
    Poems   83
The Tortuous Straightness of Charles Henri Ford   87
Muriel Rukeyser's US1   89
Foreword to Merrill Moore's Sonnets from New Directions   92
Image and Purpose (Sol Funaroff)   94
Form: The Poems of Laura Riding   97
Harry Roskolenko's Sequence on Violence   101
Patchen's First Testament   103
Letter to Reed Whittemore   105
Poets and Critics: Letter to the Editors (of Partisan Review)   109
American Writing: 1941   111
A Counsel of Madness (Kenneth Patchen)   115
A Group of Poems by Marcia Nardi   123
Preface to a Book of Poems by Harold Rosenberg   125
An Extraordinary Sensitivity (Louis Zukofsky)   129
In Praise of Marriage (Kenneth Rexroth)   132
Parker Tyler's The Granite Butterfly   139
The Genius of France (André Breton)   146
Shapiro Is All Right (Karl Shapiro)   150
Introduction to Byron Vazakas' Transfigured Night   155

A New Line Is a New Measure (Louis Zukofsky)   161
On Basil Bunting's "The Complaint of the Morpethshire Farmer"   170
Poetry with an Impressive Human Speech (David Ignatow)   171
Diamonds in Blue Clay (Peter Viereck)   173
Letter to the Editor, Richard Rubenstein   175
Mid-Century American Poets (ed. John Ciardi)   177
Discharge Note (Merrill Moore)   181
Verse with a Jolt to It (Kenneth Rexroth)   183
Letter to Robert Creeley   186
In a Mood of Tragedy (Robert Lowell)   187
Letter to Lawrence Hart and the Activists   189
A Note on Macleod's Pure as Nowhere   191
Kenneth Lawrence Beaudoin   193
Two Letters to Robert Lawrence Beum   198
On Measure—Statement for Cid Corman   202
Dylan Thomas   209
Letter to Norman Macleod   212
Letter to Srinivas Rayaprol   214
The Speed of Poetry (James Schevill)   217
A Poet who Cannot Pause (René Char)   219
A Note on Layton (Irving Layton)   222
Howl for Carl Solomon (Allen Ginsberg)   225
Charles Olson's Maximus, Book II   227
Five to the Fifth Power (Charles Bell)   232
Charles Eaton's The Greenhouse in the Garden   234
Two New Books by Kenneth Rexroth   236
Introduction to Allen Ginsberg's Empty Mirror   247
Introduction to Eli Siegel's Hot Afternoons Have Been in
   Montana   249
Tram Combs' Pilgrim's Terrace   253
Lief Ericson's Violent Daughter (Winfield Townley Scott)   255
Charles Tomlinson's Seeing is Believing   257
Contribution to a Symposium on the Beats   260
Foreword to Ron Loewinsohn's Watermelons   262
Zukofsky   264
Preface to The Roman Sonnets of G. G. Belli (trans. Harold
   Norse)   268
Introduction to Mimi Goldberg's The Lover and Other Poems   270
Robert Lowell's Verse Translation into the American Idiom   273
Introduction to Ronald Bayes' Dust and Desire   274
INDEX   275

Preface

THIS VOLUME collects William Carlos Williams' writings, both published and unpublished, on younger poets—i.e., those born after 1900. The collection includes essays, reviews, comments, prefaces, and introductions, and letters to younger poets that were published during Williams' lifetime; it does not include statements made or excerpted for dust jackets or advertising purposes. Some of the material included—e.g., Williams' comments on student poems for *The Literary Workshop* or his response to James McQuail's "Pard and the Grandmother"—will strike some readers as fairly trivial. But given Williams' own status as a major writer and his particular importance to so many of the poets who came after him, I have made this collection, within the stipulated limits, as complete as I could. With the exception of "Advice to the Young Poet," which has been placed first as a prologue, the pieces are arranged chronologically, according to date of first publication or, if unpublished, date of composition.

For unpublished material I have used what seemed to me the most complete draft in the cases where more than one draft survives. I have only changed obvious errors of spelling, capitalization, and (in a few cases) punctuation; I have also corrected Williams' transcription of quotes from texts he is reviewing. For published material I have used what seemed to me the most complete and final version published with Williams' active participation—and in all but one case this policy has meant that I have used the earliest published text. For further information about this exception, see the note to Williams' review of James Schevill's *The Right to Greet*. In the case of the one item published

posthumously—Williams' review of Olson's *Maximus* II—I
have returned to the manuscript.

After giving it some thought, I rejected the policy of
returning to Williams' manuscripts (when available) for
published texts. It is certainly true that Williams made
changes in his essays and reviews in response to criticisms
from editors and others. Two examples should be sufficient
to indicate their character. Williams sent a version of what
is now "A Counsel of Madness," a review of Kenneth
Patchen's *The Journal of Albion Moonlight*, to Stanley
Dehler Mayer, editor of *Fantasy*, whose marginal queries
reveal he did not share Williams' enthusiasm for Patchen's
book. At one point where Williams remarks that there are
passages in the *Journal* where

> the mind threatens to open and a vivid reality of the spirit
> threatens to burst forth and bloom in terrifying destruct-
> fulness—the destroying of all that we think today. The
> book threatens to break out through writing into a fact of
> the spirit [,]

Mayer responds: "the book is not clear or powerful enough
to deserve this concept of it, Bill"; Williams, in turn, an-
swers in the right margin: "No, but it approaches that and
that is its virtue" (Buffalo C28b, pp. 4–5). His defense is
ambivalent; so is his final text: "it threatens to break out
through the writing into a fact of the spirit even though it
may not often be quite powerful enough to do so."

Even more interesting are the changes Williams made in
"An Extraordinary Sensitivity," his review of Louis Zukof-
sky's *55 Poems*. Williams passed a draft of the essay along
to Zukofsky, who raised several questions in the margins
(Yale Za/Williams/286). In the opening paragraph Williams
referred to the "small excellences in Zukofsky's poems";
Zukofsky, who naturally thought better of his excellences,
suggested "detailed" or "painstaking" or "minor" or some-

thing else as a replacement. Williams opted for "painstaking." At another point Williams observed:

> I read him in a rare moment (for me) clear, quiet and alert: after a cloudy head for days, weeks—years and I found him, to my mind, clear—as if waiting just for this.

Zukofsky, naturally apprehensive about characterizing his book as such a long-range project, objected: "That's O.K. for telling me how you feel—but to hell with telling it to 'mankind'? i.e. leave out at least *years* for the public?" Williams solved the problem by eliminating the sentence altogether.

Would it be a good idea to try to look around these "intrusions," to recover what Williams "really" thought and establish a text on that basis? I don't think so. The model, frequent in editorial theory and practice, of an external, editorial coercion contaminating the author's original, pure intention is too simple; it is also based on a romantic conception of the artist as autonomous. An argument can be made that Williams revised the Patchen essay because the editor's objections spoke to doubts and reservations of his own, and that he altered the Zukofsky review not just because he was trying to please a friend (though that was probably part of it), but also because he typically thought of himself and his fellow neglected artists as bonded together in a struggle against the "public." From this point of view, the published texts actually represent Williams in a fuller, more complex way than his original statements did. In any case, my own belief is that what a writer let be published under his name during his lifetime should stand—unless there are *compelling reasons* to do otherwise; in this case there are not. Any editor who decides, say, that earlier expressions are truer to a spontaneous writer like Williams is eliminating half of what Williams regarded as the creative process (first let go; then pare down, edit) and is intruding his own aesthetic preferences into texts that properly belong to Williams.

Completing this project would have been impossible without two invaluable aids to any Williams scholar: Emily Wallace's *A Bibliography of William Carlos Williams* (Middletown, Conn., 1968) and Neil Baldwin and Steven L. Meyers' *The Manuscripts and Letters of William Carlos Williams in the Poetry Collection of the Lockwood Memorial Library, State University of New York at Buffalo: A Descriptive Catalogue* (Boston, 1978). Reference to items in the Buffalo collection will use numbers from this catalogue; references to materials in the Yale collection will use the call numbers assigned by the Beinecke Library. In using these collections I am indebted to Robert Bertholf, Curator of the Poetry Collection at Lockwood Memorial Library, and to Mary Angelotti of the Beinecke Library. I am grateful to Andrew Griffin, J. C. Levenson, Marjorie Perloff, and Michael Rogin, all of whom read my introduction and made helpful suggestions. I'm particularly indebted to Emily Wallace for her painstaking reading of the entire manuscript, her extensive knowledge of Williams, and for her valuable advice. I want, finally, to thank my wife Ramsay both for her specific ideas and for her love and encouragement.

J. E. B. B.

Introduction: The Presence of Williams in Contemporary Poetry

Has any other poet in American history been so actually *useful, usable, and influential?*[1]—*James Dickey*

He was useful in his being present, on the scene—in this country as a person. *Without him, American poetry was impoverished for me.*[2]—*David Ignatow*

In 1955 Paul Blackburn published his first book of poetry, *The Dissolving Fabric.* In October of 1956 Blackburn's work was reviewed in *Poetry*—along with books by Lawrence Ferlinghetti, Robert Creeley, and Robert Duncan—and the reviewer, Frederick Eckman, began by asserting that all of these poets "have felt to some degree the influence of William Carlos Williams, who is probably more attractive to the young than any other poet now writing."[3] Blackburn read the review, and "I thought, 'Oh, wow! I've got to read Williams!' So I got ahold of *Paterson*, and what was then his *Collected Poems.* I wanted to find out where my influences were coming from. I wanted to find out who my father was."[4] By the middle of the 1950s Williams' influence among younger poets was so pervasive that it extended even to those who had yet read him.

Now, thirty years later, a canonical figure whose life has been amply recorded in a critical biography, whose works have been collected, scrutinized, and even deconstructed, and whose centennial was officially celebrated at the 1983 Modern Language Association convention, Williams has been elevated, by the academic world he loathed, to the status of Venerable Institution; he has also become a poetic fashion whose time has gone. As early as 1970, Denise Levertov,

assessing the accomplishments of Williams' literary descen-
dants, complained that

> what began as a healthy reaction, a turning away with re-
> lief from sterile academic rhetorics, has proliferated in an
> unexampled production of *notations:* poems which tell of
> things seen or done, but which, lacking the focus of that
> energetic, compassionate, questioning spirit that infused
> even the most fragmentary of Williams's poems, do not
> impart a sense of the experiencing of seeing or doing, or
> of the *value* of such experience. . . .[5]

And in a 1976 poem Marvin Bell mocks those followers of
Williams "who took the intellect // out of poetry:/'no
ideas but the in-thing.' "[6] According to Williams, "destruc-
tion and creation/are simultaneous"; but in the sixties and
early seventies, as the New Critical hegemony collapsed,
Williams' approach to the poem lost its oppositional status
and its destructive/creative core. It became all too easy to
slip into the new mode, to *copy* the manner of Williams
without *imitating* his essential spirit. But if we have now
passed at least one phase of Williams' usefulness, we have
also attained the perspective from which to assess the extent
and nature of his presence in contemporary poetry.

A list of the younger American poets affected by Wil-
liams would contain many of the significant names in Ameri-
can poetry since 1945: Ammons, Creeley, Dickey, Duncan,
Ginsberg, Ignatow, Levertov, Lowell, O'Hara, Olson, Rex-
roth, Roethke, Snyder, Zukofsky are only the poets who
come most quickly to mind.[7] To give a full account of
Williams' impact requires familiarity with a body of mate-
rial that is just beginning to become available: the letters,
journals, manuscripts, essays, interviews, memoirs, biogra-
phies of at least two generations of twentieth-century poets.
This collection contributes to that project by providing us
with the public record of Williams' responses to some of the
younger poets who came to his attention. In some cases
Williams' recognition turned out to be the poets' only and
fingertip hold onto literary immortality; but these essays and
reviews maintain interest as statements of his evolving views

of poetic form. In other cases Williams had a deep effect on and often lengthy correspondence with poets he never discussed in public—e.g., Roethke and Levertov. So the full story can't yet be told, but I want to use this occasion to suggest some of the ways in which what we do know complicates our sense of Williams as a force in recent American poetry.

Generally, Williams is regarded in his relations with subsequent poets either as the affectionate, tolerant, and homespun patron saint of contemporary poetry or as a mindlessly indiscriminate zealot ready and willing to write a puff at the drop of a chapbook. But we do now have enough evidence to see that both the sentimental idealization and the cynical ridicule of his role are distortions of the complex human and literary relations between Williams and his successors. Studying them, in fact, will give us an expanded and more sophisticated notion of literary "influence."

At a New York City poetry reading in November of 1948 Williams interrupted his presentation of his own poems to read a poem by David Ignatow, whose first book he had enthusiastically reviewed in *The New York Times* just a few days before. The other poets in the audience, according to Ignatow, reacted to the reading of his poem with stunned silence. After the reading, as Williams and Ignatow were walking to a bar, Williams burst out: "There is no competition between poets!"[8] Williams was asserting his dream of poetry as a cooperative enterprise, transcendent of personal ambitions and egotistic triumphs. It was this vision that led to his energetic and generous quest for moments of imaginative invention that might be found tucked away in the corners of the work of unknown young writers—a critical version of his poetic quest for the sudden flashings, in obscure places, of his destructive/creative core. Yet Williams' ideal poetic community—the participants bonded in their commitment to an avant-garde writing that was grounded in the present—was a *personal* ideal which itself was premised on a hostile relation to the larger social community and which, for a long time, put him at odds with the *real* poetic community.

In a letter to Theodore Roethke, Robert Lowell takes a more candid and more realistic view of poetic rivalry.

> I remember Edwin Muir arguing with me that there is no rivalry in poetry. Well, there is. No matter what one has done or hasn't done (this sounds like a prayer) one feels each blow, each turning of the wind, each up and down grading of the critics. We've both written enough and lived long enough perhaps to find this inescapable. Each week brings some pat on the back or some brisk, righteous slur, till one rather longs for the old oblivion.[9]

Lowell and Roethke were part of a generation, coming right after the formidable Modernists, that was more unabashedly rivalrous than most. Yet it was Williams himself who grimly, and grandiosely, concluded that with "The Waste Land" Eliot "would influence all subsequent poets and take them out of my sphere."[10]

Not all writers imagine themselves as a "sphere" of influence, and those who do end up by making trouble for themselves and their fellows in the poetic community. Williams' often sputtering rage against Eliot was surely inspired by more than mere differences of poetic opinion—most deeply by an old familial battle. As an aloof, puritanical American-turned-Englishman, Eliot represented to Williams a betraying surrender to his own aloof, puritanical father; and Williams was very eager to dissociate himself from *that*. Generally, Williams' self-doubts made him comfortable in relation to sons and daughters (where he was an authority) and prickly in relation to brothers and sisters (where he was an outcast). From his marginal place in the Modernist canon, the amiable country doctor carried on an increasingly rancorous combat with the more successful male poets of his generation—Eliot, Pound, Stevens, Frost, Crane. Admittedly, he mixed affection with rancor in the case of Pound; and Williams did write enthusiastically and sometimes brilliantly about Pound, Moore, Stein, Joyce, Cummings, and H.D. His long friendship with Marianne

Moore constitutes an important exception to my point here, though late in life Williams felt betrayed by her criticisms of *Paterson* IV. Nevertheless, anger over long neglect and an inner uncertainty about his own standing in the poetic community often made Williams very touchy.

After all, what prompted Williams to declare his own ideal of poetic community—Ignatow recalls his tone as "plaintive"—was the silent manifestation of poetic rivalry.[11] For an older writer to bestow his blessing on a younger one (no matter how generous the motives) is an act of literary authority that will inevitably leave those not singled out feeling disgruntled. Writing in the privacy of his notebooks, Ignatow reveals some of the emotional complexities of these exchanges from the perspective of the younger writer. A recent letter from Williams, Ignatow writes in a 1954 entry, has "made me feel that my status . . . has been reaffirmed in his eyes."

> Nothing makes me so jittery as to think I may have sunk low in his estimate, having been "reevaluated" by him through the influence of others. I say jealousy, since I know I would be jealous and am jealous of his esteem for others. I do not know how he can abide them, I often think to myself in irritation.

Ignatow desires sole possession of his mentor; but he also realizes that his own "loneliness and unsureness" make him long for the "absolute" of Williams' validation, and with a selfishness that is at once comic and poignant he wishes a long life for Williams.

> Time, I keep hoping, will prove me right and time, I keep praying, do not take away this loving man before I can publish my second book. I want him to see it, read it, understand it, and say with me in print, in full agreement, that I, I alone, have come up to his expectations of American poets.[12]

Williams, then, was not only rivalrous in himself but the occasion of it in others. The ultimate issue raised by these

exchanges is the status and definition of the poetic imagina-
tion itself. Is the imagination disinterested, autonomous,
transcendent, thus freed of the contaminations of private
psychology and public history? Or, at the other extreme, is
the imagination, as Harold Bloom contends, a "psychic
battleground" and literary history a kind of weightlifting
competition among "strong" poets? My own view is that
it's a mistake to sever imaginative from either psychological
or historical pressures, just as it's a mistake to reduce crea-
tivity, as Bloom does, to *mere* vengeance and rivalry.[13] Like
everyone else only more so, poets are capable of complex
intertwinings of selfless and selfish motives—as the rest of
Lowell's letter to Roethke suggests. Having declared com-
petitiveness "inescapable," Lowell then proceeds to try to
bond with Roethke, now viewing himself and his old rival
as fraternal members of a pluralistic literary community:

> Well, it would be terrible if there weren't many frogs in
> the pond, and even many toads. It does make me happier
> that you exist, and can do so many big things that I have
> no gift for. We couldn't be more different, and yet how
> weirdly our lives have often gone the same way. Let's
> say we are brothers, have gone the same journey and know
> far more about each other than we have ever said or will
> say.[14]

Neither the competitive nor the comradely side of this am-
bivalent letter should be singled out as representing the
'real' Lowell, who was both. Like him, Williams combined
powerful egotism with a selfless dedication to poetry, and
his interactions with the poets who came after him mix gen-
erosity with self-interest, openness with dogmatism, warmth
with edginess, and support with doubts and reservations.

Williams' relations with younger poets can best be char-
acterized by juxtaposing him with some of his contem-
poraries. Wallace Stevens, for instance, claimed not to read
his peers for fear of being influenced by them—thereby
finding a flattering reason to ignore them—and he showed
no greater interest in the poets who came after him. Stevens
was a solitary; Frost was a more public figure who was an

equal opportunity competitor: he undercut *all* poets regardless of age, sex, or place of national origin. Donald Hall remembers Frost at the Bread Loaf poetry workshops as "cutting, sarcastic, dismissive." One day Frost read a student poem and asked disgustedly, "Who *wrote* this poem?" A woman acknowledged authorship. "*No*," said Frost, "I mean, who *really* wrote it?" The woman again identified herself. "*You* didn't write it," Frost declared. " 'You know who wrote it?'—his voice pronounced the name with the heaviest sarcasm he could summon, and he could summon sarcasm as well as anyone: 'T.S. Eliot!' " As Hall points out, Frost would have been less angry had the woman imitated Frost rather than Eliot; Frost's cruel humiliation of the student was motivated not by high standards but by professional jealousy.[15]

The case of Pound is far more complex. As a young man, Pound combined personal arrogance with an extraordinarily unselfish dedication to the advancement of good writing. As Eliot commented, "No one could have been kinder to younger men or to writers who, whether younger or not, seemed to him worthy and unrecognized";[16] Pound's practical help and promotional efforts were extended to many writers who had basic assumptions quite different from his own: Yeats, H.D., Lawrence, Eliot, Joyce, Frost, Williams. Later on, Pound was helpful to Basil Bunting and Louis Zukofsky. Then he lost interest: "after the age of fifty, one cannot be a telephone directory of younger writers," he declared, as if *any* interest would be indiscriminate and contemptible.[17] He was sent but did not read *Life Studies*, although Lowell had visited him at St. Elizabeths. Williams gave Allen Ginsberg a letter of introduction to Pound, and Ginsberg sent Pound some poems, whereupon Pound dispatched a note to Williams on the back of Ginsberg's letter: "You got more room in yr/house than I hv / in my cubicle[.] If he's yours why dont you teach him the value of time to those who want to read something that wil tell 'em wot they dont know[.]"[18] Pound's writings were an important stimulus for many younger writers after World War II, but in St. Elizabeths and after, he remained too mired in his own problems to be of any personal help. After his return to Italy, his contacts with poets such as Donald Hall and Allen Ginsberg reveal that their function was to reassure and stimulate the older poet. Devastated by self-doubt, the older Pound was like a self-preoccupied parent able only to see his children as extensions of himself.[19]

From the mid-twenties to the mid-fifties, Eliot was *the* literary authority in both England and America; in addition to the enormous prestige attached to both his creative and theoretical writings, he had, via his editorships at *The Criterion* and Faber, a practical means of implementing his authority; he became known as the "Pope of Russell Square."[20] Occupying his center of papal authority, Eliot was freed to move in ways that seemed above mere rivalry; but if he was not as greedily self-aggrandizing as Frost, neither was he as capacious as the young Pound. Eliot was certainly an early advocate of Pound's shorter poems and he was the publisher in England of *The Cantos;* he wrote influentially of Joyce's *Ulysses* and as early as 1931 he contracted for Faber to publish *Finnegans Wake*, parts of which he published in *The Criterion;* he endorsed Marianne Moore's poetry with an introduction to her *Selected Poems*. But he also kept Stevens and Williams from being published in England. After his conversion to Anglicanism, his literary judgments sometimes became frankly doctrinal, as in his branding of Yeats, Hardy, and Lawrence as heretics in *After Strange Gods*. According to Peter Ackroyd's biography, Eliot, "through his publication and support of certain judiciously chosen poets . . . determined the shape of English poetry from the Thirties into the Sixties."[21] His support of younger poets was in some ways surprisingly ecumenical, including W. H. Auden, Stephen Spender, Louis MacNeice, George Barker, Vernon Watkins, Djuna Barnes, Charles Williams, Lawrence Durrell, Ted Hughes, and Thom Gunn, many of whom worked from premises quite different from Eliot's. Stephen Spender recalls that "Eliot encouraged, talked with, wrote to young poets" and contrasts his kindness with the cruelty of *Scrutiny*, whose "frequent policy with young writers was to destroy a reputation before it was made."[22] Auden believed Eliot, of all the older writers he knew, "the most consistently friendly, the least malicious, envious, vain."[23] Spender, moreover, points out that Eliot's grave, formal manner made him personally distant but was less intimidating than the cleverness which was the standard mode of the London literary scene.[24] And among American poets Eliot clearly became a friend and mentor to Robert Lowell.

Yet there were also complaints of the chilly atmosphere in Eliot's office. "You are not a very *prolific* poet," he told F. T. Prince on one visit; on another he observed that "not everything you write is very *interesting*."[25] Social criteria clearly played some part; it is not hard to imagine the kind of reception a Ginsberg or an Olson would have received, had they ever been granted an audience in the first place. Moreover, while from the perspective of a young English poet Eliot was one of the few established writers to make himself "*present* to contemporaries twenty years younger," from the vantage point of a beginning American writer around 1950, Eliot would have appeared quite differently.[26] To an American, Eliot's reticent formality made him more, not less, intimidating. If he counseled in the *Four Quartets* that "old men should be explorers," his own literary views increasingly offered conservative positions disguised as platitudinous good sense. Eliot, for instance, told a 1947 audience at the Frick Museum:

> We cannot, in literature, any more than in the rest of life, live in a perpetual state of revolution. If every generation of poets made it their task to bring poetic diction up to date with the spoken language, poetry would fail in one of its most important obligations. For poetry should help, not only to refine the language of the time, but to prevent it from changing too rapidly: a development of language at too great a speed would be a development in the sense of a progressive deterioration, and that *is* our danger today.[27]

Apparently attacking the extreme of perpetual revolution, Eliot was really ruling out *any* revolution. The hero of internationalist Modernism, now defending High Culture against the dangers of popular linguistic energies, concluded his paper by exhorting young writers to return to Milton. Finally, as a British subject residing in London, Eliot was, for the most part, not present to those young American poets whom he was willing to direct; to them, he was an all-powerful, ubiquitous but *absent* father.

For young poets there is often something magical in the simple physical presence of an older, established writer. Meeting Eliot at a dinner party, Sylvia Plath "felt to be sitting next to a descended god; he has such a nimbus of greatness about him."[28] The first time he met Robert Frost, Donald Hall was looking through the glass doors of a lecture room: "the ground outside sank away, and Frost, approaching the lecture hall uphill, appeared to be rising out of the ground."

> He was palpable, human, in the flesh. I felt light in head and body. Merely seeing this man, merely laying startled eyes upon him, allowed me to feel enlarged. My dreams for my own life, for my own aging into stone, took reality in the stern flesh of Robert Frost, who rose out of a hill in Vermont.[29]

In meeting an established writer a younger one may seek approval, court favors, honor a hero, impress an authority, detect cracks in a monument, or measure a rival; but, as Plath and Hall suggest, such encounters have a mythic quality. A god descending into the flesh or a god rising out of the earth: the older poet powerfully embodies an abstract ideal in human reality. The ideal need not be one of personality or style—the younger poet may not even like the older one or his work—but rather it is the ideal of achieved poetic greatness: if this canonical poet is a flesh and blood person, thinks the elated beginner, then this flesh and blood person may become a canonical poet.

But in addition to any magical powers they may have projected upon him, Williams gained a special authority in the 1950s because he met many specific needs of the young American poets of the time; his presence was an *historical* presence. Williams, after all, had actually *been there* at the legendary 1910 Revolution of the Word and, converting neither to Fascism nor Christianity, he had remained rancorously committed to Modernism's founding principles. With *Paterson*, "The Desert Music," and "Asphodel, that Greeny Flower" his career was flourishing, and if the literary hegemony of the fifties still relegated him to marginal status in modern poetry, that only made him an innovator with whom young dissidents could more easily identify. Williams was, as Lowell put it, "a model and a liberator."[30] Williams thus possessed an authority that had not yet hardened into monumental granite, and he was personally available; his closest friends among younger poets were Louis Zukofsky and Robert Lowell, but Williams greeted a large number and a broad range of young poets—from, say, Robert Lowell to Allen Ginsberg—with enthusiasm, geniality, openness. From the vantage point of 9 Ridge Road it must have seemed at times as if poets, like snow, were general over northern New Jersey.

Among the prima donnas of the Modernist generation Williams stands out as a kind of blue-collar worker—living proof, as Robert Lowell put it, that one can "follow the art and be neither dry, nor crackpot, nor a stuffed shirt."[31] Writing for a local labor paper in New Jersey, Allen Ginsberg contrived an interview so he could meet Williams. Ginsberg expected "some sort of stainless steel 1920s *moderne* visage out of Brancusi and Ezra Pound and Alfred Steiglitz's American Place Gallery" but instead "found a creaky-voiced, tender-toned, soft though sharp-eyed country doc, scratching his head"—a Ginsbergian sentimentalization but one based on the vulnerable flesh and blood humanity perceived in Williams by many of Ginsberg's contemporaries.[32] Unlike Pound, Williams battled with his own generation, but for his sons and daughters in the following generations he was a tender, nurturing father who was *there*.

To put the point another way: Pound was a traditionalist whose commitment to the continuity of literature pretty much ended with his own generation; Williams was a proponent of violent discontinuity who invested much energy in the future of writing. One form this commitment took was in his willingness to help younger writers in practical ways. The introductions and reviews collected here provide abundant evidence of such assistance, and Williams was sometimes willing to do more. He tried to place Ginsberg's *Empty Mirror* with his then publisher, Random House— "I'll put every ounce of pressure on him of which I am capable to get the work accepted," he wrote Ginsberg— and he also gave the not-yet-beat poet letters of introduction to Ezra Pound and Marianne Moore, neither of whom exactly embraced the young Ginsberg.[33] I've already quoted Pound's response; Moore's pronouncement to Ginsberg on the *Empty Mirror* manuscript was: "patient or impatient repudiation of life, just repudiates itself. There is no point in it."[34] Later, when he had sent her "Howl," she instructed: "feel calmer and take more time."[35] Although Marcia Nardi was demanding, resentful if refused, and generally difficult to deal with, Williams gave her money, urged James Laughlin to do a book of her poems, and interceded with Norman Holmes Pearson to get her a small grant—all because he was convinced, however wrongly, of the quality of her work.[36]

In person, in correspondence and (to some extent) in his reviews Williams was generous with practical critical advice. What I have seen of the written record suggests that Williams was a quick, intuitive reader who was often not very skillful at articulating his literary impressions or in justifying his judgments. His remarks are typically quite general; no one would ever accuse Williams, so attentive to particulars in the poems, of getting bogged down in critical detail. Although he insists that a poem succeeds or fails in the minute workings of its words, he is not interested in discussing precisely how poems work; and when he does quote a line or passage he either admires or objects to, he is usually vague about his reasons. Williams' reviews are generally quite positive; in fact he seems to have decided that, as a matter of policy, he would publicly support younger writers, whatever his private reservations. Some may accuse him of playing literary politics here, and he did want to enlist the young in his cause, but as someone who felt himself to be a victim of both public neglect and literary snobbery, Williams was too deeply identified with the struggles of starting writers to become their harsh judge. He would encourage and nurture young writers as he wished *he* had been.

So Williams' enthusiasms were genuine enough. At times they were bravely extravagant; at others they were merely embarrassing. After reading that Marcia Nardi "is so much better at her best than some of the best known professional poets about us that I am willing to say that by moments no one surpasses her," or that Parker Tyler's *The Granite Butterfly* is "by far the best long poem of our day," or that Eli Siegel "belongs in the very first rank of our living artists," no one would accuse Williams of being afraid to climb out on any critical limbs. Yet Williams is rarely unequivocally positive; in reviews he will typically lodge what appears at first to be a minor objection but actually turns out to be a fairly damaging criticism. Both in public and in private, his method was to create a supportive context, within which he could give an instructive crack or two of the critical whip.

At times, moreover, Williams' practical advice to younger poets was astute and effective. In his letters he often worked as a loving conscience who mixed praise with an insistence on the tough standards of economy that had produced the Modernist pared-down lyric. "One active phrase is better than a whole inert page," he told Ginsberg;[37] and in a 1954 letter to Denise Levertov he urged her:

> Cut and cut again whatever you write—while you leave by your art no trace of your cutting—and the final utterance will remain packed with what you have to say.[38]

At other times, however, Williams' exhortations ran in precisely the opposite direction, urging the younger writer to break loose, to be abandoned, to let go. In 1940 Williams met Theodore Roethke when giving a reading at Penn State, where Roethke was then teaching; the two became friends and correspondents, with Williams actively taking on the

role of literary mentor. "I do owe him a debt for jibing me
in conversation and by letter to get out of small forms,"
Roethke acknowledged in 1948.[39] Unhappy with the con-
straint of *The Open House,* Williams had written Roethke
in 1941:

> I tell you you've got to write more and more fully out of
> the less known side of your nature if you are to be no-
> ticed. You are so damned much better than your position
> that I believe in you, that there is that to say out of your
> belly that can astonish—and you'll just have to astonish.[40]

A few years later Williams was still pushing Roethke in the
direction that would generate the "Lost Son" sequence:
"Make it drunker, hotter . . . more unashamed."[41] As it
turns out, Roethke was not all that familiar with Williams'
writing at the time;[42] Williams affected Roethke at a crucial
turning point in his career not by example, not by rhythm
or image or theme or theory—but by some well-timed and
well-based paternal prodding.

Roethke was not the only beneficiary of such advice. In
the late forties and early fifties, Allen Ginsberg kept journals
in which he worked on poems, recorded dreams, memories,
observations, meditations; the poems, stiff, verbose, and
awkwardly conventional, dissatisfied even Ginsberg, who
sometime in 1951 produced eleven new poems by transcrib-
ing the prose from the journals and breaking it into lines of
verse "just as experiment."[43] But he then put these poems
aside, "thinking they were nothing, thinking also I was
aimlessly trying to make poetry out of prose scraps."[44] In
February of 1952, however, Ginsberg gave the eleven poems
to Williams, who responded enthusiastically.

> Wonderful! Really. You shall be the *center* of my new
> poem—of which I shall tell you: the extension of *Pater-
> son.* . . .
>   For it I shall use your *Metaphysics* as the head. . . .
>   How many of such poems as these do you own? You
> *must* have a book. I shall see that you get it. Don't throw
> anything away. These are *it.*[45]

Ginsberg was surely aware that these poems would receive a lot warmer reception in Rutherford than his earlier Blakean effusions had, but in a letter to Williams Ginsberg at least claimed that "I don't know why I sent them to you, didn't expect that approval so much, just sent them as I had nothing else to send I felt too washed up as writer."[46] Nevertheless, the older poet's affirmation elated the young and still unpublished Ginsberg and "turned everything upside down" for him.[47] Within two weeks he had produced eighty more such poems—eventually the core of *Empty Mirror*—and was presenting himself to the old master as a young novice eager to learn:

> Important: the 80 or more poems you have are pieces of prose I selected, or rather scrambled after frantically, after receiving your letter 2 weeks ago today. They were all put in present form in last 2 weeks. I had no time for real selection or revision of material. Perhaps they are better for that, perhaps not.[48]

So, in spite of a "bog and morass of inexperience with craft,"

> I am open and capable of development. Importance to me of whatever you can show me (and I am sensitive to little details like one of shift of "don't care anymore") and have time left to show me of detail, experience in this style of last 30–40 years—your own tricks of trade, craft and method—is what I offer, and promise to continue development and whatever tradition established, as best I see fit.[49]

Williams did not draw Ginsberg aside and whisper the eternal secrets of the craft into his ear; but at this point Williams did shift emphasis, now admonishing Ginsberg to toughen and pare down the new work: "If you cut down everything no joking, no looseness—your book has a chance of making some kind of impression different from the general run";[50] Williams also provided suggestions for the elimination and revision of particular poems, most of which Ginsberg adopted.[51] The result, *Empty Mirror*, may not be Immortal Poesy or even Ginsberg's mature idiom. But at a

time when Ginsberg had reached a creative dead-end
("washed up"), Williams helpfully steered him away from
the self-consciously literary works he produced whenever
he sat down to write a poem and steered him toward accept-
ing his more spontaneous writings as embodying his real
creative energies—a crucial advance in Ginsberg's artistic
development.

When Williams first met poets like Levertov, Roethke,
and Ginsberg, they were unformed, struggling young poets
who shared his animosity toward the New Critical hege-
mony. When Williams first met Robert Lowell, he was its
already dazzlingly successful creation; in fact, Lowell was
then, at thirty, the Poetry Consultant to the Library of Con-
gress, a position the sixty-four-year-old Williams had not yet
been invited to hold. Lowell, who asked Williams to record
a reading for the Library of Congress and who regularly
reviewed in such New Critical strongholds as *Sewanee Re-
view* and *The Kenyon Review*, was in a position to do favors
for the older poet—a role reversal that could easily have in-
censed the volatile Williams. In this context it's surprising
that the two men had anything good to say to or about
each other, much less that they became close friends. Wil-
liams had confided in a 1946 letter to Roethke that "Lowell
is turgid . . . very dull."[52] But Lowell's warm praise of
Paterson I in a 1947 review apparently caused Williams to
think better of his admirer's work. A grateful Williams
wrote Lowell that

> it is a satisfaction to me when a person of distinction, par-
> ticularly one who is skillful and accomplished in some
> craft which I myself employ, in the first place notices the
> work I have done and in the second place speaks out con-
> cerning it.[53]

Shortly thereafter, Williams was congratulating Lowell on
his ability, in *Lord Weary's Castle*, to employ "local place
names" without creating "bathos."[54] Whatever reasons of
personal psychology or literary politics may have prompted
Williams' critical reassessment of Lowell, his writings about
younger poets reveal a somewhat—not vastly, but some-

what—more complicated view of traditional verse forms than some of his polemic explosions might lead us to expect. There is his extraordinary *mea culpa* on the sonnet form in his "Foreword" to Merrill Moore's *Sonnets*—a well-based retraction which Williams promptly forgot. But more typically Williams will detect a restlessness with the constraints of external forms; and if at times this perception was simply a projection of his own impatience with such means, at others he was quite accurate, as in his review of Lowell's *The Mills of the Kavanaughs*. Moreover, in the Lowell of 1951 Williams had a poet who was willing to listen, though not to accept all that he had to say.

The Lowell of *The Mills* possessed a formed poetic style; for many, including Lowell himself, the style had become a bit too well-formed: rigid, narrow, and predictable. So Lowell, less needy and less eager to please than the young Ginsberg, approached Williams with a healthy combination of independence and receptivity. What Williams offered Lowell was a benign alternative to the severity of his earlier New Critical fathers like Allen Tate. At times Lowell did look up to Williams as an admiring disciple: "I have no master, only masters, you are about the first among them";[55] and it always remained clear who was the authority figure in their relation. But the correspondence between them reveals a strong sense of mutual respect, affection, and even love; though thirty-four years separated them, both men liked to think of their connection as a fraternal bond based on acceptance of difference. As Williams wrote to Lowell in 1948,

Cal, we're not alike but that's a good thing. I think we annoy each other the less for that and I can speak freely to you whereas if we were more similar I couldn't do it. What I have to say requires a large frame of reference, that it can include two people as far apart as we are is its greatest virtue—as it is its main reason for being.[56]

Six years later, Williams was observing that "in spite of differences in our poetic styles I feel that we are close brothers under the skin."[57] Lowell eagerly agreed:

Of course we are brothers under the skin; I've felt that since my first visit in Rutherford, and these last rapid years have increased the feeling. In a funny way, though I've really seen little of you, I feel more love for you than for any man of your age—but you are younger than us all.[58]

Much of the correspondence between the two men consists of friendly but firm expressions of their differing basic assumptions. In his review of *The Mills* Williams places a few critical depth charges beneath the positive surface.

In his new book Robert Lowell gives us six first-rate poems of which we may well be proud. As usual he has taken the rhyme-track for his effects. We shall now have rhyme again for a while, *rhymes completely missing the incentive*. [Italics added.]

Or,

When he does, when he does under stress of emotion break through *the monotony* of the line, it never goes far, it is as though he had at last wakened to breathe freely again, you can feel the lines breathing, the poem rouses *as though from a trance*. [Italics added.]

Lowell's response was neither resentful nor fawning:

I like particularly the parts about rime and my meaning—the two are the same but most people won't understand that. One difference—I certainly see rime as joy and colour, not just an obstacle, or perhaps, when the obstacle is accepted there is colour, joy and a certain sad glory.[59]

Eliot and Pound also became points of disagreement, with Lowell attempting to persuade Williams to a more complex assessment of his rivals and Williams reluctant to budge. But, as was so often the case in the 1950s, "free verse" became the ground on which a range of moral, political, and literary values were contested. All through the decade Lowell remained ambivalent, but he gradually shifted his primary loyalty from the conservative to the liberal side of his ambivalence. Even in his response to Williams' review of *The Mills*, Lowell, after defending rhyme, admits that, having just read *The Collected Later Poems*, "I've been wondering if my characters and plots aren't a bit trifling and cumbersome—a bit in the way of the eye, and what one lives."[60] Still, in 1951 Lowell could only conclude by drawing back: "But I'd feel as unhappy out of rime and meter as you would in them."[61] Six years later in *Life Studies*, Lowell had joined Williams with his "first unmeasured verse,"[62] but he was still insisting that "there's no ideal form that does for any two of us,"[63] and asserting a well-balanced view that dissented from Williams' absolutism:

> I wouldn't like ever to completely give up meter; it's wonderful opposition to wrench against and revise with. Yet now that I've joined you in unscanned verse, I am struck by how often the old classics get boxed up in their machinery, the sonority of the iambic pentameter line, the apparatus of logic and conceit and even set subjects. Still, the muscle is there in the classics, we reread them with joy, and in a sense wherever a man has really worked his stuff outbraves time and novel methods.[64]

As early as 1952 Lowell had wished, in a letter to Williams, "that I could absorb something of your way of writing into mine."[65] Rather than experiencing a self-annihilating literary conversion, Lowell re-formed his poetic style by absorbing some of the poetic realism and rhythmic inventiveness of Williams' way of writing into his own. Williams *was* "a model and a liberator."

Not all literary influence is strictly literary, as the case of Williams plainly shows; and the taxonomies of Harold Bloom barely begin to identify the possibilities. Williams affected younger writers simply by *being there*—as well as by his practical assistance, critical advice, and psychological support. When Lowell sent *Life Studies* to Allen Tate, his New Critical mentor reacted with the alarmed disapproval of an austere Republican father whose son has just joined a union. Tate pronounced the poems "definitely *bad*," so

much so that he urged Lowell not to publish them. Their
"free verse" was "arbitrary and without rhythm," while
their autobiograhical details, "presented in *causerie* and at
random, are of interest only to you. They are, of course, of
great interest to me because I am one of your oldest friends.
But they have no public or literary interest."[66] Tate was so
alarmed that he started a rumor that Lowell had written the
poems during one of his manic episodes.[67] Williams, who
was more or less the shop steward in Lowell's new union,
naturally adopted a more supportive position.

> Floss has just finished reading me your terrible wonder-
> ful poems. You have lost nothing of your art, in fact you
> have piled accomplishment upon accomplishment until
> there is nothing to be said to you in rebuttal of your
> devastating statements or the way you have uttered them.
> I'm trying to be not rhetorical but to approach the man
> you are with all defenses down.[68]

Such acts of support have a special meaning for writers.
Unlike doctors, lawyers, or Ph.D.'s, poets have no formal-
ized processes of initiation and certification; nor do they
have shared, stable criteria for assessing achievement, as the
differing judgments of Tate and Williams attest. Poetry is
thus a vocation pervaded, from start to finish, with self-
doubt, so that the affirmation of an older, recognized poet
has powerful psychological consequences for a younger
one, particularly for poets, unlike the Lowell of *Life Studies*,
who are anxiously starting out. "It's a beautiful book!" Wil-
liams wrote to Denise Levertov of her *Here and Now:*

> It's a wise book and reveals a mind with which I am in
> love. . . . I am really amazed and a little in awe of you.
> I didn't realize you were so good though I had an in-
> timation of it on that day in our front room when you
> were reading to me and I saw that you really were a
> poet.[69]

Even more significant are *public* acts of the laying-on-of-
hands, as in Williams' adoption of Ginsberg as the son of
Paterson, his quotation of Gilbert Sorrentino's prose in

Paterson or Olson's "Projective Verse" in the *Autobiography*, or in the introductions and reviews collected in this volume. When David Ignatow read Williams' review of his first book, he says, "I felt I was confirmed as a poet."[70] It was an important moment for someone in a profession in which many are called but few are confirmed.

Many critics and poets have judged Williams far too lax in dispensing his support, as if he were a wayward bishop willing to confirm anyone able to stumble to the altar. It's not just that he was nowhere near as acute as Pound had been in the 'teens, it's that Williams often takes a literary pratfall. It's one thing, and even a noble thing, to read the little magazines and encourage promising young writers; but it's another thing to declare, say, the poems of W. J. Pemble "major work."[71] To his credit, Williams was an early admirer of Louis Zukofsky, George Oppen, Muriel Rukeyser, David Ignatow, Charles Olson, Charles Tomlinson, and Allen Ginsberg (to stick to names from this collection), but many of his other enthusiasms were not the best minds of their, or any other, generation. Williams' praise, hyperbolic and overextended, loses credibility.

Yet nothing has been damaged but Williams' own reputation. Western civilization is not going to slip into the Atlantic Ocean merely because a few poetic grubs have been advertised as butterflies; besides Williams was unable to find any buyers. In other words, he may have had the power to confirm but not to canonize. Moreover, to be fair we should remember that older artists are often flabbergastingly inept in their choice of younger writers to take up—Yeats and Dorothy Wellsley, Stevens and Samuel French Morse being two examples; perhaps many aging poets are more comfortable with nonthreatening mediocrities. In this context, Williams' record looks both better and worse than the norm.

The important point, however, is that Williams' errors were not accidents; they occurred for reasons, and not just because he was too nice a guy. The reasons were both psychological and theoretical. The psychological, having to do with his use of younger poets to vindicate himself to himself, I will be discussing shortly. Now I want to emphasize

the role of his theoretical commitments. Williams was more
worried about the dangers of repression than those of chaos.
His model of the creative process, as we've seen in his advice
to Ginsberg and Roethke, stressed the need, first, to let go,
expand, explore unknown areas of consciousness, then to
discriminate, pare down, perfect. He viewed the historical
evolution of poetry as a similar kind of process and thus
wanted to create an atmosphere of risk-taking and permis-
sion in the present, with the polished achievements to come
later.[72] So committed was he to uncovering the new in
obscure places that he sometimes hallucinated the promised
land when he was actually still wandering in a poetic desert.

Of course, Williams' impact was also, to a considerable
extent, a literary one; his presence, advice, and support de-
rived their authority from his work. In the fifties, more-
over, Williams' writing assumed an historical role. Robert
Lowell wrote of T. S. Eliot that "his influence is every-
where inescapable, and nowhere really usable."[73] Many
young poets found Williams "usable" precisely because he
had opened a kind of underground railroad route out of the
domination of Eliot. More specifically, Williams established
a creative alternative to the domestication of Modernism
accomplished in the 1950s by the Anglicanized Eliot, the
New Critics, and the young formalist poets. Together, they
produced the reign of the well-wrought symbolist poem—a
detached, genteel, and attenuated mode of writing that soon
created a literary impasse.[74] Williams' impact in this histori-
cal context is revealed in a letter Allen Ginsberg wrote to
his father. Traveling in Italy in 1957, Ginsberg met W. H.
Auden in a cafe on the Isle of Ischia and opened the con-
versation by quoting the beginning of "Song of Myself":

> and Auden said, "O but my dear, that's so *wrong*, and so
> *shameless*, it's an utterly bad line—when I hear that I feel
> I must say please *don't* include me". . . . All this gives
> me the conviction, or strengthens the conviction I have
> had, that the republic of poetry needs a full scale revolu-
> tion and upsetting of 'values.' . . . In all this scene, with
> the great names like Auden and Marianne Moore trying

to be conservative, and Eliot ambiguous, and Pound partly nuts, Williams stands out as the only beautiful soul among the great poets who has tearfully clung to his humanity and has survived as a man to bequeath in America some semblance of the heritage of spiritual democracy in indestructible individuality.[75]

Williams' "indestructible individuality" affected a diversity of young poets and affected each of them differently, but the general character of his literary presence can be defined by a tribute in a letter from James Dickey:

I have been familiar with your own work for as long as I have known about poetry, and have admired its concreteness and the way the work seems to be letting the world have its own say, instead of serving as "material" for a "work of art."[76]

Dickey here identifies two of the key generative features of Williams' work: (1) concrete physicality—his literary realism; and (2) a conception of form as a process of unfolding which the poet lets happen *to* him—his poem as a field of action. Williams' notion of form, moreover, entails two further and more radical consequences: the purification of poetic speech—his American idiom; the re-making of the poetic line—his variable foot.

What may strike us, and probably struck his younger adherents, as an attractively loose and flexible set of principles are, however, different ways of making a single point—i.e., that the creative source is hidden in the moment, an energy that is at once present and absent. As Williams eloquently put it in an interview,

there's a lot yet to discover in the way we behave and what we do and what we think. And the way to discover it is to be an iconoclast, which means to break the icon, to get out from inside that strictly restricting mold or ritual, and get out, not because we want to get out of it, because the secret spirit of that ritual can exist not only in that form, but once that form is broken, the spirit of it comes out and can take again a form which will be more contemporary.[77]

Williams liked to think of himself as a secular poet; but his
remarks here reveal the basis of what became *the* obsession
of his old age: a sacred principle resides, hidden, in the
speech of the day, the American idiom. Unlike Eliot, Wil-
liams wanted popular linguistic energies to *restore* poetry.
His remarks also pose a double challenge. In the first place,
they require of subsequent poets that they find a way of
relating to Williams without ritualizing him; as Olson
wrote—more to himself than Williams—"let's love, not imi-
tate, you and ez."[78] But in an excruciating way, Williams'
conception of the progress of poetry challenges him to view
his own work as an icon that will in its turn be broken so
that the "secret spirit" it houses can live on.

Such detachment from one's own achievements is prob-
ably too much to ask of anyone, especially from a poet, like
Williams, rankled by long neglect. Williams' critics have
long accepted his self-idealization as someone who, at an
early age, attained an "inner security" that allowed him to
let things be.[79] But Williams was no Zen master; he was in
fact beset by all the self-doubts organic to his vocation of
poetry, exacerbated in his case by personal insecurities and
by the world's mystifying refusal to grant him much liter-
ary recognition, much less to realize his messianic dreams
for his own poetry. "I never had an audience until I was
past fifty," he bitterly remarked.[80] As he grew older, his
worries were aggravated by the mixed reception of *Pater-
son* and by ill health, but one way he cheered himself up
was by deferring to the next generation: "the whole future
of letters is in youth," he said.[81] The remark is a statement
of the obvious—but one we cannot imagine being made by
Eliot or Pound or Stevens or Frost. Still, the future was not
something Williams was prepared to leave to chance—or
the opposition. If at one moment he speaks of breaking "the
mold or ritual," at another he is imagining that "if we suc-
ceed" in inventing a new form, "others will cast their work
in the same mold."[82] One side of Williams was a tenderly
nurturing influence—a *maternal* father; another side was
strict, impositional—a *Puritan* father of the sort he most
despised. Williams wanted to "mold" youth, not just to let

them be; and the reason he was so involved with them was that their mission was to vindicate him and allay his self-doubts.

In 1944 Williams published an imaginary dialogue between Washington and Lafayette during the night following their victory at Monmouth. Just after the battle, Washington had furiously condemned a treacherous subordinate, General Lee, but he is now having second thoughts. The heroic liberator thus exposes his self-doubts to the younger man, who responds with an odd combination of boyish adulation and mature perspective.[83] In this allegory of intergenerational relations, written at the crisis point of Williams' sixtieth year, the function of younger men is to love, respect, and reassure their troubled elders, especially when they are betrayed by comrades who abandon the cause of freedom and, in effect, go over to Europe. So at 9 Ridge Road, support was a reciprocal affair, for younger writers were Williams' first real audience, compensating for the traitorous neglect of his own generation. A gratified Williams wrote to Lowell in 1948:

Whoever takes the trouble to read so carefully? I am deeply indebted to you. For even having read, who could have written so well? No one else that I know. It makes me think of my old friend Ez who knowing me since childhood, you might say, has never really digested anything I have put down. Never. All his favors have been "friendship." And you know what that means. Where in his Cantos which mention hundreds of intimates have you ever seen my shadow?[84]

Particularly satisfying for Williams were capitulations from the enemy camp; if Eliot had taken away all the younger poets of the twenties, now Williams could return the favor, plus inspiring a few desertions. The conversion of Lowell, thought to be Eliot's heir apparent in the late forties and early fifties, was Williams' prize catch, and when he read Life Studies he frankly admitted to Lowell that "this book in unrhymed verse brings one of my dreams for you into full fruit."[85] Similarly, he confessed to Denise Levertov that

> I have never forgot how you came to me out of the for-
> malism of English verse. At first as must have been in-
> evitable although I welcomed you I was not completely
> convinced, after all I wasn't completely convinced of my
> own position, I wanted YOU to convince ME.[86]

With moving candor, Williams here reveals both the uncer-
tainty behind his belligerent public polemics and his de-
pendency on young poets to justify him to others and to
himself.

Williams was not just looking for foot soldiers who would
march forward, lockstep, under his command; he wanted
something more like a band of zealous guerrillas loosely
bound by their hatred of a common foe. But he was still
sensitive to possible insubordination, which he sometimes
defined as anything like a dramatic show of independence.
More and more, he fretted over Ginsberg. "He went back,"
Williams said. "His longer lines don't seem to fit in with the
modern tendency at all. Retrograde. I don't like them at all
in *Howl!*"[87] Like many embarrassed prophets, Williams felt
impelled to declare some of his professed disciples to be
schismatics. "You don't feel then that to any extent you
have been a father of the Beat generation," an interviewer
asked him.

> No. No. It has been accidental that I knew Allen Gins-
> berg. My only association with him was that he had some-
> thing to say and I wanted him to say it. And I wanted to
> befriend him. But I am not thoroughly satisfied with
> what he has done. I have told him—I mean I am disgusted
> with him and his long lines.[88]

In a letter Ginsberg tried to reassure Williams:

> Don't worry also about my use of long line, the Whitman
> un-measure. I am trying to find it, I mean find a way to
> use it, how it can be varied and built into measured,
> measurable, visible, symmetries, without violating the nat-
> ural speech breath. It seemed to me 5 years ago logical
> next thing to approach scientifically, after all your experi-
> ence (and my little) with short line phrase and breath
> units.[89]

Ginsberg is conciliatory and he persuasively views his versi-
fication as the next evolutionary step out of Williams, whose
response remained that of an aggrieved and exasperated par-
ent: he had done *so* much for that boy, but—those long
lines! Even Lowell's literary pilgrimage had not brought
him all the way to Rutherford; and in a letter in which he is
trying to approach Lowell "with all defenses down,"
Williams can't resist a gentle reminder:

> Your use of the words is aristocratic—sometimes you use
> rhyme—but thank goodness less and less frequently and
> that is an improvement, you speak more to us, more di-
> rectly when you do not have to descend to it, your lan-
> guage gains in seriousness and ability in your choice of
> words when you abandon rhyme completely.[90]

Williams had difficulties letting go of the younger writers
he had finally won over. A testy individualist himself, he
resisted granting his sons and daughters their full indepen-
dence, and he most admired in them what he felt he had
placed there himself. For this reason, his introductions and
reviews—the more so as time went on—became occasions
for Williams to reiterate some of his favorite obsessions, es-
pecially his crusade for the American idiom; often the cost
of being confirmed by Williams was being appropriated as
the text for one of his sermons. Williams' correspondence
with younger writers was *voluminous*, so vast, so urgent, so
insistent in its repetitions of critical ideas that it becomes
hard not to realize that these letters served his needs as much
as any recipient's.[91] David Ignatow says that he read Wil-
liams' letters on two levels: on the one, that they were per-
sonal and "addressed to me," but on the second, "that of his
critical theories that virtually raged through the letters," it
was "as if he was addressing others beyond me . . . the
world of literary dogma." At the time Ignatow was uncon-
cerned with this world, but he sensed that

> Williams was in need of and in constant search of an au-
> dience that could listen and absorb what he had to say,
> in contrast to the silence he was meeting in the literary

world, that in singling me out for this excited, intellectual
discussion, he had found another potential adherent. . . .[92]

At such moments Williams was actually addressing himself
to at least three audiences: the young writer, the poetic and
human communities he felt shunned by, and himself. His
letters thus curiously combine intimacy with obsessive the-
oretical ruminations, warm encouragement with second
thoughts and grim warnings of the struggle ahead; they
urge openness—but they often do so dogmatically. In a
letter to Denise Levertov, Williams wrote,

> The presence of poetry is an evasive thing. Don't speak
> again of what I have written here but forget it. But go on, as
> I don't need to urge you to do, writing of those things of
> which you have written in this poem.[93]

At first Williams is instructional; then he tries to efface him-
self and tells her to forget what he's said—but this is itself a
directive; then he returns to the more explicitly directive
mode, while claiming he is only telling her what she already
knows. At other times Williams could be downright patron-
izing, as he is in another letter to Levertov:

> You need a book of your closely chosen work. I think, if
> you thought out and selected your choice very carefully,
> it would be one of the most worthwhile books of the
> generation. It would have to be a small book squeezed up
> to get the gists alone of what you have to say. Much
> would have to be omitted. You may not be old enough
> yet to know your own mind for it would have to be a
> thoughtful, an adult book of deep feeling that would re-
> veal you in what may not want to be revealed. I am
> curious to know what you are thinking—you never say.
> But you reveal more by your poems than can be easily
> deciphered and that is what draws a reader on. Perhaps
> you will never be able to say what you want to say. In
> that case you make me feel that the loss will be great.[94]

As we've seen, Williams could be supportive, tolerant, and
acute in his correspondence; here his praise ("one of the
most worthwhile books of the generation") is immediately

qualified by his emphasis on how much needs to be omitted from this book, then further eroded by his fear that Levertov may not be equal to the task. At first his doubts about whether the thirty-one-year-old poet is "old enough to know" her "own mind" and produce "an adult book of deep feeling" are merely condescending; later, they become fairly devastating: "perhaps you will never be able to say what you want to say." Williams' reservations, moreover, have a lot to do with the fact that Levertov is a woman; at the heart of his apprehensions is his lifelong fascination/frustration with woman as mystery ("I am curious to know what you are thinking—you never say")—with Levertov here imagined as the elusive Kora and Williams an anxious Pluto, eager to possess her. Williams is not cutting, as Frost had been with his Bread Loaf student, or vituperative, as Pound had been with Ginsberg, but he does make clear who is the master, who the subordinate.

Williams' motives in his engagements with younger writers were thus neither selfless generosity nor personal aggrandizement but a mixture of both. His private insecurities and his public battles made him eager to enlist, to instruct, to direct, and so to triumph. Yet, whatever his motives, his interest, along with his writing, stimulated, encouraged, and in many cases profoundly altered the work of new poets. If youthful displays of independence sometimes made him nervous, he still had no more the power to excommunicate than to canonize. So by the late fifties Williams himself had become an icon, which subsequent poets have been free to worship, break, or recast. The styles of *Life Studies* and "Howl," to mention just two examples, bear no resemblance to each other—or to the style of Williams. Early in his career, Williams had shrewdly observed that "the only way to be like Whitman is to write *unlike* Whitman."[95] Sometimes the doctor-poet wrote prescriptions for his young patients that were really remedies for his own ills, but at his and their best he helped two generations of American poets to realize that, by learning to write unlike Williams, they could *be* like him.

J. E. B. B.

Notes

[1] *Babel to Byzantium* (New York, 1971), p. 191.

[2] *Open Between Us,* ed. Ralph J. Mills, Jr. (Ann Arbor, 1980), p. 127.

[3] *Poetry,* 89 (October 1956): 52.

[4] *The Craft of Poetry,* ed. William Packard (New York, 1974), p. 11.

[5] *The Poet in the World* (New York, 1973), p. 90.

[6] "Someone Ought to Say Williams," *Iowa Review,* 7, 4 (Fall 1976): 83.

[7] In this essay I confine my remarks to American poets, although this collection demonstrates Williams' positive response to British poetry (Tomlinson and Thomas), French poetry (Breton and Char), Canadian poetry (Irving Layton), Italian poetry (G. G. Belli), and Chinese poetry (the Rexroth translation).

[8] *Open Between Us,* p. 175.

[9] Ian Hamilton, *Robert Lowell, A Biography* (New York, 1982), p. 336.

[10] *I Wanted to Write a Poem* (Boston, 1958), p. 30.

[11] *Open Between Us,* p. 175.

[12] *The Notebooks of David Ignatow* (Chicago, 1973), pp. 75–76.

[13] *Poetry and Repression* (New Haven and London: Yale University Press, 1976), p. 2.

[14] *Robert Lowell, A Biography,* pp. 336–37.

[15] Donald Hall, *Remembering Poets* (New York, 1978), pp. 48–49.

[16] "Ezra Pound," in *Ezra Pound, A Collection of Critical Essays,* ed. Walter Sutton (Englewood Cliffs, N.J., 1963), p. 18.

[17] Michael Reck, *Ezra Pound, A Close-Up* (New York, 1967), p. 95.

[18] The letter, n.d. but soon after May 25, 1952, is in the Williams collection, Beinecke Library, Yale University. Subsequent references will be to the Yale collection.

[19] See the Pound chapters in Hall's *Remembering Poets* and Allen Ginsberg, "Encounters with Ezra Pound," *City Lights Anthology* (1974): 9–21.

[20] For an account of Eliot as an editor, see F. V. Morley, "T. S. Eliot as Publisher," in *T. S. Eliot, A Symposium,* ed. Richard March and Tambimuttu (Chicago, 1949), pp. 160–70.

[21] *T. S. Eliot, A Life* (New York, 1984), p. 182.

[22] *The Thirties and After* (New York, 1978), pp. 207–08.

[23] According to Stephen Spender, *T. S. Eliot* (New York, 1975), p. 51.

[24] *The Thirties and After,* p. 208.

[25] Quoted in *T. S. Eliot, A Life,* p. 224.

[26] *The Thirties and After,* p. 208.

[27] "Milton II," *Selected Prose of T. S. Eliot,* ed. Frank Kermode (New York, 1975), p. 273.

28 *Letters Home,* ed. Aurelia Schober Plath (New York, 1975), p. 381.

29 *Remembering Poets,* pp. 47–48.

30 "William Carlos Williams," in *William Carlos Williams, A Collection of Critical Essays,* ed. J. Hillis Miller (Englewood Cliffs, N.J., 1966), p. 158.

31 Robert Lowell to William Carlos Williams, Feb. 15, 1959, in the Yale collection.

32 Alison Colbert, "A Talk with Allen Ginsberg," *Partisan Review,* 38, 3 (1971): 295.

33 For Williams' efforts to persuade Random House, see the letters from Williams to Ginsberg, April 7, 1952 and May 24, 1952, in the Allen Ginsberg Archives, Columbia University. Subsequent references will be made to the Columbia collection. The quotation is from the April 7 letter; the letters of introduction were enclosed with the May 24 letter.

34 Marianne Moore to Allen Ginsberg, July 4, 1952, in the Columbia collection.

35 Marianne Moore to Allen Ginsberg, Jan. 24, 1957, in the Columbia collection.

36 For Williams' relation to Nardi, see Paul Mariani, *William Carlos Williams, A New World Naked* (New York, 1981), pp. 586–87, and Theodora Graham, " 'Her Heigh Compleynte': The Cress Letters of . . . *Paterson,"* in *Ezra Pound and William Carlos Williams,* ed. Daniel Hoffman (Philadelphia, 1983), pp. 164–93.

37 Allen Ginsberg to me, in conversation, August 4, 1984.

38 William Carlos Williams to Denise Levertov, August 23, 1954. This and subsequent letters from Williams to Levertov are quoted with the kind permission of Denise Levertov.

39 *Selected Letters of Theodore Roethke,* ed. Ralph J. Mills, Jr. (Seattle, 1968), p. 146.

40 William Carlos Williams to Theodore Roethke, Sept. 26, 1941, in the Yale collection.

41 William Carlos Williams to Theodore Roethke, Nov. 14, 1944, in the Yale collection.

42 *Selected Letters of Theodore Roethke,* p. 146.

43 Allen Ginsberg to William Carlos Williams, March 10, 1952, in the Yale collection.

44 *Ibid.*

45 William Carlos Williams to Allen Ginsberg, Feb. 27, 1952, in the Columbia collection.

46 Allen Ginsberg to William Carlos Williams, March 10, 1952, in the Columbia collection.

47 *Ibid.* The poems were taken from the "Notebook, 1950–1952," in the Columbia collection; once Williams had affirmed the poems, keeping the journals became a less spontaneous activity for Ginsberg. Just before the entry for March 11, 1952, Ginsberg notes: "Here Williams told me poems from Journal were poetry. Henceforth everything has added self-consciousness."

48 *Ibid.*

49 *Ibid.*

[50] From a conversation with Williams transcribed in the "Notebook, 1950–1952," June 28, 1952, in the Columbia collection.

[51] See William Carlos Williams to Allen Ginsberg, May 24, 1952, in the Columbia collection, and "Explanations," by Ginsberg, n.d., in the Yale collection.

[52] William Carlos Williams to Theodore Roethke, n.d., in the Yale collection.

[53] *The Selected Letters of William Carlos Williams*, ed. John C. Thirlwall (New York, 1957), p. 260.

[54] *Ibid.*, p. 262.

[55] Robert Lowell to William Carlos Williams, Jan. 22, 1958, in the Yale collection. The text actually reads: "I have no masters, only masters, you are about the first among them," and my transcription assumes that the "s" in the first "masters" is a slip.

[56] William Carlos Williams to Robert Lowell, November 12, 1948, in the Lowell collection, Houghton Library, Harvard University. Subsequent references will be to the Harvard collection.

[57] William Carlos Williams to Robert Lowell, March 16, 1954, in the Harvard collection.

[58] Robert Lowell to William Carlos Williams, March 19, [1954], in the Yale collection.

[59] Robert Lowell to William Carlos Williams, April 26, [1951], in the Yale Collection.

[60] *Ibid.*

[61] *Ibid.*

[62] Robert Lowell to William Carlos Williams, Dec. 3, 1947, in the Yale collection.

[63] Robert Lowell to William Carlos Williams, Sept. 30, 1957, in the Yale collection.

[64] Robert Lowell to William Carlos Williams, Feb. 19, 1958, in the Yale collection.

[65] Robert Lowell to William Carlos Williams, n.d. [1952], in the Yale collection.

[66] *Robert Lowell, A Biography*, p. 237.

[67] *Ibid.*

[68] William Carlos Williams to Robert Lowell, Nov. 24, 1958, in the Harvard collection.

[69] William Carlos Williams to Denise Levertov, n.d. [1957].

[70] *Open Between Us*, p. 127. Philip Whalen recalls the similar impact Williams had on a visit to Reed College: Williams "was interested in what we had to say. He made us feel like poets, not students any more; he talked to us as if we were his equals. It was at that point, I think, that I really could begin to take myself seriously as a writer." " 'Goldberry Is Waiting'; or, P.W., His Magic Education as a Poet," *The Poetics of the New American Poetry*, ed. Donald M. Allen and Warren Tallman (New York, 1973), p. 455.

[71] Williams' statement: "He can go anywhere and indeed shows a will to go SOMEwhere—if he can keep focussed on what he reveals here. . . . This whole poem is possessed by a deep feeling which gives the poem the impact of unity. I don't seem to be able to get over that poem, I think it major work, it should be at least in one of the

more important magazines, it is so much better than what I see printed anywhere there that I am astonished." Quoted in *Nimrod*, 1, 3 (Spring 1957): [7].

72 In a 1939 letter to the editors of *Furioso*, Williams wrote that Pound "has taken the attitude of being little interested in the intermediary steps, his attack and thoughts being occupied with nothing but the peaks of interest," while he urged the young editors of the new magazine to "print the kids—print 'em bald, fragmentarily, scattered, in part, a line, a bit and paragraph FOR THE GOOD IN IT . . . eliminating everything but the good piece which MAY appear later as a considered work." *Selected Letters*, p. 182.

73 "T. S. Eliot," unpublished essay [1965] in the Harvard collection.

74 For a fuller account of this historical crisis, see my *From Modern to Contemporary: American Poetry, 1945–1965* (Chicago, 1984).

75 Allen Ginsberg to Louis Ginsberg, Sept. 1, 1957, in the Columbia collection.

76 James Dickey to William Carlos Williams, Nov. 22, 1957, in the Yale collection.

77 John W. Gerber and Emily M. Wallace, "An Interview with William Carlos Williams," in *Interviews with William Carlos Williams*, ed. Linda Wagner (New York, 1976), pp. 25–26.

78 Charles Olson to William Carlos Williams, April 21, 1950, in the Yale collection.

79 *The Selected Letters of William Carlos Williams*, p. 147.

80 Dorothy Tooker, "The Editors Meet William Carlos Williams," *Interview with William Carlos Williams*, p. 31.

81 *Ibid.*, pp. 34–35.

82 *Ibid.*, p. 34.

83 *The University of Kansas City Review*, 11 (Autumn 1944): 26–28.

84 William Carlos Williams to Robert Lowell, June 12, 1948, in the Harvard collection.

85 William Carlos Williams to Robert Lowell, Dec. 4, 1957, in the Harvard collection.

86 William Carlos Williams to Denise Levertov, Feb. 11, 1957.

87 Walter Sutton, "A Visit with William Carlos Williams," *Interviews with William Carlos Williams*, p. 41.

88 *Ibid.*, p. 56.

89 Allen Ginsberg to William Carlos Williams, Jan. 23, [1959], in the Yale Collection.

90 William Carlos Williams to Robert Lowell, Nov. 24, 1958, in the Harvard collection.

91 Among other, lesser-known figures, the younger poets Williams corresponded with included Mary Barnard, Cid Corman, Robert Creeley, Richard Eberhart, Allen Ginsberg, David Ignatow, Denise Levertov, Robert Lowell, Charles Olson, Theodore Roethke, Gilbert Sorrentino, Charles Tomlinson, and Louis Zukofsky.

92 *Open Between Us*, p. 177.

93 William Carlos Williams to Denise Levertov, Jan. 6, 1954.

94 William Carlos Williams to Denise Levertov, Aug. 23, 1954.

95 "America, Whitman, and the Art of Poetry," *The Poetry Journal* (November 1917): 31.

Advice to the Young Poet

View, 1942

ALL OUR *efforts as writers and as men must be to release the enchained dragon within us. That it may not exist is no concern of the critic, we presume that it does. Enchained by whom? By ourselves, naturally, who else?*

There in all the colors of shells and crystals, as certain as chemistry, lives the thing we are, its connection with our senses afferent and direct. Subconsciously we cannot lie.

But to give it efferent channels is another matter. It is an unwilling witness and there is no easy way to bring it to time—it is convenient to be a liar and too often the mark of culture—no way for the poet to unleash it but one open to all the destroying winds of the world and the world beyond the world.

By words only can it be called up. Give your dragon the words and it will bear witness.

Since when in modern times must we condone the effrontery of him who would predetermine the mold and complexion of the supernatural, delimiting that only as good which to him seems desirable?

Your business is to see that all avenues of egress are kept open between what is inside you and the page. To do otherwise inaugurates a steady process of deterioration in a writer. And that isn't the half of it—unsuitable for this letter.

Select the good! Certainly we must select the good—as

Essay in *View,* 2, 3 (Oct. 1942): 23.

*witnessed by our dragon from within. As poets we must se-
lect what is pertinent to us as poets. Unless you follow that
order in full belief you will come into contact with right-
eousness of a sort you may not be prepared to face.*

*No one cares what blinders you choose to wear and you
may call good what you will. But unless the dragon speak
it. . . You may blather in Greek of the wisdom of the an-
cients to your heart's content and wear the motley of the
very church, but if as a poet you do not rouse the dragon
within you, unscathed! you are by that so much more the
fool.*

*Consciously, sitting before a piece of paper with only
words as our weapons every trick of the imagination offers
itself to defeat us. Our job is to reveal what we are by what
we have apprehended. It must be sensual for that is our only
contact with the world. And there it IS, crouching within
us—a mold packed with the images of ten million minutes
before we have learned so much as to drink from a cup.*

*The art is to get through to the fact and make it eloquent.
We have to make a direct contact, from the sense to the ob-
ject (within us) so that what we disclose is peeled, acute,
virulent . . . But we too easily get to thinking of the effect.
The effect! On whom? The effect has nothing whatever to
do with the matter. It is an accidental by-product of the
work, to focus there is to say that the eye is simply not on
the object.*

*For words are dangerous principally to the users of them.
Sometimes they work release in a man young enough not to
have learned the trick of being a liar. Wait a while, the
words will soon bring lies enough for him, generations of
lies have been bred into them by careful selection. Like it or
not words for a poet are everything. And there the lies
begin.*

*Yet the unlying dragon within us can only be called up
by an incantation of words. How? Shall we go learn the
words at an academy? Shall we?*

Academies are the cemeteries of all dragons. Avoid them.

There behind fences they stand on the defensive, protecting knowledge—as they would have it, clerks at the best, awaiting a master—shoved there to be rid of them. At the worst unmentionable.

But wait a minute. Avoid scholars but do not avoid their knowledge. Be sure only that it is not conditioned by their assumptions of learning. Infamous blackguards when too far gone "willing" themselves to their maimed attitudes. Remember that as degree men they are no more than clerks locking knowledge in awaiting a master. Get what they have, at your peril! Get it if you have to murder them for it. For without knowledge and its coinage of words, born in you or stolen, you will never raise anything by your abracadabras but straw.

Get what you need, get it if necessary the way Bill Suckaround got his, through a horse's head. They have never forgiven him for it, stealing their bacon. Within us lies imprisoned the infinitely multiplex quarry, only a channel of words will release it, words related to the senses, not learned at school—whose witness will be the instinctive movements of a nascent thing, a variety, living and firm—not those of a hack or a seal trained to say papa.

An "Objectivists" Anthology

Edited by Louis Zukofsky

The Symposium, 1933

THE DIFFICULTY in facing a "new" work, critically, is first to see then to say something about it that in its particularity will be new also, certainly something that will be at least of an equal freshness with the work itself. But most often we set in motion an antiquated machine whose enormous creaking and heavy and complicated motions frighten the birds, flatten the grass and fill the whole countryside with smoke. Zukofsky's present work will yield nothing to that approach.

His "Objectivists" Anthology of modern poetry is faulty, the poems presented are of uneven interest (he did not have a world of time, material or resources at his disposal) but it presents a new and valuable viewpoint toward the subject, a maximum objectification of the poetic means, together with some strikingly original work including the whole, to date, of his own long poem "*A*." He has had something to say and has made a book of it, excellently. The preface should be read also but not stodgily.

Had *he* not said it it would not have been said. It is the presentation, simply, of certain new objects without obvious connection with the classics and which he entitles "poems." These poems being in many cases outside the recognized limits of that which has been done before have, therefore, a

---

Review of *An "Objectivists" Anthology*, ed. Louis Zukofsky (Le Beausset, Var, France and New York: To Publishers, 1932); in *The Symposium*, Concord, N.H., 1 (Jan. 1933): 114–16. Williams himself contributed seventeen poems to the anthology.

tendency to emphasize the classical. And so, for the same reason, they suggest to the mind a classical which would be modern and which, in a sense, they represent. Certainly, unless it be discovered that out of that which has been accepted as classic excellence in the past a way has been found for an expansion of the sense to include the present, the former classic excellence must be said to be merely dead. But the new having emerged it affirms as no copy could the continued existence of the old.

> Then appeared
> like a seal through a paper hoop
> the scarlet egg of the lunation
> roaring through the sky
> uprooting the brass trees
> passing noiselessly
> over the deserted cities
> over the ghosts in nickel shrouds
> over the moss green and purple headlands
> over the grey sea.

> *Kenneth Rexroth, "Fundamental Disagreement with Two Contemporaries"*

By taking words, of which writing is solely made, and words which in the classical have been supposed to have an exact meaning and movement among themselves and by using them in a way (as stated above) to emphasize the *worth* of that which has existed before while differing from it in *form* a purely objective method is at least intimated.

> The further room
> the root of light
> the staff
> given in the asian night
> carried across Europe
> planted in Glastonbury
> the unguent

> broken on the hair
> Bread figs cheese olives grapes wine
> the swords rest
> mustered for war on the field of law
> glories of kingdom
> o lord of herds
> and these
> objects
> the plume of mimosa
> brushing the roof
>
> *Rexroth, "The Place, for Yvor Winters"*

It is a poetry of conviction. It is not, surely, the law. Nor is it a treatise against the law. But it presents, with objective purity, that of which the law is made. These pieces, these lines, these words, neither are they fragments but their power is cumulative rather in tension than in story. There is nothing here that seductively takes us up—as a man might carry a child. Nor is reason used to cudgel the mind into unwilling submission. The attack is by simple presentation, perhaps confrontation would be the better term.

If Rexroth is the prime example, Rakosi reiterates the intent from a warmer level—

> An ideal
> like a canary
> singing in the dark
> for appleseed and barley
>
> *Carl Rakosi, "A Journey Away"*

Zukofsky's own long poem is of a similar choice but, again, a variant. It refuses to be understood as a series of pictures. It seems broken, over-abbreviated. But unless I am mistaken, though a "scene" is often indicated, a "scene" which is nearly always absent in Rexroth's poems, the aggregate tonality, as with Rexroth, is the major objective. It is to make this up that the word-characters have been united and from it in each poem they take their connotative significance in that case.

> On that morning when everything
>   will be clear,
> Greeting, myself, Rimbaud
>   with glasses,
> The world's earth spread a rose,
>   rose every particle,
> The palm of the hand lie open
>   earth's lily,
> One will see
>   gravel in gravel
> Stray bits
>   of burnt matches
> Glass,
>   disused rubber,
> Scrape heels of shoes,
>   and not trip,
> Not that one will get, see,
>   more than particulars,

> *Rest thee softly, softly rest.*

> Preparing to receive the captain of industry,
> Emptied one full clothes closet and, when he came,
> Said—"My dear Magnus, here is entirely to yourself
> A closet for your suspenders."

> *Louis Zukofsky, "A"*

Poems by Basil Bunting, Mary Butts, Robert McAlmon, T. S. Eliot, Frances Fletcher, Ezra Pound, George Oppen, Charles Reznikoff, Jerry Reisman, R. B. N. Warriston, and W. C. Williams complete the list.

All through the anthology an objective level is sought.

The collaborations are added to show that the personality of the writer must be suspect. If a poem is made of words those words are not sacred. They may be arranged (provided they are capable of retaining any meaning at all) in a somewhat new order and the sense *perhaps* be clarified.

It is the gesture of collaboration, infuriating to nearly all writers, which is more important than the particular success of the pieces which have been used for the exercise.

And so, the poems making up this anthology and which Zukofsky has selected to point his purpose are various but they are successfully displayed to hold an objective view of poetry which, in a certain way, clarifies it, showing it to be not a seductive arrangement of scenes, sounds and colors so much as a construction each part of which has a direct bearing on its meaning as a whole, an objectification of significant particulars.

The music of Bach has been adopted by Zukofsky in his own poem particularly as a pattern. In Bach, not as with the music of some other later composers, it seems not to be the purpose to seduce the sense by leading it away from the value of the notes (words) as musical particulars. On the contrary, though a sequence of sounds is attained it is never a "burden" of necessity less than themselves.

The Element of Time: Advice to a Young Writer

The Harvard Advocate, 1934

IF GENIUS has anything to say in America it had better be strongwinded. Because a life, contrary to the classic opinion, is endless. There is plenty of time. And no hurry. Nobody ever overtakes anybody else. Longwindedness is always a competitor and has to be lived down but even that dies finally from living in its vacuum. Then genius has its chance. Nothing grows old.

The only thing necessary is to have something to say when at last the opportunity comes to say it. But most blurt it out, or try to, breathlessly before or during puberty, and then look around for the next opportunity. It has passed.

Certainly, let everything there is to be said go into it, any time. That's probably everything there is in you—so rottenly imperfect that God himself couldn't make head nor tail of it till he'd worked on you for a few years longer. Using the figure of "God."

In youth the violences usually have a great element of justice about them. Maybe it's only drink. There's a whole philosophy in that too. But it's a tough career. Taking something of a lesser sweep, or a greater one, it's no matter, the good of it, I wish to say, comes only to full flavor by intense doggedness.

Essay in *The Harvard Advocate*, 120, 4 (Feb. 1934): 10; reprinted in *Harvard Advocate Centennial Anthology*, ed. Jonathan D. Culler (Cambridge: Schenkman Publishing Co., 1966), pp. 197–98.

I'd go so far as to say that everything a man can be taught in his youth has only this value, that unless he is a man it will kill him. Whatever he sees, whatever is brilliant to him, closest, most significant, no matter what anyone else says about it, that is the thing he's got to work with till he disproves it or makes it into a satisfying whole. And for this, there is an ocean of time.

I emphasize, it isn't the mass of difficulties that need unhorse a genius. It is the slipping, sliding wastefulness of useless rushing about. There isn't much to do. It's just the flip of a word sometimes. One doesn't have to live this kind of life, that kind of life. The only thing that has ever seemed to me to be important is never to yield an inch of what is to the mind important—and to let the life take care of itself. Sure, go ahead to Paris. Why not?

Life gets to be a battering down of the inessential. But if something doesn't come up out of the scaffolding when that is removed. And if that hasn't been essentially there from the time the first hair sprouted on the belly—in spite of all the whackings it got. Then, why not have stuck a flag at the peak of the lumber after all and called it a day.

And nobody can't tell you nothing about what you gotta do. Listen to them and take a lesson. You'll see what I mean.

The writer has an opportunity in this country that is unequaled elsewhere. But he's got to live through being a worm in the manure heap. Nowhere is there the intensity of uninformation that, I am assured, will be found in the House of Representatives. Nowhere else on earth. Not even China where childishness was, at least until quite recently, a glamorous spectacle in the adult. But in this country everything is still broken apart.

If anybody can hold to anything and cling to it long enough to have it be beaten into some shape by the holding and the onslaught, it will at least be refined enough for one to make out clearly its original futility. And even that would be a distinction.

It's not likely, though, that anyone with any intelligence

at all will be able to hold to something wholly futile throughout a lifetime. He might though. If he is a supreme genius.

But there's no way of eliminating stupidity, the way it will take, from any instructions.

Anyone who has survived to this point, and finds the times rather tough—though I was referring more to the preceding paragraphs than the times—might profit by the following and realize that today is a comparatively enlightened era after all. Tomorrow writing may be even more highly honored for the indestructible accuracy reflecting the adjustment between the page and the unbeaten mind of the writer there is in it.

No, I don't think I'll tell that story after all.

Sequence and Change

The Literary Workshop, 1934

I HAVE been asked to criticise the five poems in Vol. I, No. 1, of THE LITERARY WORKSHOP, the national organ for student expression. The poems are, "Earth Bound," by Ellen Saltonstall; "Tilden Street," by Mary Helen Jones; "Pictures in a Mirror," by Evelyn Marjorie Brown; "To Walt Whitman," by Raymond Nathan, and "The Park," by Myra Dixon. I find them free from obvious inversion of phrase, free from "poetic" diction, passably idiomatic, that is to say, fairly sensitive to the spoken American language, and their authors reasonably alert to the malevolence of "standard" metrical effects. But in respect of an advanced feeling for use of words in the poetic line I do not think any one of them is as expert as that by Elizabeth Gallagher, "Thistle in the Desert," which won the *Forum Prize* this year, the best student poem submitted in competition with about three thousand others:

Along the arid ridges of this waste
Only the thistle twists its bitter roots.
In water-courses long-dry freshets traced,
The reeds lie sere with dust in all their flutes.
Even the wind is lured to hidden death

Comment on student poems in *The Literary Workshop*, New York, 1, 2 (1934): 50–53. Williams had been asked to comment on five poems in the previous issue of *The Literary Workshop* but instead attends mainly to a student poem by Elizabeth Gallagher he had seen in *The New York Times*.

Here where the sun makes brittle the airiest bones.
There is no green thing here, no fugitive breath
Of life but the thistle springing among bare stones.
When will the wild heart learn, and be appeased
For its loneliness by the thistle's purple flower?
The transient bloom that death has already seized
Knows victory for one precarious hour.
What would the heart ask more than its ancient dower?—
Thistle in the desert, and once a purple flower.

Therefore, to get the most out of a few words, such as I
intend, and to avoid direct comparisons, which I do not care
to make, let me speak indirectly of the five poems in ques-
tion by attempting to evaluate Miss Gallagher's prize-
winning sonnet from at least one elementary viewpoint.
Being in the same class with the poems under discussion I
may possibly be able to throw a little light upon those.

I saw Miss Gallagher's poem in *The New York Times* as
a news item. This was particularly fortunate to my present
purpose, since it gave the precise matrix which all poems,
when they are published, must face in the world; a quite in-
different, quite irrelevant tissue of "general interest." That
the newspaper comment is typically valueless as criticism
need cause no astonishment in itself. But that the attitude of
mind revealed there may possibly have an influence on those
none too sure of themselves in a field which few succeed in
crossing to solid achievement, gives me my opportunity.

"College Jazz Era at End, Poets Show," begins the col-
umn. "Conservative Type of Student Revealed in Contest,
Editor Says." "Rhyme Scorned no More." Then among
other things it goes on to say that, "Ninety per cent of the
poetry received was rhymed." "The iconoclastic brooder
and gin drinker" has been displaced by a more conservative,
optimistic type of college student, to whom rhyme is natu-
ral, no doubt. The co-eds' verse is about "home, babies and
the emotions of motherhood." And so it goes on. It has, to
be sure, the tone of William Lyon Phelps commenting on

Gertrude Stein's opera, *Four Saints in Three Acts*, but for all that it has nothing to do with poetry.

Now take one of the line pairs from Miss Gallagher's sonnet, very irregularly rhymed, by the way:

> There is no green thing here,
> No fugitive breath
> Of life but the thistle springing
> Among bare stones.

There is about them, I would agree with the judges, something distinguished, as is the whole poem, for one clear reason: a sensitive musical integrity of the words to the emotion *and* the speech of our day.

There would be little reason for me to go further had it not been for the bad context in which I found the poem I have quoted in the newspaper. Let it be understood that the term "radical" as associated with what is apparently loosely constructed verse and "conservative" as associated with regular rhyme forms, have no legitimate meanings. "Radical" has to do with a return of the understanding to the root of a matter, while "conservative" signifies an intention to conserve the basis, or roots, of an understanding. They are identical in purport. Both have as their objective not an essential opposition to each other, as supposed, but an intention mutually to destroy mediocrity, sham and general stupidity, the fear of excellence, underlying the journalistic exhibition to which I have just referred.

The true situation, as I attempted to indicate in the title to this writing, "Sequence and Change," as they are related to the writing of poetry, would be something as follows: Twenty years ago rhyme was largely discarded in the writing of verse for a very good reason. This was that all manner of trite rot was thought to be poetry "in the best circles," unfortunately those with the greatest economic influence, merely because it disclosed some recognizable rhyme scheme. And what rhymes! The meager resources of the English language in this respect had been completely ignored. The words had been so man-handled, hackneyed and generally made vulgar that the final effect to any sensitive ear was the very opposite of that probably intended. And under this grease of trite rhyme, for this is the point of most importance, the most banal of line structures was permitted to fill the page. Poetry was then thought to be all "meaning" to which the rhyme added a grace, "so you could know it was poetry." When it came to a question of capable *structure*, nobody knew what you were talking about.

It became imperative under the circumstance to let rhyme go, not only to let it go but to drive it out. One might have thought with some confidence that the "influences" would have at once guessed the point of the project—thinking as they could not have helped doing of the history of English poetry.

Much was made apparent once the dirty draping of rhyme was torn down and the light let into the line itself, which poetry is. No amount of "radical" "conservative" talk should permit that gain, a true sequence, to be lost today, as it may very well be. Perhaps Miss Gallagher has some knowledge of and feeling for Latin or even Greek poetry or maybe she has heard of the "experiments" of Robert Bridges who was the English Poet Laureate. In any case her ear seems to be attuned to what in verse is called quantity. Perhaps it is only when that true sense for the quantity of a poetic line is lost that poets turn to rhyme as a last resort.

At least this sense for quantity Miss Gallagher has. She is moved by it to avoid certain worn-out cadences which brings as a result the use of the "natural" word. There is, in short, thank God, some acceptable correlation evidenced between feeling and the words in position in the line, an indispensable consonance.

This comes, I should say, first from having intensely "seen" the object written about. And when I say "seen" I have reference to a complex process: it is the point of fusion between an object and an emotion. For this reason poems, to exist at all, must be and are essentially sensual. The senses have perceived an identity between something in their world and a "reality," if you wish to call it that, within.

The thing thus "known" becomes a personal possession. And this personal possession of knowledge is the thing that the reader looks for in what has been put on the page without which he finds nothing for him of deep interest. This is revealed by the variable quantity of the line (not wholly so, of course) of which I have been speaking. It is revealed above all by slight variations, slightly displaced emphases in the line structure.

Thus a poem is made up of peculiarly feeling observation and a sensitive musicality, variability and balance of emphasis in the line to match that. Rhyme may help but it may just as well ruin this effect. Accuracy to sight (or other sensual function) coupled with an accurate adjustment to the emotion engendered (tho' it more probably causes the vision than comes from it) are the foundations of excellence.

All bad poems are inaccurate poems.

There is in a bad poem either inaccuracy in observation or the construction of the vehicle which is to contain it— one fitted artificially to the other. The nearer this dual process comes to perfection the likelier is the individual to come to that which makes for lasting excellence.

All this to say that though times change it would be wise, always, for the young writer not to believe all that he hears glibly spoken. But to discover, if he can, by personal observation the reasons which prompted his immediate progenitors in the art to do as they did. Thus he will be in a position to preserve the great sequences of poetry, even by differing with them.

The New Poetical Economy

George Oppen's Discrete Series

Poetry, 1934

MR. OPPEN has given us thirty-seven pages of short poems, well-printed and well-bound, around which several statements relative to modern verse forms may well be made.

The appearance of a book of poems, if it be a book of good poems, is an important event because of relationships the work it contains will have with thought and accomplishment in other contemporary reaches of the intelligence. This leads to a definition of the term "good." If the poems in the book constitute necessary corrections of or emendations to human conduct in their day, both as to thought and manner, then they are good. But if these changes originated in the poems, causing thereby a direct liberation of the intelligence, then the book becomes of importance to the highest degree.

But this importance cannot be in what the poem says, since in that case the fact that it is a poem would be a redundancy. The importance lies in what the poem *is*. Its existence as a poem is of first importance, a technical matter, as with all facts, compelling the recognition of a mechanical structure. A poem which does not arouse respect for the technical requirements of its own mechanics may have anything you please painted all over it or on it in the way of

---

Review of George Oppen, *Discrete Series* (New York: The Objectivist Press, 1934); in *Poetry*, 44, 4 (July 1934): 220–25. The Preface to Oppen's book is by Ezra Pound.

meaning but it will for all that be as empty as a man made of wax or straw.

It is the acceptable fact of a poem as a mechanism that is the proof of its meaning and this is as technical a matter as in the case of any other machine. Without the poem being a workable mechanism in its own right, a mechanism which arises from, while at the same time it constitutes the meaning of, the poem as a whole, it will remain ineffective. And what it says regarding the use or worth of that particular piece of "propaganda" which it is detailing will never be convincing.

The preface seems to me irrelevant. Why mention something which the book is believed definitely not to resemble? "Discrete" in the sense used by Mr. Oppen, is, in all probability, meant merely to designate a series separate from other series. I feel that he is justified in so using the term. It has something of the implications about it of work in a laboratory when one is following what he believes to be a profitable lead along some one line of possible investigation.

This indicates what is probably the correct way to view the book as well as the best way to obtain pleasure from it. Very few people, not to say critics, see poetry in their day as a moment in the long-drawn periodic progress of an ever-changing activity toward occasional peaks of surpassing excellence. Yet these are the correct historic facts of the case. These high periods rest on the continuity of what has gone before. As a corollary, most critics fail to connect up the apparently dissociated work of the various men writing contemporaneously in a general scheme of understanding. Most commentators are, to be sure, incapable of doing so since they have no valid technical knowledge of the difficulties involved, what has to be destroyed since it is dead, and what saved and treasured. The dead, granted, was once alive but now it is dead and it stinks.

The term, technical excellence, has an unpoetic sound to most ears. But if an intelligence be deeply concerned with the bringing up of the body of poetry to a contemporary level equal with the excellences of other times, technique means everything. Surely an apprentice watching his master sees nothing prosaic about the details of technique. Nor would he find a narrow world because of the smallness of the aperture through which he views it, but through that pinhole, rather, a world enormous as his mind permits him to witness.

A friend sticks his head in at the door and says, "Why all the junk standing around?"

The one at work, startled perhaps, looks up puzzled and tries to comprehend the dullness of his friend.

Were there an accredited critic of any understanding about, he might be able to correlate the details of the situation, bringing a reasonable order into these affairs. But the only accredited critics are those who, seeking order, have proceeded to cut away all the material they do not understand in order to obtain it. Since man has two legs, then so also must the elephant. Cut off the ones that are redundant! Following this, logically, they describe a hollow tail and a tassel sticking out just above the mouth. This is my considered opinion of the position of the formerly alert critic, T. S. Eliot.

Then there are the people who do reviews for the newspapers. They haven't the vaguest notion why one word follows another, but deal directly with meanings themselves.

An imaginable new social order would require a skeleton of severe discipline for its realization and maintenance. Thus by a sharp restriction to essentials, the seriousness of a new order is brought to realization. Poetry might turn this condition to its own ends. Only by being an object sharply defined and without redundancy will its form project whatever meaning is required of it. It could well be, at the same time, first and last a poem facing as it must the dialectic necessities of its day. Oppen has carried this social necessity, so far as poetry may be concerned in it, over to an extreme.

Such an undertaking will be as well a criticism of the classics, a movement that seeks to be made up only of essentials and to discover what they are. The classics are for modern purposes just so much old coach.

And once again, for the glad, the young and the enthusiastic, let it be said that such statement as the above has nothing to do with the abiding excellence of the classics but only with their availability as a means toward present ends. In the light of that objective, they are nostalgic obstacles.

Oppen has moved to present a clear outline for an understanding of what a new construction would require. His poems seek an irreducible minimum in the means for the achievement of their objective, no loose bolts or beams sticking out unattached at one end or put there to hold up a rococo cupid or a concrete saint, nor either to be a frame for a portrait of mother or a deceased wife.

The words are plain words; the metric is taken from speech; the colors, images, moods are not suburban, not peasant-restricted to serve as a pertinent example. A *Discrete Series*. This is the work of a "stinking" intellectual, if you please. That is, you should use the man as you would use any other mechanic—to serve a purpose for which training, his head, his general abilities fit him, to build with— that others may build after him.

Such service would be timely today since people are beginning to forget that poems are constructions. One no longer hears poems spoken of as good or bad; that is, whether or not they do or do not stand up and hold together. One is likely, rather, to hear of them now as "proletarian" or "fascist" or whatever it may be. The social school of criticism is getting to be almost as subversive to the intelligence as the religious school nearly succeeded in being in the recent past.

> The mast
> Inaudibly soars; bole-like, tapering:
> Sail flattens from it beneath the wind.
> The limp water holds the boat's round
>   sides. Sun

Slants dry light on the deck.
                              Beneath us glide
Rocks, sand, and unrimmed holes.

Whether or not a poem of this sort, technically excellent, will be read over and over again, year after year, perhaps century after century, as, let us say, some of Dante's sonnets have been read over and over again by succeeding generations—seems to me to be beside the point. Or that such a test is the sole criterion of excellence in a poem—who shall say? I wish merely to affirm in my own right that unless a poem rests on the bedrock of a craftsmanlike economy of means, its value must remain of a secondary order, and that for this reason good work, such as that shown among Mr. Oppen's poems, should be praised.

Notes on Norman Macleod

Mosaic, 1934

9/16—THERE ARE several seriously conflicting elements in Macleod's style which would make a detailed analysis of his poems profitable from the writer's viewpoint—and interesting too. There is neither time for it nor space here for such a study. To give point to what I say, however, there is a plainness of phrase, complete lack of literary ornament, coupled with something which is not at all straight in the diction; there is an affecting preoccupation with the desert and the people of the American desert with all the elemental symbolism involved, "death," "beauty," etc. over against "the revolution" and its peculiarities in the literal modern sense. He occasionally touches rhyme but more often eschews it while even in his loosest line forms he still allows a disturbing feeling of many disused poetic conventions to come through.

I like the intention of the poems, a tying up of the past with a today, on the ground—in what should be a plainness of speech. But—it leads to the struggle in a poet between his art and what they're trying to make him do with it. There is really a terrific confusion here. Maybe that's the good in the book. It certainly is something by itself. If my enjoyment is marred by what I don't like, I at least like and applaud the struggle of an enormous humanity trying,

---

Review of Norman Macleod, *Horizons of Death* (New York: The Parnassus Press, 1934); in *Mosaic*, New York, 1, 1 (Nov.–Dec. 1934): 27–28.

brokenly, to come through what is probably a lyric talent—unwilling to be relegated to the purely antiquarian—and succeeding.

The following random notes were done several days ago.

9/15—I can't write about these poems. They confuse me. I like them and I don't like them. I think I know what it is but I don't care to say. Here are some favorable notes I wrote two days ago—but I'd have to modify them if I went on.

9/14—I can't place these poems; I've read them over half a dozen times but I'm still confused as to what I see. It may come from the format in which they appear. I dislike books making a great show of white paper. I wish good work might be more frequently printed—on butcher paper if necessary. It seems particularly out of place to print Macleod preciously—unless some preconceived notion of him as a "revolutionary poet" is disturbing me.

9/13—The best in a poem is in its smaller parts. Their character is the determining factor toward excellence. It should take apart well. The parts in themselves should arouse interest.

If it takes apart well and the parts are not shoddy it is time to look at the rest.

What I find in Macleod is commendable. But to begin with what I do not find: I do not find obvious padding. The fabric hasn't been filled with lead and glue—not for any reason! I do not find verbiage come of an attempt to follow a meaningless metric. I do not find a loose resort to easy words merely because previous thought, hidden there, resents a damage from later, better thought—better because more accurate, as present day astronomy is more accurate than that of the fourteenth century or 1890. I do not find, in short, meaningless words put there for the sound alone.

I do find that the phrase makes a definite attempt to attain to the clarity of good prose. It shows, in its regard for the contours of words, some realization of the work done in the despised "laboratories" of the present generations. The phrase is compact, meaningful—and if not always, at least often enough to be important, bent upon the thing spoken of. This gives it pregnant sound instead of mere noise. The constraint, in that all poetry is constraint, lies in a fidelity to the object, the thought about it and their passionate welding. It is the movement of this constrained passion, limiting itself to the objective of its immediate purpose, which creates the meter as the obstructions in a river create the pattern of its flow.

Taking the poems in the large: They are today. Death may be the remote title of the book, as the image of man, beast or bird may appear upon a coin, but the value is in the spending. Life is the burden.

Alive as an Indian in the desert. That's the whole of it. Or the beginning rather. Macleod carries it up out of a cliff-dweller's past to the cities of the world and the deaths of which they are largely constituted. Inevitably it goes over into a revolt reaching to a man's very guts at the spectacle.

This is the essence of poetry. Upon this theme of life it is all based. Only a damned fool could mistake the revolution implied.

Tea Time Tales: Comment on James McQuail's "Pard and the Grandmother"

Trial Balances, 1935

Two COURSES seem open to me in criticising this poem. One would be to throw it out completely as a sort of Red Book-Sat Eve Post hand-me-down, rather better than its prose equivalent because shorter. The other would be to take it seriously for what good may come of that. I choose the latter course.

The poem belongs to the romantic category. As such it employs the usual stresses, paraphernalia, situations peculiar to what is known in the U.S. as "the nineties." The cards would have to be gilt-edged, the old woman's fingers bony and the clock ormolu. The old woman recalls a life the height of which seems to have been the love of a horse and the fact that a man of distinction once admired her as she stood in her riding habit. No doubt people did things in those days but they found it improper to talk about them in an understandable manner. Hard to make a woman come alive under such circumstances. It would have been more fitting had there been less stress upon "period," less intention to write beautifully with only the result of turgidity, less of, "He stopped and bit his lips," and more of rough, outspoken candor in the old gal such as one might reasonably expect from the horsy old bitch if poetry is to be concerned with her.

McQuail can be apt in his images but it's too, too lugu-

Trial Balances, ed. Ann Winslow (New York: The Macmillan Co., 1935), pp. 196–97.

brious, too over-strained, too "poetic" for modern concep-
tion, note that I did not say "modern poetry." Decoration, if
well done, has a place but it's a very minor place today. I
skip the dexterity or lack of it in the rhyme. But there is one
passage that I like:

> Pard stood up. "An idiotic trick in the New York *Times*,
> Printed on page twenty-eight, or perhaps Ripley
> Will illustrate it with his clever pencil. Nut rhymes,
> Letter for letter, and sound for sound, with nut."

The reason I speak seriously of this poem is that at least
McQuail has chosen to speak about a human being without
falling into a psychologic, soul-searching method. He has
put down a situation as he saw or thought he saw it, de-
scribing, expounding, explaining as he was able. He himself,
McQuail, does not appear, thank God! It is upon this plain
writing with an undeveloped human interest, but an appar-
ently real one, that I have counted in paying this penny for
the show. If McQuail will take language as he finds it today
and has the imagination to see the real situations about him
as they live and not as he falsely imagines they were fifty
years ago—he might write poetry—if he wants to undergo
the pains of it. I'd advise him rather to take up arboriculture,
unless he is so extraordinarily devoted to writing at its most
difficult that even newspaper reporting doesn't attract him.
Poetry is worse than cyanide of potassium to a young man
unless he wants to die that way.

Norman Macleod's Thanksgiving Before November

Not previously published, 1936

IF THERE's a literature addressed justifiably to the working class then there must be a criticism to go with it. Such a criticism will begin by throwing out the criteria which preceded it. Headings will be sacrificed as well as heads in the revolution thus implied. The whole concept of poetic excellence will be altered. There will be no "perfection" in the old sense. There will be only—?

In this spirit, one may begin to search for something on which a criticism will fit. One may begin by taking the poems of Norman Macleod. For these are definitely poems of "the revolution." It begins curiously enough with the American Indians. How shall the word be used? How the image? The line? Is there in this new *any* relationship [with] an older verse? If not then what is "good" and what "bad"? Is clarity still a virtue, or a fault—since it falsifies the predicament of an awakening but not awakened class? What kind of clarity? Should it be an excessive simplicity of statement, of syntax, of image? Should it be a primitive mode? And if so what sort of primitiveness? Subject or method? Or both? And unity? What should be the attitude toward locality? Should the mode be plain as a plowshare

---

Previously unpublished review of Norman Macleod, *Thanksgiving Before November* (New York: The Parnassus Press, 1936). The text is Buffalo C23, four typed pages with corrections in ink.

or should it have a primarily universal appeal? Should the assistance of rhyme be courted or abjured?

And if it has a justifiably new quality, what is that quality? And to what degree do these particular poems possess it? For it is to be presumed that whatever the new criticism may be its objective must still be excellence or, at least, abundance in the qualities it respects.

Take one of Macleod's poems which I enjoy in the first group: —What's the use. That's the hangover of the old that tries to dissect for analysis. It's not for these things—they don't work that way.

I'd say here was no art at all. Not even any great clarity. No metaphors. No rhyme. A sort of movement rather than a meter—iambic in feel perhaps. A rather bare language at least best when it is so. The whole first section is one. It's a childhood and youth with a mood of defeat and loss over it that sees in the Indian a firmness, the feet growing into the ground like maize. There's a parallel between what the growing youth misses, desires and the stolid persistence of the Indian. This is shown to be good. The Indian waiting for the machines to become useless, to break down and pass. A feeling that machines, made for the enslavements that they now represent, will break down and pass. And that something that the Indians have, only something new, something that can be had again, will come out of it. It is the vague feeling of the boy of the west. It paints a somewhat vague, empty picture of the west—the west toward which Horace Greeley told young men to go.

So the young western man goes east: to the cities. And there he finds less than he found among the Indians. "There is torpidity of pain and worry" about the world. "Thanksgiving Before November," a poem in this second section, which is one poem: Details of a place where a person is living are brought to the attention one by one, as by a man sitting pointlessly in the "cradle of an easy chair." A sort of satisfied waiting. Alert to what there is—to a degree. But no wish to go elsewhere, to succeed. To do anything. It implies the same waiting, waiting—for what? This seems to me a good poem. Waiting. For what? The very question at least projects a sort of answer. It is, "For what?" Something at least which now is definitely not. There's a purpose in that.

It is a curious torpidity that isn't awake, refuses to accept anything that is as real. The poems do not seem real. They seem in a mist. That's their defect. And if they have a virtue, it is their virtue. The western boy thanks you, but doesn't accept. There is nothing to accept. He can't be bothered to be brilliant or to write that way. Why should he? What for?

Then in the third poem, or section, he begins to get communications from somewhere, the revolution. It isn't any longer from the farm or his mother or Horace Greeley. He begins to grow clearer. He moves about and sees a design: It is a design in white. Niggers doused in cotton—lost in it. It's a symbol of himself in a sense. At least it's some sort of a design. Even if it merely ends by decorating their graves. Steel mills. Red Furnace.

In the end he gets talking to a lot of people who are definite and seem to be in the same condition he is in. They are professional fishermen along the Pacific: they've just had a dirty deal worked on them which they don't know how to get away from. We see a government man-of-war in the harbor beyond the tied up fishing fleet flying red flags.

The poet has abandoned all pretence at formal poetic structure and uses capitals instead for his emphasis.

As poems many of the earlier ones could be made more effective by drastic cutting. It would make them snappier, more pithy—but without improving them much relative to the new use which a present-day criticism might put them to.

I don't see what you're going to say any longer. I don't think any worker will read these poems much. They have an aggregate meaning to a reader mostly by what they're not than what they are. They seem to me a maze, a lost quality over them gives them their best meaning—and who much will care for that?

A Twentieth-Century American

H. H. Lewis

Poetry, 1936

WITHOUT hesitation, I say that there is no question here of high art. Lewis has read from many of the well-known English and American poets and frankly copies their forms, using them as they come ready to his hand. It might be anything from Gray to Whitman, including the book of limericks, nursery rhymes, popular songs, Poe—anything you please, even back to Shakespeare; he'll borrow the form and turn it to his purpose. Once in a while he makes the form ring with meaning. Sometimes the attempt falls flat. But through all runs the drive that might strike fire, actually, in a word, a phrase, bringing the mind to sudden realization. At moments the charge is so great it lifts the commonplace to lyric achievement:

> Russia, Russia, righting wrong
> Russia, Russia, Russia!
> That unified one sovereign throng,
> That hundred and sixty million strong,—
> Russia!
> America's loud EXAMPLE-SONG
> Russia, Russia, Russia!

The use of the word "Russia" resembles that of Aragon's "S.S.S.R." It goes to Lewis' head, as he says repeatedly; it

---

Review of four booklets by H. H. Lewis: *Red Renaissance* (1930), *Thinking of Russia* (1932), *Salvation* (1934), and *Road to Utterly* (1935), all published by B. C. Hagglund, Holt, Minn.; in *Poetry*, 47, 4 (Jan. 1936): 227–29. The manuscript is Buffalo C21. The next two reviews are also about H. H. Lewis.

maddens him with hope, with conviction, with certainty, with belief—the belief that sets him singing.

Lewis knows what he wants to say. He is convinced of its importance to a fanatical degree. He has been hurt and he yells outright the how, why, and wherefore of it. And what he would do in retaliation. The booklets show little or no progress in form that I can discern. If anything, I think the earlier ones are better because more forthright, cruder, from a more patently outraged conscience.

The influence of Lewis' work on other writers cannot but be good. For whatever his merits as an artist may or may not be, he has the one great strength without which there can be no art at all—belief, a belief in his own songs, in their absolute value, the power of their words to penetrate to the very bones of his listeners. This is a superlatively good thing, that must come as a blast of healthy wind among the frailer stuff or more cultivated—no, positively *not* more cultivated, but less cultivated—writers.

I am speaking of poetry. It is quite essential that one stick to pure poetry, in fact, when talking of it—whatever the incentive to its writing may have been. But it is quite possible that those who, traditionally, might be inclined to slight Lewis—from an eminence of culture—might be doing so from what is really an eminence of bad practice. Without saying that Lewis is important as a poet, which is a point that will have to be very carefully considered before a proper opinion can be arrived at, I will say that he is tremendously important in the United States as an instigator to thought about what poetry can and cannot be for us today.

This isn't Auden or Spender. This is a Missouri farmhand, first cousin to a mule, at one dollar a day. If Lewis' subject matter should distress some readers, it's about time they learned what makes their fruits and vegetables come to ripeness for them—and what kind of thoughts their cultivation breeds in a man of revolutionary inheritance.

An Outcry from the Dirt

H. H. Lewis

Not previously published, 1936

TAKEN ALL in all, I'd rather hear what a man has to say, in America, when I know his ancestors crossed the Cumberland Gap into Kentucky with Boone—than to listen to another whose people did not have that advantage. I won't say the first is a better man. I'll say, merely that it is my belief he's more likely to know what he's talking about than the other fellow. Certainly what he's talking about will nine times out of ten be more interesting to me.

Let the subject [be] Marxism as it may be applied to our country or anything else you please. When you've gathered a certain sort of energy in your bones—through generations of the same thing you are not likely to get it confused with what it ain't. That's what's so good about Lewis. He isn't buying what they tell him is good. He's taking it into his own hands and fitting it into what he knows—on the site. I like that. It's a growth. It has roots. It stands solidly on the specific history of the place. It doesn't aim to destroy anything. It's a righteous, hard-headed, hard-handed taking hold of things and a courageous matching up the material with the job. No particular excitement about it, but a lot of furious disgust—that things haven't worked out—and the truth's beginning to be known about it.

Why Lewis should have hit onto verse for his protest—is

Previously unpublished review of a fifth pamphlet by H. H. Lewis, *Midfield Sediments* (Holt, Minnesota: B. C. Hagglund, 1936); the text is Buffalo C22, six typed pages with corrections in pencil.

perhaps not too hard to discover. Verse is terse, it's succinct. And Lewis' reasons for his beliefs are not abstract. Verse has a lilt too, a capacity for slogan, for compact statement and for hard left hooks to the jaw—in the manner of Kipling who put over more of what he had to say that way than in acres of prose.

Again, as in the earlier booklets—it's the fervor of the belief rather than the subtlety of the lines themselves that makes what Lewis has to say good. For years poets have been fighting to get out from under the implications of the older verse forms and practices. There's something about most poems that is sickening, verse such as that of T. S. Eliot (as the peak of what I mean) but to a diminishing extent it runs down through many lesser craftsmen. I'm not speaking of the ambitious nonpoet, the inept. I'm speaking of men who should know better. I'm speaking of myself.

It's the language that's at fault and the way the words are put together. In the U.S. it comes largely from thinking we still speak English and trying to act accordingly. It stinks, really. In the proletarian poet as among the others. It's what they would call "poetry." That is, the stink of it is what the ordinary person calls poetry. When you don't write that way they tell you, Oh yes, but that isn't poetry!

You may talk all you please about propaganda and verse, but the only propaganda that's worth a dirty pair of lady's drawers—if any—is a proletarian *style*. And that has to be discovered, has to be invented. Has to be made. That requires an artist—not just a garbage wagon.

The answer is, Do you call Lewis an artist?

And the answer to that is, NO! No. No. I don't call Lewis an artist. But I say that he has, by the fervid sincerity that flows in his blood, found a way which many a would-be artist might well seek to imitate. Mostly Lewis goes across poetry as if he were following one of his mules across a clayey pasture he was turning. But at least he isn't afraid of poetry, he doesn't reverence it for itself or the illustrious examples of its past. He uses his own language for it, and he

uses it because he has something to say. He has, let me re-
peat, something to say. He uses American. And he has a
feeling for the line. He doesn't often hit it off. It's pretty
damned flat at times but—occasionally he makes the drab
stuff flare—

He's a descendant of the crowd that followed Boone
across the middle-west. And now he finds himself, among
others who inherited the country, stranded. He doesn't have
to follow the details of the economic puzzle. He doesn't
have to know how or why government has failed him—
though he surmises it's those who want to grab off the coin
and do nothing for it—he isn't even concerned with the
niceties of HOW it should be brought to an end. He simply
yells, END it! Now. It's being done in Russia. Then I'm for
the same thing here. End it. And, by God, why don't we?
WORKERS OF THE WORLD UNITE. If it must be
Communism, very well. It wouldn't need to be. If ten mil-
lion of us stood up on Tuesday, September 1st, 1936, at ten
o'clock in the morning and said, This is the end, it would
be the end.

That's all I think Communism means to H. H. Lewis. And
in that I agree with him.

(But I'm not going into the brand of Lewis' Communism.
He calls himself a Communist and cries toward Russia.
Rightly. I merely happen to be interested in his writing.)

It won't do anybody any harm to study what Lewis has
to say. There's no use splitting hairs over him, because he
isn't this or he isn't that. He's what he is where he is. Get
what there is. It's a breath of fresh air—and a lesson in pros-
ody—of the simplest sort.

America was destined to be free. It was promised us from
the first. We have been lied to. Both parties lie, both are in
the hands of those who own our credit. Politics, as Steffens
pointed out years ago, uses crime, and government uses
politics. This sort of thing:

American Etiquette

The "American" Legion, banker-led,
Drums through a street in Miami,
Belgarno usurer at the head:—
Hats ON, the flag is passing by!

Whether to uncover
Depends
Not upon the Flag itself
But upon who shows.

If that be some Tory-buffaloed group willing to abolish
the Bill of Rights for further benefit of plutes,
Then keep your hat on—
From respect for what did serve the Jeffersonian major-
ity and what does stand today against complete
fascism.

But when the paraders are such evolved Jeffersonians that
they would remove the red from between the white
and the blue and flaunt it alone,—
Then decisively
Off with the hat,
Though you be bald as Lenin!

All I say is that that is a good poem. Particularly good is
the second quatrain. That sort of direct statement—*about*
a matter of serious importance, thoroughly *meant*—is all too
rare in contemporary verse. It's always rare.

Again, as I did previously, I make the plea for distribu-
tion. Hagglund is willing to undertake the job of printing
work of the Rebel Poets for a ridiculously small sum. But
the distribution of it is the problem. What good to have
good verse, trenchant verse, even if not the most marvelous
in the world—but verse to be read and heard—what good,
if we can't get to it.

Instead of fighting among ourselves and spitting in each other's faces—let's try for a united front on that. I for one haven't an idea. I've tried as I have been able to do but there's no outlet that I can see. I've always felt that the real difficulty here is communication between interested parties. It's by keeping us from getting together into *any* sort of front, for good verse, for good prose, for good pictures that the subversive forces who play on a really asinine public hold sway.

The problem is greater and simpler than we imagine. We all want to be so right and so profound that we forget the plainest simplicities. Why did and does France get ahead with its art? No other reason than that all of it is centered in Paris and that Paris is a café town.

We're all lost in America. The Communist Party should be bigger than it is. In spirit, I mean. In the just spirit of Lewis. No use being so narrow, so bigoted. If it could really form a united front, on common sense, on the *general* congruence of all the best, fightingest ideas of America, if there were centers, trading posts where men and women, not a lot of patent leather hyenas could get together on a general basis of our common disinheritance and disgust with the obvious inadequacy of our times—

I'd say, for the moment, have a ban on the word Marxian—for ten years, so that we could get under the weight and get to know each other. We'd get somewhere.

This is the sort of feeling Lewis was born to uncover. He's too valuable a man to throw aside because you don't just exactly find that his color of thought doesn't match the latest importation from Moscow. Can't it be seen that nothing will fit America that isn't bred of America? We've got to work it out ourselves helped as we may be by extrinsic circumstances and ideas.

Anyhow, Lewis is a voice, shouting out of the dirt in no uncertain tones. Here's luck to him.

An American Poet

H. H. Lewis, Missouri Dirt Farmer and Song Maker,
Evaluated as an Instigator to Thought About
What Poetry Can and Cannot Do.

New Masses, 1937

DURING THE past ten years or so a man named H. H. Lewis, a persistent dirt farmer and dairyman of Cape Girardeau, Missouri, has been thinking for himself about his condition as a "free" American citizen, descendant of some of the most famous of Kentucky pioneers. And he's been thinking of others too, like himself, trying to make sense out of what confronts them today in their enjoyment of life, liberty, and in their pursuit of happiness.

Like the pioneers Lewis hasn't been content merely to think. Nor has he been willing to accept a parochial viewpoint. He has wandered for years up and down the country for a look-see. Then he returned home to work and to become vocal. His medium is, curiously enough, verse. He has published four cheaply printed, paper-covered booklets. They constitute a phenomenon worthy of widespread consideration. They are entitled, *Red Renaissance, Thinking of*

Review of four booklets by H. H. Lewis: *Red Renaissance* (1930), *Thinking of Russia* (1932), *Salvation* (1934), and *Road to Utterly* (1935), all published by B. C. Hagglund of Holt, Minnesota; in *New Masses*, 25, 9 (Nov. 23, 1937): 17–18.

Williams' earlier published review of these four pamphlets, "A Twentieth-Century American," *Poetry*, 47, 4 (Jan. 1936): 227–29, is either extracted from the manuscript of the *New Masses* review or the *New Masses* review incorporates the much shorter version. Although the *Poetry* version is organized differently, all the sentences in it are, with minor changes, in the *New Masses* review.

Russia, Salvation, and *The Road to Utterly.* It is the begin-
ning of a definitely new sort in American literary history. It
is an important beginning. It might lead to extremely im-
portant results.

In the first place, the format of these issues is forever
right. This is the way poems should be printed. It is closest
to word of mouth, next to Homeric singing and a universal
stage. It attacks the problem of style at the source: directly
in the exigencies of publication. Publication is the weak link
in the essential process of conveying undamaged writing
from writer to reader today. And that comprehends style.
The thought of publication is at the source that which
beckons most writers to destruction. Because they must
write, then, under implied restrictions making publication at
least possible, a cheap pamphlet is more likely to rest upon
some depth of style for its appeal, the truth personal.

A man has to write in a certain way in order to be pub-
lished in the accepted mode—his book selling for not less
than a dollar. That forces his hand; it ruins his style. It
transforms truths to lies. Given cheap books—if the purvey-
ing of them can be solved also—there will be in fact a re-
naissance. Woolworth is the logical medium, advertising be-
ing definitely out. Woolworth might make money hiring
the right sort of literary sales manager. It could be done.
Books like these of Lewis's at ten cents—not twenty-five
cents—each, widely distributed, would free the intelligence
from the tyranny of bought and sold profit printing.

Better than all conventions, all resolutions, all associations:
to be published and distributed cheap and fast, volumi-
nously. That, all but the last, I'd say is Lewis's first contribu-
tion. Later the *deluxe* editions, on parchment, of Villon, of
anyone come with time, savored with time. But today dis-
tribution and availability are the pressing needs while there
is yet time to know what is thought and said with a direct
bearing on the day.

This has been solved in Russia where one can, apparently,
read infinitely. Here we are starved, choked—writer and
reader both. Our tastes dictated to us by cash, by the power

held to limit what we shall know and express. This is no question of obscenity or sedition: there is legitimate news to be handed about. Lewis's cheap editions, though not cheap enough, are the right sort of gesture (before having once looked into them). Already this very shape of the books carries a mark of what should be inside.

Without saying that Lewis is important as a poet, which is a point that will have to be very carefully considered before a proper opinion can be arrived at, I will say that he is tremendously important in the United States as an instigator to thought about what poetry can and cannot do to us today. He speaks in no uncertain terms. He speaks with fervor, a revolutionary singleness and intensity of purpose, a clearly expressed content. He knows what he wants to say; he is convinced of its importance to a fanatical degree. He has been hurt, and he yells the how, why, and wherefore. In all this he resembles the American patriot of our revolutionary tradition. There is a lock, stock, and barrel identity between Lewis today, fighting to free himself from a class enslavement which torments his body with lice and cow dung, and the persecuted colonist of early American tradition. It doesn't matter that Lewis comes out openly, passionately, for Russia. When he speaks of Russia, it is precisely then that he is most American, most solidly in the tradition, not out of it, not borrowing a "foreign" solution. It is the same cry that sent Europeans to a "foreign" America and there set them madly free.

Again and again Lewis comes back to it with that brain-bursting elevation which men believe in, believe in and believe that America represents.

That *is* America to the whole world, that cry:

> Russia, Russia, Russia, Russia
> Roaring with each for all. . . .

That's pure American revolutionary stuff. I should say that that is the first important thing to establish about Lewis

as a poet in this second quarter of the twentieth century.
There is no one that as directly expresses the mind of the
United States as Lewis does now.

This isn't Auden or Spender. Nor is it Aragon's *Le Front
Rouge* of an essential, if unobserved, French background.
This is a Missouri farmhand, first cousin to a mule, at one
dollar a day. On the other hand, all of these have one thing
in common—the content of the poems involved is the essen-
tial matter; all are united in being definite movements to-
ward political action communistic in nature. Or, to be more
specific, action. The content of the poems constitutes the
avowed weight of them.

There is a movement in the practice of poetry (avoiding
identifications of the *worth*, the content, spoken of above)
largely in opposition to the character of the poetic impetus
of the first quarter of the century in America (as else-
where), which constituted a revolt in the form of the poetic
matter, a clearing away of the formal impediments—for
what? Implied in the work of the best writers of the first
quarter of the century was a barrier in the forms themselves.
It was necessary to break them down, invent new ones. And
it was for an important reason that this had to be done.

Was this work a preparation for Lewis and the second
quarter of the century? If so, has he been able to profit by
what was offered him? Or has he missed the significance or
been unable to seize the reins, going astray into charged
doggerel, poetry having been pushed aside?

Taking the familiar clock-face of the statisticians as the
whole of poetry, as written in the widely separate ages of
its greatness in the world: how much of it will represent the
best poetry of this century and how much of it is Lewis?

This brings his strength at once forward. Fervor, intensity
comes to a focus by the singleness of his purpose; the clear
objective, Communism, as a great desideratum to a fooled
and betrayed people. This the first quarter of the century
lacked.

Let it be noticed that I am speaking of poetry. It is not necessary to defame the ancient practices of the art to praise Lewis or anybody. It is quite essential that one stick to pure poetry, in fact, when talking of it, whatever its incentive may be. But it is also quite possible that those who, traditionally, might be inclined to slight Lewis—from an eminence of culture—might really be doing so from what is really an eminence of bad practice.

The great segment of all poetry is belief, from which springs the rhythmic nature of the created work, and this belief, when it is at its full, asserts life, with fervor, with confidence (directly or indirectly), not death. Here Lewis excels, and this may be the determining factor of the new quarter of the century and the one after it. Lewis may be the very essence of the innovator, and so, *good*—in spite of a total lack of all other excellence: his work good *poetry*.

It may be that the new of today *must* strip themselves for action, must divest themselves of much that the first quarter of the century poet could afford to carry. They cannot be so burdened and *go* as they must. Perhaps this is the inevitable step. Not that there is an inevitable clash between the two stresses—one complements the other—but because it must be so, for reasons of poetry, to have poetry get ahead, to have it mean its full.

Looking at Lewis' books, in the poems themselves one will find what he uses of the poetic means, what he has carried over from the work immediately preceding him in his own country, because he has the fervor, and by that and whatever else he has will be measured his poetic worth and by that again the importance of his contribution to the cause he loves, the kind of work he does for it.

But whatever *his* interests may be in writing poetry, there can be no doubt about what the critic's attitude toward him should be, solely to determine the worth of his poems as poetry.

Without hesitation I say that there is here no question of high art. Lewis has read from many of the well-known English and American poets and frankly copied their forms, using them as they come readily to his hand. It might be anything from Gray to Whitman, including the books of limericks, nursery rhymes, popular songs, Poe—anything you please, even back to Shakespeare—he'll borrow the form and turn it to his own purpose. Once in a while he makes the form ring with meaning. Sometimes the attempt falls flat. But through it all runs the drive that might catch fire, actually, in a word, a phrase—bringing the mind seriously to the task of realization. At moments the charge is so great that it lifts the commonplace to lyric achievement.

> Russia, Russia, righting wrong
> Russia, Russia, Russia!
> That unified one sovereign throng,
> That hundred and sixty million strong,—
> Russia!
> America's loud EXAMPLE-SONG,
> Russia, Russia, Russia!

The use of the word "Russia" resembles that of Aragon's "S. S. S. R." It goes to his head, as he says repeatedly, it maddens him with hope, with conviction, with certainty, with belief, the belief that sets him singing. His songs are songs, as good as he can make them, of triumph, realization. A poet's vision of a real future.

From the work of the first quarter of the century he has taken one positive thing, his dialect. Once in a while we come upon the inversion of Milton and hymn books. But in general he uses words with the confidence and the natural ease of a native speaking his own language as he hears it spoken in his own place and day. It adds to the impact of his seriousness.

He uses rhyme, but unaffectedly. Therefore, he uses it well. He does not let it take him for a ride for effects. He uses it in songs obviously intended for mass singing in trucks and in marching about "on business." There rhyme marks lines usefully, gives the pace and the measure.

He takes a direct interest in his day. He speaks of the political situations existing at the time he writes. He speaks directly, and so automatically does away with the putrescence of symbolism with which the first quarter of the century was cursed. He might fall into simple allegory, but it is so plain that it goes for fact simply.

He has picked up from Joyce—or out of his own head—the valuable time-saving trick of inventing words, compressing them to give a new twist to the meaning: Joyce Killer, flagrags, dailybathism, demockratism, dogmatrix, Rusevelt.

He can write, though, with the effectiveness of the expert craftsman when he does a thing like this:

> Uh needs a pair o' breeches,
> Mirandy needs a skuht.

Then he speaks of the donkey, "used to middles," which is afraid to ruin the rows of growing cotton the farmer is forcing him to plow under, saying at last: "Sumpin' sho' is rotten!" Then the piece goes on:

> I'll say,
> Phew, for Chrissake,
> The brains of the "Brain Trust,"
>   that's it,
> Rrrrrrotten!
>
> Pity the poor American donkey,
> Pity the poor American farmhand,
> The one nervously zigzagging,
> The other compelled to jerk him back
>   to the row,
> Plowing under cotton!
> Such an "assinine"
> Torturing
> Strain on the sound sense of both!

In our need plowing under "what would be wealth in Russia." To this he comes back again and again. Here his convictions have forced him to write well.

The four booklets show little or no progress in form that I can discern. If anything, I think the earlier ones are better, more forthright, cruder with a more patently outraged conscience. Lewis has let go, seeming to be repeating himself. Not that there can be too much repetition if his purpose— to bring about the revolution which will be the consummation of his effort—is to be achieved. He may dig up a richer nugget any day, some hot song that may force itself to everybody's lips—the *Marseillaise* of tomorrow. Maybe something he has written already will catch on and be carried to the front.

The influence of Lewis' work on other writers cannot but be good, for whatever his merits as an artist may or may not be, he has the one great strength without which there can be no art at all—the sincerity of belief in his own songs, in their value, and in their power to penetrate to the very bones of the listeners. This is a good thing that must come as a blast of healthy wind among the frailer stuff of the more cultured—no, positively *not* more cultured but less cultured—writers.

If Lewis' subject matter should distress some readers, it's about time they learned what makes their fruit and vegetables grow for them, what kind of thoughts their cultivation breeds in a man, and, finally, what the meaning of poetry is.

Introduction to Sydney Salt's Christopher Columbus and Other Poems

1937

SYDNEY SALT has created a character which interests me in Gaspar Gorricio of the long poem, "Christopher Columbus," the most important work here presented. It is a gentle character whose notes framing the poem are either translations of authentic documents or inventions of amazing merit, it hardly matters which. More important is it that the person so clearly revealed by them is the perfect foil for the turbulent soul which they have been used to frame. This gives the poem its fresh character, bathing the great adventure which is portrayed in the subdued light manifested by the saintly Gaspar, his holy attitude toward the world, and so emphasizes in Columbus what Salt wishes us to feel and to see. This is well done. It is Salt at his best. I think he needs something established, a definite but modulable ground over which to work to bring out his own effective appeal. It is principally of this poem, to which I shall return in a moment, that I wish to speak here.

The same definiteness of outline one finds also in the briefer poems. "Capri Parade" has it and "Two Horses," "Young Lilting Bough," "About Stones," though I doubt that many would agree with my taste.

Unique in the book there is also a short prose form en-

Introduction to Sydney Salt, *Christopher Columbus and Other Poems* (Boston: Bruce Humphries, Inc., 1937), pp. 7–10. Manuscript is Buffalo C78.

titled "It," deserving of far more attention than Salt seems to have awarded it. It represents vividly a state of mind, a construction in which the contrast between illusion and sharp objectivity is so well maintained that we are deeply affected by its oppressive reality. But I return, as in reading the book, to the Columbus.

Here is a subject as stereotyped as any that could well be found. Salt follows the well-known Journal—but the treatment is curiously seductive. Salt puts his own faith in a naive gentleness to the test and—an antiphony between it and the violence of heroic adventure creeps in on us, somehow subduing the violence and showing Columbus to have been the poet that he was—or he never could have held the tiller so unfailingly and for so long. A practical man would have turned back. The same naive faith discovered the new world, that's what Salt seems to say. For myself I never tire of the Columbus story—provided it isn't made to drag. Salt has discovered a way that it moves always forward gently but surely.

After all, for Americans the conditions surrounding our establishment in history are all we should ever need to know to keep us straight. And every twenty years or so should have its own telling. In the Columbus legend lies the one opportunity all Americans can have to feel together as brothers. We together are the New World and there can never be another.

The movement of the poem is, as I have said, easy, and Salt has found an easy meter in which to embody it. There is quietness in the lines and a continuous sense of wonder moving forward as the three ships moved always to the west—not overloaded with metaphor or burdensome profundity of thought. The whole is to be read for the pleasure of it and the enlightenment of its placid beauty.

In the following imaginary conversation some further implications of the poems are taken up:

"Why do you moderns write so beautifully and then spoil everything by some eccentricity? Many of you could be successful writers if you would adopt more accepted modes of expression. Why do you do it?"

"That you may not enjoy . . ."

"But . . ."

"Wait a moment, if you please. That you may not enjoy as you would like to. What do you think beauty is, since you speak so glibly of the beautiful? You think it's a partial thing, something here against something 'ugly' there. Impossible. It's the whole thing at once. Or nothing."

"So you refuse to write what we like, for us?"

"Yes, we refuse. Because what you think is lovely is in reality horrible. You don't know this because you aren't equipped to know it. But I am an expert. Do you want to force me to be a liar also?"

"I am not perfect, I know that. Make me nearer to perfection, then. It is the ideal which you should hold before us. Everything in the arts should be beautiful—as we wish to be."

"Horrible, horrible, horrible—as you are! But art is beautiful except not—as you wish to be. The ideal, which you imagine, you see in reality through the backs of your heads but it is your eyes through which you should be looking. You have looked so long from the back that you cannot look ahead now. You recognize nothing. The ideal is a lie and in the end it will kill you."

"But I'm not blind. Neither am I stupid."

"No, you're not stupid. But are you sure you're not blind?"

"I'm not blind to good soup. I trust my senses."

"Ha, ha, ha, ha! Do you have a chemical analysis of every plate of soup you eat?"

"Of course not. Nor of every poem that I read."

"Then how can you know there isn't a tasteless poison in it?"

"I trust the cook."

"Don't confuse the issue. But I am a chemist and I tell you your life is your soup and that if you put something in there

that should not be in there—it will be poison. Your life is
made of vegetables, of meats, of water and of salt . . ."

"Is that a joke?"

"It belongs to the soup. Your life is one thing all together.
It is a whole. And what you see in a work of art is like that.
It is a whole."

"But what has that to do with this book?"

"This book and other books. Do you think there is some-
thing poetry cannot touch? Yes, you do think so. Because
they are not 'lovely' things. There's your old lie again.
Nothing is lovely but the whole. You want the world to be
flat, you do not want to see that it is round—you do not
want to see back of the picture. And that is what you want
us poets to write. We can't do it, our feet are too heavy. . . .
You smile! Yes, we are not afraid to say now that our feet
are too heavy, like our hearts. They break through. *Nuevo
Mundo!*"

The Tortuous Straightness of Charles Henri Ford

The Garden of Disorder and Other Poems

1938

IN READING these poems through, from beginning to end, at one long stroke, a special condition of the mind is generated which to me seems the gist of the poems, and the only way to understand them particularly or generally. They form an accompaniment to the radio jazz and other various, half preaching, half sacrilegious sounds of a Saturday night in June with the windows open and the mind stretched out attempting to regain some sort of quiet and be cool on a stuffed couch. . . . The poems form a single, continuous, running accompaniment, well put together as to their words, to a life altogether unreal. By retaining a firmness of extraordinary word juxtapositions while dealing wholly with a world to which the usual mind is unfamiliar, a counterfoil to the vague and excessively stupid juxtapositions commonly known as 'reality' is created. The effect is to revive the senses and force them to re-see, re-hear, re-taste, re-smell, and generally re-value all that it was believed had been seen, heard, smelled, and generally valued. By this means poetry has always in the past put a finger upon reality.

This sort of particularly hard, generally dreamlike poetry is inevitable today when the practice of the art tends to be seduced by politics. As always you find the foil immediately

---

Introduction to Charles Henri Ford, *The Garden of Disorder and Other Poems* (London: Europa Press, 1938), pp. 9–11, reprinted in *Selected Essays* where it is misdated 1939. Buffalo C142 has one draft.

beside the counterfoil. Poetry must lie against poetry, no-
where else. So this book can be enjoyed immediately beside
whatever hard-bitten poet of "the revolution" it is desired
to place it and there fecundate—in active denial of all the
unformed intermediate worlds in which we live and from
which we suffer bitterly.

To me the sonnet form is thoroughly banal because it is
a word in itself whose meaning is definitely fascistic. To use
it subverts most intelligences. I object to its use even here,
as I always object to its use other than for doggerel. But for
Ford's sake I am willing to ignore the form as unimportant
and look for the small excellences of tenuous but concretely
imagined word appositions which are contained in them.
They can be read in that way.

What I like best are his "Late Lyrics." For in every man
there must finally occur a fusion between his dream which
he dreamed when he was young and the phenomenal world
of his later years if he is to be rated high as a master of his
art.

In these later lyrics it seems to me that Ford shows evi-
dence of this important fusion—sometimes with loss of his
keenest intuitions where his sympathies have been too
roughly aroused—but then again with all his best faculties
retained. I always look for such lines as these—"I, Rainey
Betha, 22, / from the top branch of race-hatred look at you."
That's hard material to handle. It tests every resource of a
poet to do it well. Ford's method of handling it is interest-
ing. One should look for these differences of handling of the
today conventional theme—as one looks at the handling of
the Crucifixion—by Bellini, Raphael, and El Greco.

But in the last poem of the book Ford seems to return to
something he had begun to forget—a fantastic drive out of,
while in the very process of entering the banal: using the
banal to escape the banal—and by this, placing accurately a
value upon that which is excellent and good.

Muriel Rukeyser's US1

The New Republic, 1938

THIS BOOK is all to the good, three longish, subdivided poems and a group of lyrics relating almost without exception to the social revolution. There are moments in the book that are pretty dull, but that's bound to be the character of all good things if they are serious enough: when a devoted and determined person sets out to do a thing he isn't thinking first of being brilliant, he wants to get there even if he has to crawl—on his face. When he is able to—whenever he is able to—he gets up and runs.

Muriel Rukeyser doesn't know everything about writing—Lorca, Pound, Eluard—but she does show that she has a respect for some of the battles won for it in the recent past. So much so that her book is strong enough to stand up to critical attack.

In her first poem, "The Book of the Dead," her material, *not* her subject matter but her poetic material, is in part the notes of a congressional investigation, an x-ray report and the testimony of a physician under cross-examination. These she uses with something of the skill employed by Pound in the material of his *Cantos*. She knows how to use the *language* of an x-ray report or a stenographic record of a cross-examination. She knows, in other words, how to select and exhibit her material. She understands what words are for and

---

Review of Muriel Rukeyser, *US1* (New York: Covici, 1938); in *The New Republic*, 94 (March 9, 1938): 141–42. Buffalo C35 has three drafts.

how important it is not to twist them in order to make "poetry" of them.

This poem relates to big business and its "innocent" effects on the men it employs. If drills in silicate ore can work twice as fast dry as wet but, if dry, the dust they raise ultimately kills the men from a disease known as silicosis—then it still remains good business (if you can get away with it by bribery and other felonies of the sort) not to wet the drills. Inspired by her moral indignation Miss Rukeyser seizes upon the documentary facts of the cases in such a way as to make her points overwhelmingly convincing, so much so that a very real beauty results.

Miss Rukeyser's work is still very uneven. In some of her descriptions of natural loveliness in this poem and later she appears to forget that the beauty of a poem is not in what the poet sees but in what he makes of it. Plain statement is not quite enough in that case; nothing results but a piling up of words.

To me the best writing of the book aside from the use of the documentary evidence referred to above, is in the shorter poems of the second section. Here, because of the compactness, perhaps, the artist has been forced to select her words more carefully. The effect is satisfying. The third section, of the ship without a port, is an allegory too hastily written for my taste. The poet, possibly Hart Crane, is better handled than most of the other characters, but the effect of the whole is enlightening. I prefer the newspapers for that sort of thing. They at least have the correct date at the top. Nothing comes up clear to me; it seems insufficiently studied. The same for the fourth section, the removal of the group of foreign athletes from Barcelona for France at the outbreak of the fascist rebellion. Harder, sharper pictures are required. We see the man left behind on the dock, we get a glimpse of the Russian sailors, but we do not get them sharply enough to make their significance vocal; they are lost in a tangle of intervening words.

I hope Miss Rukeyser does not lose herself in her injudicious haste for a "cause," accepting, uncritically, what she does as satisfactory, her intentions being of the best. I hope she will stick it out the hardest way, a tough road, and invent! make the form that will embody her rare gifts of intelligence and passion for a social rebirth the chief object of her labors. Her passion will not be sacrificed, on the contrary it will be emphasized, by the success of such attention to technical detail. So will the revolution.

Foreword to Merrill Moore's Sonnets from New Directions

Merrill Moore's Sonnets, Present Total, Steadily Mounting, 50,000

1938

MERRILL MOORE'S sonnets are magnificent. Never in this world did I expect to praise a living writer because of his sonnets but these have been a revelation to me. For years I have been stating that the sonnet form is impossible to us, but Moore, by destroying the rigidities of the old form and rescuing the form itself intact—an achievement of far-reaching implications—has succeeded in completely altering my opinion. The sonnet, I see now, is not and has never been a form at all in any fixed sense other than that incident upon a certain turn of the mind. It is the extremely familiar dialogue unit upon which all dramatic writing is founded: a statement, then a rejoinder of a sort, perhaps a direct reply, perhaps a variant of the original—but a comeback of one sort or another—which Dante and his contemporaries had formalized for their day and language.

What Moore has done is more or less what we have all been striving to do in America since Whitman's famous "Me, myself"; he has broken through the blinding stupid formality of the thing and gone after the core of it, not of

---

Foreword to Merrill Moore, *Sonnets From New Directions* (Norfolk, Conn.: New Directions, 1938), pp. [5–6]; reprinted in three other books by Moore: *The Noise that Time Makes* (Boston, 1938), *M, One Thousand Autobiographical Sonnets* (New York, 1938), and *The Dance of Death* (Brooklyn, N.Y., 1957). Buffalo C93 has four drafts.

the sonnet, which is nothing, but the sonnet *form* which is the gist of the whole matter. That's what is so seldom understood. It's not a matter of destroying forms so much as it is a matter of observation, of resensing the problem, of seeing, of comprehending that of which the form consists as a form, of rescuing that essence and *re*-forming it.

Moore cleaned house. I am impressed and delighted. I had been slovenly enough in my thinking and unimaginative enough to believe that a sonnet was a matter of numbered lines and rhymes. I should have known better with Shakespeare as a preliminary example, but the British copyists had obscured the point again after him. It's hard to keep the imagination at its proper structural labors. I hadn't the alertness of mind which Moore had to realize that it wasn't the sonnet itself which was at fault in our day but the bad artists who used it that were the calamity. If sonnets of importance can now again be written, it is Merrill Moore who has made them possible. Moore's insight in cracking this toughest nut among the dynamics of contemporary verse-making is to me a major achievement.

Image and Purpose

Sol Funaroff's The Spider and the Clock

New Masses, 1938

THERE IS no democracy of taste relative to literary matters in America, least of all relative to poetry. Writing is judged, as it must be judged by the uninformed and the badly informed, purely by its token value as a success plug. Such things are to be taken for granted.

But limiting the attention to poetry, how can we expect anything else, even in those of good intention? It puzzles and bewilders them. It takes a sharply objective mind but also an agile mind to jump from the concrete to the general and from that back again to the personal application necessary to get the most out of a poem.

It is harder to read poetry than it is to read music, even for a completely literate and highly intelligent person.

But when excellent modern poetry, such as that of Funaroff, has to face and overcome besides everything else its dedication to a socially unacceptable viewpoint, then taste breaks down completely. I ask Funaroff to be patient.

So here we have a few good poems, the best characterized by a technical smoothness, a loveliness of jointure in the words—that may possibly seem out of place in dealing with the coarseness of some of the subject matter. But it is the essence for me of what Funaroff does: a verbal facility, an ear for the music of the line which is outstanding, a good outline to the image, and a clearly indicated relationship of the image to the purpose of the poem. Besides, the mind is clear and at ease back of all the rest. All this over against

---

Review of Sol Funaroff, *The Spider and the Clock* (New York: International Publishers, 1938); in *New Masses*, 28, 8 (Aug. 16, 1938): 23–25. Buffalo C20 has two drafts.

the present-day social impasse.

The result is tranquillity in strife, a direct, unconfused intention, well integrated—that spells final conviction and the peace of mind which it brings. This is the poetic impact: the storm but also the quiet above the storm—good flying weather there. I like that. Funaroff is sure. He sees for the most part the good which poetry has securely in its grasp down the ages—just as good today as ever.

But Funaroff tends to waste his best effects when he forgets, as he does at times, that it is words that are his materials and *not*, as a poet, states of society. It seems strange that no one has grown tired of hearing that said of him to an extent sufficient to make him pay lasting heed to it. Not that states of society and the conditions governing words cannot be semblable but you *cannot* write a poem paying primary heed to social conditions, you cannot write a poem with anything but words, words that will do their part, as much as words can do, for what you wish to put over while retaining the conditions necessary to a poem—if you think that worthwhile. In his ardor to drive ahead Funaroff sometimes forgets that. It is the mistake of a young man—sufficiently counteracted in this case by better work, to indicate that he may, possibly, get over it.

No matter what the "school," a poem implies a specific use of words in a special manner for the attainment of a definite complexion of meaning. It isn't easy. But without it the Marxian climax would resemble a man made of dough. Funaroff accomplishes just that meaning in "The Bellbuoy," "A Worker," but especially in "A Love Poem About Spring." There are other good poems and some not so good in the book. When I don't like a poem it is because it jumps the track. Energy is only wasted when a poem goes with a hell of a lot of noise—into the social ditch. Not that ditches aren't of social value, mind you. Imagine if we didn't have ditches! But the thing is to keep the car, as a car, rolling. We cannot allow ourselves to forget the first principle of the Marxian dialectic: to use *poetry*, also, to forward the universal purpose. Poetry, mind you. That's where the emphasis lies. Not to junk poetry wholesale in the semi-comic

Wilsonian sense nor to junk it piecemeal through the body of the poem itself. Why, e. e. cummings is a better Marxian than that!

"The Bellbuoy," the introductory poem, gives the key—the sound of that bell over all the tragedy that the sea implies, like the sound of the poems Funaroff asks us to hear in his words.

There's always an undiscoverable felicity in the best of things. To me the fact that Funaroff is so delightful to read, while I cannot discover what makes him put his words together so very simply, so very directly without any strain at all—is the secret! I can think of all kinds of poets who would give their best false teeth to be able to do that.

Take the perfectly clear statement underlying an image in the first widely separated lines of "A Love Poem About Spring." Nothing trite, nothing overstated, never too much. Just enough. That too is good writing. How is it done?

All such things come from inside, from conviction, from ease in the spirit of the man. Not the vaguest wobbling here. He knows what he is about and why. He carries the reader to willing discoveries. Funaroff is interested also, deeply interested, in those discoveries.

Such a well put image, summative of a state of mind, as "unhappy between kiss and kiss," as Funaroff uses it, is difficult to praise. The mind at once says, What's to that? Well, the simplicity of the approach, the natural language molded without strain or distortion to an acute purpose—without weariness or boredom—that a freshness comes of it. That's good writing. And in this case it says everything. Everyone who writes strives for the same thing. To say it swiftly, clearly, to say the hard thing that way, using few words. Not to gum up the paragraph. To know when to quit when you've done. And not to have hangovers of other ideas sifting in unnoticed. Good writing is precisely like good dressing. Bad writing is like a badly dressed woman—improper emphasis, badly chosen colors. But bad writing is also the lack of freshness in the impossible copying of good taste wholesale. Invention, well focused invention—while still retaining clarity of means, honesty of expedient.

Form: The Poems of Laura Riding

Not previously published, 1938

THERE ARE those who might say, with some justice, these are monochromes painted by a lame person; they suggest colors and movements—but nothing distinguished. That should not, in Laura Riding's definition, limit them as poems. The "reasons for poetry" are neither painting nor the dance. It is a dour theme—an undifferentiated, albuminous femaleness of art—at its worst but ably defended as a poetic womb-darkness, where only a few aimless kicks are permitted, by Laura Riding.

But then, she is right and serious and—voluminous. Weak poems may be ignored. The good in the blend is of high

---

Previously unpublished review of Laura Riding, *Collected Poems* (New York: Random House, 1938). The text is Buffalo C33, six typed pages with corrections in pencil. This ms. represents the one case in which I have adopted a more active editorial role. The typed ms. begins with what is here paragraph four. At the bottom of ms. p. 3 there is a handwritten version of what is here paragraph one; in the ms. this paragraph is marked "(1)"; at the bottom of ms. p. 5 there is a handwritten version of what is now paragraph two and it is numbered "(2)"; and at the top of the first ms. page there is a handwritten version of what is here paragraph three, numbered "(3)"; and the first (typed) paragraph of the ms. has a handwritten "(4)" beside it in the left margin. All the handwritten additions appear, typed, with a few changes and in the numbered order, on the last of the ms. pages. My conclusion, based on the numbering, is that Williams intended to add these paragraphs to the beginning of the review and I have so printed it; this way of ordering the ms. was first suggested to me by Emily Wallace.

value. This good is the basis of all poetry and all art: form—
life, love, clarity and singleness—as overwhelmingly final as
a child in the womb.

As Laura Riding says in her preface to the poems they
are perfectly lucid when properly read, with the "reason for
poetry" in mind. As must happen when any work of art is
improperly applied the poems become incoherent when any-
thing but the "reason for poetry" in reading them is before
the mind. Laura Riding would wish them to be not only in-
coherent but completely incomprehensible under such a cir-
cumstance if I judge her rightly. She is a purist: either read
as I require or remain unenlightened might be her directions
to the book.

From what I see, reading on the line, literally, Riding is
constantly seeking and arriving at, point by point, a station
beyond what might be termed common sense. This is achieved
though she may not agree with my way of putting it by a
deliberate alteration of the word sequence from daily usage
which constitutes her own peculiar form.

By this, perfect literalness and lucidity of phrase may be
maintained but the form, an addition to common sense, (by)
the new relationship results in a new meaning from a bur-
densome deficient meaning underlying it, submerged by it—
till there emerges lightness, relief—a fresh smelling, delight-
ful atmosphere. Poetry.

In that perhaps is a return, the real return to poetry as
satisfaction, assuagement from debased meaning, a break-
through, which poetry should and must always be, a cleans-
ing—a recovery of meaning in the best sense. The highest
sense. Form is the operative agent.

No matter about what the woman is concerned, the poet
says it doesn't matter—except love! love beyond any par-
ticular love, though in particular. Lose or win: it doesn't
matter. Only poetry matters, built out of love.

The effect I experienced on reading the poems though I
began them with indifference was relief. I skimmed through
the preface unmoved and little enlightened. But the poems

served as a better definition of the intent. They were extremely simple—lucid and at peace. I started disliking the woman. No doubt I am right in doing so. It doesn't matter. At her best she is a poet only to be understood one way. Find the meaning of—

But to go back to a further consideration of the difficulties of poetic form: The thing that few artists realize, if any but one or two realize it as Laura Riding may be presumed to realize it, is that form is the major significance in a work of art: to dislocate ordinary sense and to achieve extraordinary sense the form of the writing, to speak of writing, must change. This the "new" that is always reviled in art or lauded to the skies.

Thus to emphasize, form is a "word," a complex but definite meaning compressing into itself all the major aspects of the intelligence in its day. So that when an old form is reinflated for contemporary use what in reality it amounts to is a word of archaic significance, unseen, unnoticed almost always by the writer, a word which he does not know is in his sentence, modifying what he says by a film of meaning to destroy him and his work together. Form is the operative agent.

The words contain the traditional literalness. The form on the other hand in all its changes contains the new, our world today. Together they link up to a complex world with the past and give it its full articulateness. The form is the invention or the perception—the form is the discovery, the adventure, the greatest achievement of the poet, of poetry in its time. It is the form that is the work of the genius. The words that bespeak a talent. The form is that quality of words by which their arrangement gives them a significance beyond their literal (common) meaning. But Riding might try to deny that in her insistence on literalism.

Very well. Poetry is that branch of writing of which form is the primary character, a return to the pure use of words—induced by freeing them from other significances than their literal meaning. If so then there can be no other

way to do this than by a formal arrangement through which
they are divorced from a lesser sense. —To dislocate ordi-
nary sense: thus to emphasize that form is a "word" in itself,
one of the major words of the poem, which by its archaic
significance unwittingly employed violates every—

This applies to the poems of Laura Riding—not obviously
but plainly when perceived.

—The form, the new form that is, in this case clears the
words of old connotations pasted upon them by old forms
with their quondam contemporary meanings (of another
day) and allows the present, eternal, clear meaning of the
word in our day to come through clean. That, as I take it,
would be the special significance of form in Laura Riding's
case, her insistence on what she terms "literalness" as I
should say, unsmudged by the lamed, uninvented form—the
obsolete which might surround it.

Naturally "form" in the sense I use it is a very broad term
including even formlessness as part of its mathematical (and
practical) appurtenances. There is a school of form by con-
venience which would and does oppose everything I say.
This is the class of mind which though poetically well inten-
tioned cannot see in form the be all and end all of the poet—
but a sort of wagon, rather to carry the salt hay in from the
marsh. Or else there is the strictly limited class and mind
which had already limited form to a few exercises, a child-
like innocence which believes form to be something too like
a house—but form is anything formal that modifies a work
of art to the dimensions of its times. It might be grossly
physical, it might relate to theoretical mathematical con-
cepts, have sociological connotations etc. etc. But in a poem
this comes off as relationships between the words. Well,
there's no quarreling with the partial because it isn't the
whole. Let it go. Form today is protean, elastic, unsure in
temperature so that whether solid, fluid or gaseous it still re-
mains the same thing.

Harry Roskolenko's Sequence on Violence

Not previously published, 1938

IF THERE's any virtue in this book it's in such things as—

> *Begrudged, Defiled—*
> *By the world exiled—*
> *And fortune quite disabled.*

and—

> The dancer has left the scene,
> the audience remains with broken mirror,
> the lights smashed by a blind spectator.

It's pretty hard to say that this is poetry but it about expresses what Roskolenko has to say. I've never quite been able to make it out. If anything, I suppose, that would be the answer. It isn't to be made out. It's about what you'd find after a bomb had been dropped from 10,000 feet on a crowded subway entrance.

I don't know what poetry is for if not to be read. And damned if I can see who would want to go to the theater to see the lights smashed by a blind spectator after the dancer had left the stage—or who would want to read this book but a misanthrope.

Previously unpublished review of Harry Roskolenko, *Sequence on Violence* (New York: Signal Publishers, 1938). The text is Buffalo C34, two typed pages with corrections in pen and pencil. Yale Za/Williams/292 contains one draft.

I can't say that I make much sense out of Roskolenko's forced rhymes or his unnecessary inversions of phrase. Such recurrences as "Timeless are not those" instead of "Those are not timeless" annoy me beyond words. It's all right to be broken up but, hell, that doesn't prove the whole to have been any good of which we pick up only the pieces.

Dull, badly imagined surfaces—do not spell tragedy by violence. I see the dulling that may be produced by repeated blows on the head. I am even moved to pity but I am not moved to a conviction that the result has been poetry.

Not that the solution is easy. I have every respect for a man who will not write what he does not feel, a man who detests the facile, limping and lilting in the beautifulest of lovely lines all velveted with deepest feeling about the sorrows of man. I can respect a man who knows that it is in the structure of a piece that its true meaning lies, that today in the poison-gas atmosphere in which we live bruce-bartoned at Congress, we feel apathy before slaughter merely because it occurs in Spain—until it is accepted in silence. I say I can respect a man who knows that the form of the verse must show this brokenness and this despair—But I must say that it is not mastery to make a bad statue out of plaster and think to give it pregnancy by smashing it to bits by the blow of a maul.

I can see what Roskolenko is at. I don't think he has succeeded. Yet, in spite of all that, that the book will never be read, that it doesn't get anywhere, that there isn't a well-made poem in it, that his words are as flat, often as the debacle he holds up to our disdain—the book is so bad, that by its very depravity it is impressive. It is senseless.

Patchen's First Testament

Not previously published, 1939

LOVE IS Patchen's great theme, divine and human, and, un-winking, what our life has done to it. To this he brings a structural device filling the page at its best for what he wants to say—scattered, jagged, irregular, with long explanatory titles—burdened with uncertainty.

Critically speaking a poet's structural devices reveal not only his competence as a poet but his intentions. Seek there.

The object is brutal and public. Stop or be stopped by the red signal at 52nd St. and Broadway going west just after sundown and you will see! Aside from the buildings with their tops blown off, nothing whatever! no one thing to penetrate the encased mind, but a whole, startling to the attention:

An eviscerated woman whose jeweled guts fallen down, sparkling with garish splendor, cars drag wildly up and down the avenue while over them her eyes and scattered hair, the rounds of her pale breasts and buttocks spattered with blood, hover tormented and obscene.

I have said Patchen resembles John Donne. But there is a university of disaster to love between them. Alike in inmost reverence both are explicit in their poetic form. Donne be-

---

Previously unpublished; probably intended as an introduction, these comments on Kenneth Patchen, *First Will and Testament* (Norfolk, Conn.: New Directions, 1939) are Buffalo C27e, two typed pages (carbon) with corrections in pencil. C27 also contains four earlier drafts. Excerpts from Williams' essay were quoted on the book's dust jacket.

hind bars, shaking them, remains confined to bespeak his disaster. Patchen in his day, to shouts in his ears also, no doubt, of Order order, order! rising angrily about him, builds upon the same theme of love divine and human but after a different pattern.

Does anyone forget that Bartholomew's Eve was also a call to order?

Order, order, order? What other order can there be but this: to embrace the theme in the construction and follow through unrestrictedly to a conclusion, stopping at nothing, slipping nowhere but blasting aside restraints to the full and present revelation. To discover love's full reaches and its ways.

And so I reach the extraordinary conclusion that the structure of Patchen's verse is the revelation of his love, the attempt to stretch arms about the difficult object to hold it close within his warm embrace.

Letter to Reed Whittemore

Furioso, 1940

DEAR WHITTEMORE:

I've got a subject, you write, that I don't know anything about. It may have been covered a lot before but it certainly should be covered right now in *Furioso*. Propaganda in Poetry. Poetry that tries to influence people. In other words, just what is the function of poetry? What has a poetry magazine to do with a war, with a country's policy, with a new bunch of quintuplets, etc.? In publishing *Furioso* I think that's one of the things we've been trying to find out, and so far I haven't found out anything. Pound says that everything he's written has economic implications. Everything (nearly) that Genevieve Taggard writes says "better read Marx." In other words most of the modern poets *think* they're pointing toward something which they believe is right. And I want to know if they've picked the right medium. Why not write an article for *Liberty?* My idea is that poetry deals with the generalities of human conduct, with questions that

---

Williams had been asked by editors James Angleton and Reed Whittemore to contribute to the first edition of *Furioso* and had sent them three poems, "The Cure," "Last Words of My English Grandmother," and "In Sisterly Fashion." He liked the first issue when he saw it, though he urged the editors to play it less safe and publish unknown writers; see note 72 to my Introduction. His letter is in *Selected Letters*, pp. 182–83; apparently Whittemore responded to Williams, who in turn answered with this letter, published in *Furioso*, New Haven, 1, 2 (New Year Issue, 1940): 21–23.

are important for more than ten minutes, with movements greater than the French occupation of the Saar Basin. Then all I can do is say, So what? I wonder what's the good of writing an article for *Liberty* either, except that we're still a neutral country. . . . I've read several poems of yours that are precisely about what I'm trying to get at, etc., etc. —To all of this my answer would be, Yes.

Take an extreme case, take the concepts that walk around as T. S. Eliot. We know they are completely worthless so that aside from Eliot's being a poet we do not have to pay much attention to him. He is strictly limited even as a poet but for all that we may speak of him as a good poet, good, that is, far beyond his other limitations.

That, I think, if true, would leave a certain irreducible minimum which we may designate as the poetic quantum.

Taggard may entertain certain concepts but these do not by any stretch of the imagination make her a good writer. Pound, you say, believes that all his writings have an economic implication. So, by the way, does the peanut vendor at a ball game. It is obvious that unless Pound's writings have other implication, the poetic quantum, he would be of far less use to us as Pound than a lucid text on the subject he believes he is expounding, the lucid text he is always dreaming of. Should his concepts ever clarify themselves, that is to say, his economic concepts, and he be able to transcribe them . . . it might be the end of him. Horrible thought.

Peter Cooper said a number of years ago, Exorbitant rent (commonly called interest) silently but surely devours the substance of the people.—I think this, in one sentence, says more succinctly than Pound ever dreamed, everything he ever conceived of economics. But Peter Cooper was not a poet. Pound is a poet, so we forgive him.

We all like to believe that we are master minds. But what men seldom seem to learn is that the end of poetry is a poem; I don't know a thing about the value of a poem as such or of a hunk of gold as such or of a man himself as such but I do know *that*.

Some exposure to the sharp edge of the mechanics of liv-
ing—such as blindness, political exile, a commercial theater
to support and be supported by, a profession out of neces-
sity, dire poverty, defiance of the law, insanity—is necessary
to the poet. It doesn't matter what the form is, these are all
of a class, to give the poet his sense of precision in the appre-
ciation of values, what is commonly spoken of as "reality."
They force him to observe and to weigh, they prompt his
choice of the means of expression and give his words pun-
gency and a charge. In themselves they have nothing to do
with poetry.

Notice clearly, this is the sole use of these focusing stimu-
lae; they are not in any way related to the poet's function as
a poet. He must know this without possibility of a doubt.
The end of poetry is something apart from all that.

A blind singer for bed and board, an altar thief, a starve-
ling—if they for one moment forget, prodded as they may
be by death, disease or economic pressures, that their work
as poets is completely alien to all that—if they permit them-
selves to be caught in the snare of their own lives and let
that affect their decisions touching their workmanship in the
faintest possible manner—they are lost. It is a balance as to
the push of reality's either stimulating them to excellence or
killing them outright—but they must never forget that the
real significance passes beyond such incidentals. It lies im-
bedded indestructibly in the body of the poem itself, if. . . !

This being true the poet who mistakes the function of the
propaganda he practices, taking it overzealously to heart, is
his own dupe. Let's have no more jerked measures. To the
poet it is plain that all stimulae are and must be one, he is
the Jesuit of his own mind, the end always justifies the
means if he produce a good poem. But he must be more re-
sourceful than all that, he must still remain a Jesuit even in
giving up the Church. No matter what the propaganda and
no matter how it touches him, it can be of no concern to
the poet. To hell with it as soon as he has finished with it,
when it's worn out he'll find some other propaganda.

Be the Shakespeare of your own day, write well, skillfully, covertly, deceitfully, with every faculty under a hood or blanket concealed from public view, write of that which is nearest to the skin (to hell with the heart!) but write well.

So what, huh? After all, man being human must believe himself at times a great conceptualist (read your Spanish lit.: "just savages" E. P.), at least for home consumption, or lie down and die of disgust at the sights he sees about him. I don't blame anyone for wanting to teach his fellows to "blow hard" when Papa wields the rag. 's O.K. by me.

Then occasionally we get someone who can write. It's a *double entendre* that goes something like this:

> See the little angels
> Ascend up! ascend up!
> O! see the little angels
> Ascend up to Heaven!

There's something deeper to it than most people imagine. Ha!

WILLIAM CARLOS WILLIAMS

Poets and Critics: Letter to the Editors

Partisan Review, 1940

SIRS:

I think you've committed a blunder in bunching your notices of books of poems received under one title, as you have done in this last issue of PR, and allowing them to be "criticised" in the offhand manner assumed by your Mr. Jarrell. It does not seem like you. I am wondering how it happened.

Don't you think it would have been more in keeping with the spirit of PR to have given Patchen's verse, the best of it, for instance, or the work of some other one of the group you have dealt with, a bold spread in your pages rather than to have aired such a wastebasket full of such trite flippancies as these you sponsor?

A man whom one respects because of his achievements is entitled to make unsupported critical remarks, even silly ones, at times, because what he says refers back to his established reputation. But such a condition does not pertain to your critic in this case. This seems to be just another of those professional literary sophomores who turn up from the universities every now and again to instruct us out of the book in our errors. I for one detest them as I detest plant lice.

Letter to *Partisan Review*, 7, 3 (May–June, 1940): 247–48. Randall Jarrell later wrote the Introduction to Williams' *Selected Poems* (Norfolk, Conn.: New Directions, 1949).

I'm not blaming Mr. Jarrell, I'm blaming you. Unless I'm very much mistaken you've been beautifully taken in by just another one of these flagrant literary classmen, to make a show of your reputed partisanship. I hope he hasn't nailed you so prettily for here is sentimentality of the most barren sort, that of the academic instructor toward his assigned subject.

Mr. Jarrell attacks me for my praise of Patchen as a poet, taking exception to my catch phrase "a hawk on the tomb of John Donne" and replacing it with his own phrase "a parrot on the stones of half a cemetery." Let the two phrases lie side by side—and go to Patchen's verses.

Sorry to see this sort of thing.

Sincerely,

WILLIAM CARLOS WILLIAMS

—Dr. Williams protests that Mr. Jarrell's review was "academic" and "trite," but the tone of his letter suggests that what really disturbed him was, on the contrary, the fact that our reviewer failed to treat these young poets with the genteel tact and forbearance customary in the critical press. We think that Mr. Jarrell's review was witty rather than flippant, that its virulence was matched by its good sense, and that it let some fresh air into the poetic hothouse. There is a tendency these days to regard young poets as sacred beasts, surrounded by awful sanctions. While we applaud Dr. Williams' constant encouragement of and interest in young poets, we suggest that sometimes they will profit more from unsparing criticism than from blanket endorsements.—ED. [Partisan Review]

American Writing: 1941

Not previously published, 1941

QUIT HYPNOTIZING yourself over the headlines, quit reading the papers. Pay attention to the bulletins of your art, the news is *there*. Read good verse, if you can find any, that is to say verse that is pertinent to the day. Read especially, at this moment and as an example, the verse in Edmund Wilson's "American Writing: 1941." There are secrets latent in every craft, explicit there also in the best work. They are structural and when they can be deciphered tell volumes as to the significance of the moment and the age. Find them.

Edmund Wilson in his preface to "American Writing: 1941," says "there are [today] unmistakable signs of the revival of an interest in literature for its own sake—that is, as a department of activity which has its own aims, techniques and rights. Writers who have been mesmerized . . . are beginning to see the world for themselves again, etc. etc." What follows here is no more than approving commentary on that point of view.

If England collapses (as Athens and Rome did finally) or uniquely survives the next year or two, what is the signifi-

---

Previously unpublished review of a Supplement to *The New Republic*, 104, 16 (April 21, 1941): 547–78, edited by Edmund Wilson. Contributors to the Supplement were Rolfe Humphries, Elizabeth Bishop, Randall Jarrell, Vladimir Nabokov (translating Pushkin), Edmund Wilson, Philip Rahv, Babette Deutsch, Morton Dauwen Zabel, and Henry Miller. The text is Buffalo C6a, five typed pages with corrections in pencil.

cance of such a collapse or survival interpreted in terms of poetic form? What today remains important and what, in the form of its verse, paralleled the weakness which paved the way for a downfall? For a downfall did not occur without weakness, an inability to contend with factors which were eating away the foundations. The counterparts of these should be found in all activities of the period. That is, formal counterparts in the writing of the period—whether of Auden, Eliot, Pound or whoever it may be—cannot but be found if we will look for them, divergent tendencies which reveal wherein the collapse was accelerated or might have been written off with forethought and energetic application of talents. These things I say—formally expressed.

On the other hand, if the German Triumvirate is to triumph—or collapse, what in formal terms of literature but especially in verse forms will be involved? It is necessary to know these things or at least to be aware of them and their significance in our moment to moment living if we are ourselves to survive—as poets or, at one remove, as critics. Which is the thing of value and what shall we do about it—formally? If we do not know that we shall not know where to base our constructive effort or our comments. We shall on the contrary go on believing that the "meaning" of a poem is what it "says," that the frivolity or gravity of its announcements are its significance, completely forgetting that it is only by its formal necessities that it has any meaning at all. Wilson does not sufficiently stress this point.

To take a childish example, we do not care, formally, which is to say as artists, which is to say as those speaking a certain hierarchic language, "why," that is to say, involving the wishes of the people in it, an airplane leaves the ground. Perhaps the pilot is coming out of a drunk and wishes to be alone, perhaps this, that or the other. What he thinks or intends to do in the plane is of no direct importance—besides, we know all about that anyway. The important thing to know is how, when and why the plane lifts and carries at command and comes safely down again, how fast it can go in relation to other planes and what weight and for how long it can bear it.

In English literature, since that is under discussion principally because of its intimate relationship with our own, there were elements, formal elements which we should embrace and others which we should beware of or at least with which we should be intimately familiar if we are to know what they and as a consequence we are doing today. Instead of applying ourselves to that we have been led astray too often by unrelated detail.

Coming back to my take-off, in the supplement of *The New Republic* of which I have spoken, there are three groups of poems, by Elizabeth Bishop, Rolph Humphries, and Randall Jarrell which, I believe, EdmundWilson selected for his assembly because of formal qualities he thought significant in the poems themselves. This pleases me immensely no matter what I may happen to think of the poems themselves. In itself that is a good piece of work on Wilson's part.

Limiting myself briefly to a comment on the poems of Mr. Jarrell—with Auden lingering somewhere above my left eye—and though I strongly dislike certain of Mr. Jarrel's critical attributes—I find myself forced to pay attention to his poetic line. What are the formal qualities of this line? It is important that I should recognize the qualities of this line, much more important than that I should pay any attention to what Mr. Jarrell "says" in the poems.

It is a well-handled conventional line, but not the usual conventional line, using good tasty words in a "normal" sequence, consonant with the tactile qualities of speech. There is an equally good use of the pause in the line, well varied and placed, again, with sensual distinction. I do not feel that the sense or the correct choice of the word has been sacrificed to keep the line intact, rather the line has been strained, properly, to meet the necessities of the correct word. All this is first rate. How far does it go toward penetrating the formal urgencies presented for our attack in 1941? That is not a matter about which I have set out to comment here. The approach should be more deliberate. My stress is solely upon what I take to be important matters of form.

Matters of this sort, I repeat, are very closely related to our general offensive or defensive attitude. What is worth having and how are we to keep it? All these things are to be answered before we can say that this or that poem is good. They lie proven in the secrets of the verse itself which rouses us to feel an authenticity and then, gradually, to know it. If Mr. Wilson implies in his preface to this supplement, "American Writing: 1941," that an art is disarticulated from its day and the stresses of its day when it retires most into itself I flatly disagree with him. I am certain that at precisely such a time its intimate identification with its period may be most pronounced and most fruitful, that is, at that time when it is most concerned with its own, innate and particular formal necessities.

A Counsel of Madness

Kenneth Patchen's The Journal of Albion Moonlight

Fantasy, 1942

WHITE MOONLIGHT, penetrating, distorting the mind is a symbol of madness. It denotes, negatively, also an absence of the sun. The sun does not touch the pages of Kenneth Patchen's *The Journal of Albion Moonlight*. So that what virtues are to be found here may be taken for madness. Could we interpret them we should know the cure. That is, I think, Patchen's intention, so, in reverse, to make the cure not only apparent, but, by the horror of his picture, imperative.

By such exhibitions the paterfamilias of fifty years or more ago, showing the horrible effects of syphilis, would seek to drive his sons to chastity. The age is syphilitic, cancerous, even leprous in Patchen's opinion—show it then, in itself and in its effects, upon the body and upon the mind— that we may know ourselves and be made whole thereby. And of it all, says Patchen, perhaps the only really normal and good thing remaining is the sexual kiss of two bodies, full-fledged.

In criticising such a book one should pay Patchen at least the compliment of being as low down as he is himself—and as outspoken. If he has attempted drastic strictures upon his age may we not demand of him by what authority he does

Review of Kenneth Patchen, *The Journal of Albion Moonlight* (Mount Vernon, N.Y.: Walpole Printing Office, 1941); in *Fantasy*, Pittsburgh, Pa., 10, 26 (1942): 102–07. Buffalo C28 has six drafts.

so? Is his picture a true one? And does he prove himself suf-
ficiently powerful as a writer to portray it? To scream vio-
lently against vile practices does not dispose of them. Fur-
thermore, though this book is full of violent statement, is
it violent, really? Violence overthrows. Does this succeed
in overthrowing anything at all or is it not, lacking full abil-
ity, no more than a sign of the author's and our own defeat,
hiding itself in noise? Shall not one say, finally, that this
book is erotically and pornographically sound; if it lives at
all it will be for no more than its lewdity that it does so?
That is the danger.

Everything depends upon the writing, a dangerous genre:
either to the minds of those who read it, it will work toward
the light or burrow in the mud. It can't be half good. It
can't do both.

For myself I ask for no authorities, so likely to be gutted
of any worth in our day, if not positively rotten. There is
no authority evidenced in this but the man himself. If there
are others like him, if we are not all somewhat as he is,
provided he write truthfully and out of a gifted mind, he
has a right to speak and needs no other authority. But if he
belies himself and us, overpreens himself and makes use of
devices that are shopworn and cheap, that's a different
matter. We owe Patchen nothing as Patchen. But if he's a
man and we feel a great fellowship with him, a deep sym-
pathy, then we can tolerate his vagaries, his stupidities even,
even his screaming. But if he shows that he enjoys that more
than the cure, that would be bad.

For what we're after is a cure. That at its best is what the
book's about. A man terribly bitten and seeking a cure, a
cure for the bedeviled spirit of his day. Nor are we inter-
ested in a Punch and Judy morality with a lily-white soul
wrapped in a sheet—or a fog, it doesn't matter which. We
are ready and willing to accept a low-down human spirit
which if it didn't have a hip joint we'd never be in a position
to speak of it at all. We know and can feel for that raving
reality, bedeviled by erotic dreams, which often enough is
ourselves. This book is from the gutter.

The story is that oldest of all themes, the journey, evangelical in purpose, that is to say, with a purpose to save the world from impending doom. A message must be got through to Roivas, read the name backward.

May 2. It starts under a sky of stone, from the region about New York City, in a countryside where an angel lies in a "little thicket." "It couldn't have hurt much when they slit its throat."

There is a simple statement of faith at the beginning:

> He was the Word that spake it;
> He took the bread and brake it;
> And what the Word did make it,
> I do believe and take it.

He must get through a message to the people such as they are who have lost hope in the world.

It gets up to August 27. And that is all. It ends. It ends because it has never succeeded in starting. There is—after a hundred thousand words—nothing to be said.

Albion's heart is broken by the war in Europe. Surely his message has to do with that. That is the message. But it is not advice to go in or to stay out. It is order lost. For the war has been caused by humanity, thwarted not by lack of order but by too much. Murder is the desperate theme. Murder out of despair.

The chief defect of such a book lies in the very plan and method of it, one is locked up with the other.

Patchen slams his vivid impressions on the page and lets them go at that. He is investigating the deformities of truth which he perceives in and about him. Not idly. He is seeking, the book is seeking, if I am correct, a new order among the debris of a mind conditioned by old and persistent wreckage. Patchen is seeking a way through among the debris and, as he goes, seeks also to reveal his meaning by truthful statement—under conditions of white moonlight. From that to reorder the universe.

There can be no checks, taboos or revisions permitted to

such a plan since the only chance it has of laying down positive values comes from first impressions, and they distorted. What else, in the writing, could a man do or say other than to put down the moonlight delineaments of the landscape he is witnessing? Could any traveller through a jungle do more? Or less? All that we demand of him is that he do not see and put down what is not there. Also that he do not fail to put down what is there. It is, in fact, one mind, his tortured own, that Patchen is travelling through and attempting to reveal to us by its observed attributes. In treating of that there can be no deleting, no pruning no matter how the initiative may wander.

Where does the journey take place did I say? In America? Why not? One place is like another. In the mind? How? What is the mind? You can't separate it from the body or the land any more than you can separate America from the world. We are all one, we are all guilty. No accusation is here permitted—Moonlight himself must, is forced to, take part in the murder no matter how he would escape it. All he can do is take part *willingly*.

The journey does traverse the mind. Therefore it gets to Chicago, Arizona, Galen. The dream which is more solid than the earth. And out of the cauldron of thought the earth itself is reborn and we walk on it into the small towns of Texas and Missouri.

There can be no graph except the map you pick up at a gas station—but as we hold it the graph becomes vertical also and takes us up into the tips of the mountains of Galen. People expand and shrink to the varying proportions of those in *Alice in Wonderland*, and every day but—desperately. We are at war, we are insane.

Reality? Do we think that America is not reality or that human beings are excluded from it? Death Valley appears. It is the mind itself, where Jackeen lies murdered. By Moonlight himself. It rots and stinks and is arrested and hung up—while one foot drops off on the gallows and a geranium sprouts from its left ear with roots in the heart of that corpse. Who is doing the hanging? It is again—Moonlight. Moonlight. He himself must be identified with the foulest crimes he imagines. He must. He cannot separate himself and be alone. Such is his journey.

Naturally everything observed will not be significant or new and it is the business of the writer to be careful of that. Yet, I shouldn't wish to advise him—at the edge of the thicket may lie a discovery, no matter how small it will seem at the time, which holds that quality of coming out of foulness faultlessly clean, a new order of thought shucking off the old which may justify a thousand redundancies. That's the chance taken by such a method. Tortured and perverted as we may think it, the book represents the same outlook over the world as did the Vita Nuova—reversed.

It is a book come of desperation, the desperation of the thwarted and the young. Write and discover. Go, move, waggle your legs in more terrible jungles than any primitive continent could ever afford, the present day shambles of the Mind. Tortured as you may be, seek cleanliness, seek vigor, unafraid. Seek love! Such is the New Life dimly perceivable through the medieval horrors of Patchen's hell. This is the order he is seeking.

Oh, we had a call to "order" some years ago, dead now or nearly dead now, fortunately. Its warts, like the hair of corpses, continue a separate existence, in the academies, and breed others of the sort from year to year; but the body has hygienically rotted away. This is not what Patchen is thinking of. Such an "order" consisted mainly in amputating all the extravagances, all the unimaginable offshoots of the living thing to make it conform to—those very restrictions from which, at its best, the present day is an almost miraculous escape. What they attempted was like that Nazi "order" now familiar in Europe which already in order to maintain itself has found it necessary to commit three hundred and fifty thousand murders among the civilian population.

Whether or not this book is a good one (let's not talk

prematurely of genius) I believe it to be a right one, a well
directed one and a hopeful one. It is the sort of book that
must be attempted from time to time, a book to violate all
the taboos, a racial necessity as it is a paradisiacal one, a
purge in the best sense—suggesting a return to health and
to the craft itself after the little word-and-thought pansies
have got through their nibbling. I don't say it's the best *sort*
of book, as the world goes, but it is the sort of book some
one should write in every generation, some one writer—let
himself go! and drop it for at least twenty years thereafter.

Patchen lets himself go. Such a book will rest heavily on
the character, ability and learning of the man who writes it.
If it is a failure, not clear or powerful enough to deserve the
concept of it I am suggesting, that is his hard luck. But the
book should be written, a book that had better perhaps have
been postponed to a maturer period of the man's career—
but which had after all to be written *now*.

That's precisely it. Even though it acknowledge itself to
be a foregone failure—the book must still have been made
as it is, the work of a young man, a new man—finding him-
self unprepared, though vocal, in the world. He voices the
world of the young—as he finds it, screaming against what
we, older, have given him. This precisely is the book's prime
validity.

Though Patchen is still young, still not ready, shall he be
silent for that? That is the significance and reason for all his
passion, that he is young, the seriousness and poignancy of
it. And it does, whatever its failings, find a crack in the ar-
mament of the killing suppression which is driving the
world to the only relief it knows, murder! today. It is itself
evidence, as a thing in itself, of our perversity and failure.

We destroy because we cannot escape. Because we are
confined. There is no opening for us from the desperate
womb of our times. We cannot get out. Everywhere we
turn, to Christ himself, we are met by a wall of "order," a
murderous crossfire which is offered us by "learning" and
the frightened conformists of our world.

For once a writer insists on the maddening facts of our

plight in plain terms; we grow afraid, we dare not pretend that we know or can know anything, straight out, in our own right. We have to be "correctly" educated first. But here and there, confronting Christ with Hitler—you won't believe it can be done—there are passages in this book where the mind threatens to open and a vivid reality of the spirit to burst forth and bloom in terrifying destructfulness—the destroying of all that we think we know in our time. It threatens to break out through the writing into a fact of the spirit even though it may not often be quite powerful enough to do so. I cannot specify these knots of understanding, of candor that—are the book's high places. The feeling that is experienced at those best moments is of an impending purity that might be. This is the order that I speak of.

What might it not do to the world if ONCE a universal truth, order, of the sort glimpsed here could be made free. It is as if it were too bright and that that is the reason no one has yet glimpsed it. Too bright! Van Gogh went mad staring at the sun and the stars.

I say all this in approbation—but writing is also a craft and we have to look well at that in this book. Florid and uncontrolled as Patchen's imagination may be, his images foetid, the passions of his Honeys and Claras funnelled into the socket of sex, compressed as a bomb to explode in colored lights—the writing must not be florid in any loose sense. And I should say, tangential as the thought may be, the writing is, in general well muscled, the word often brilliantly clear.

Many devices are used at times successfully, but not always so. There are lapses, disheartening lapses, and though I have said that in this sort of writing a man cannot stop for corrections yet, as readers, we have a right to object.

However we face it, one must still hold to the writing. Writing is not an instrument. The best writing happens on the page. It is the proof, with that stamp of the man upon it signifying it alive to live on independent of him, a thing in itself. The Word. We are responsible finally to that.

The book's defects are glaring, conjoined, as I have said,

inextricably with its virtues. It must have been written hap-
hazard to unearth the good. Whether or not there is enough
good to carry off the method will remain the question.
Many will doubt it, find the book to be no more a journey
than that taken by a dog trying to catch his own tail.

One of the chief weaknesses of the book is its total lack
of humor. Certainly the style is green and needs seasoning—
but having said that, one has begged the entire question—
nevertheless it must be said. The book would benefit by re-
visions and rather severe cutting. Sometimes the effect is fat
and soft, even spotted, when Patchen confuses his subject
matter with the workmanship to bad effect. These things
make it at times difficult for the reader to plow ahead. But
if, in spite of that, he is willing to face and cross these sap-
less spaces he will come to patches of really astonishing ob-
servation, profound feeling and a strongly imaginative and
just use of the word which, to me, give the book a highly
distinctive character.

A Group of Poems by Marcia Nardi

New Directions, 1942

MARCIA NARDI, now in her early thirties, is that woman you remember who disappointed her shocked parents by insisting on art school rather than college—and came to grief because of it. The woman who watched the sun come up in the morning with grave anticipation. She is the woman who refused to give in following her first defeat and came to the city with determination and lively expectation of working into the world of letters by her own hard efforts.

She is that woman who got a job in the office of The Liberal Weekly, did a few reviews, spoke out of turn a few times and found herself working on tables in a cheap restaurant. Her feet and her hands bothered her. She's the one who was given the review to do, needing some extra cash, of a book by the editor's wife—and nobody told her why she was expected to praise it. The one who contradicted the man who gave the books out for reviewing, and had him discover that he was wrong later.

She's the woman who lives in the single room at the floor rear who might do better if her mind were worse. The woman who taught herself French because of an admiration for Gide and Corbière. The woman who wears glasses and is terrified by the police on the slightest provocation. The

---

This "Introduction by William Carlos Williams Who Discovered Her" was printed in *New Directions*, 7 (1942), 413–14, but did not appear in her book, *Poems* (Denver: Alan Swallow, 1956).

one who wanting love, with or without, finds herself embarrassed by her own courtesy breaking her brain on the hard stone of necessity.

This is the woman, this you will not remember, who never learned to write English. The one whose poems falter over the speech about her as if over a stony path at night where she is footing it to get to a place to lie down in. She uses the language for a purpose, the purpose is to make poems which in themselves tell what her whole body is screaming to make clear but nothing comes of it. She goes ahead. Occasionally you see her full of dignity and imagination. Then she falls. That is her poems. They are completely successful.

Marcia Nardi, here and there in her work, produces a line or two as fine as anything that anyone, man or woman, writing today can boast of. She is so much better at her best than some of the best known professional poets about us that I am willing to say that by moments no one surpasses her. There are lines, I claim nothing else, in that rubble that can have come from nothing other than a fine mind, courage and an emotional force of exceptional power.

Preface to a Book of Poems by Harold Rosenberg

Not previously published, 1942

IN POETRY, we have gradually discovered, the line and the sense, the didactic, expository sense, have nothing directly to do with one another. It is extremely important to realize this distinction, between what the poem says and what it means, in the understanding of modern verse—or any verse. The meaning is the total poem, it is not directly dependent on what the poem says.

The distinct separation of these two elements in a poem is not in itself the importance. But where the formal make-up is too heavily ridden by what is said we are likely to get into bad habits of thought. The line becomes an implement merely for stressing the explanatory statements and we fall inevitably into the error, so recently popularized by the English exiles to America, especially Auden, when he says that all writing is an instrument, an appliance. As a matter of fact no first-rate work of art can be described as an appliance. Man is the instrument; the poem, the whole poem— when it is "realized"—subordinates man and becomes "the word." We need only to visualize this to see its truth.

Thus to separate the patter from the line, from rigid and always suspicious conformity to the line, is an important part of the poet's occupation today; in painting the color and the outline frequently have the same relationship. The statement, no matter how embellished by metaphor, today

---

Preface intended for Harold Rosenberg, *Trance Above the Streets* (New York: Gotham Bookmart Press, 1942), but not used, possibly because Williams could find so little favorable to say of Rosenberg's poems; Rosenberg later became well-known as the art critic for *The New Yorker*. The text is taken from a manuscript in the Yale collection, Za/Williams/201, six typed pages with no corrections.

runs over, irrelevant to the metrical pattern, from one line to another.

No need to carry this further, more than to say that by this common expedient, of separating the expository narrative importance from the structure the poem, the metrical movement is taken out in a purer form for further study and adjustment. We are better able to see the structure of the poem, as sounds and stresses, as a thing in itself and so are enabled to focus ourselves on that for enlightenment.

It is certain that sooner or later the sense and the total meaning, in some later work, will have to be rebound, reunited, reassociated. But never in the way these two elements were united formerly. We are still in the stage of incomplete realization (as Auden's premature syntheses indicate) of what the coming syntheses must be. So that the separation is still an imperative upon us for we know it cannot be what is behind us.

One of the first incentives, following a complete concentration on the sheer making of a poem apart from what it "says," is the language. I should say that there would be no better discipline for a young poet than to pledge himself by his mistress' thighs or whatever else is holy to him, never to use a word of archaic connotation or direct meaning when one of contemporary meaning is at hand. But how am I going to make it conform to the *line?* he may wail. That (archaic) word exactly fills the structural place I want to inflate. Exactly. By this we see that the *line*, the meter, the pace, the structural element is tyrannically ruling this poet's functioning brain. He is succumbing to the poem, not mastering it. But what is more important, he is being made a supine instrument to total meanings he hasn't suspected even exist. He is being used as an appliance of a subversive order (Eliot's call to order must not be forgotten for what it revealed of him some years ago), he is being made a dupe. Are these points the splitting of hairs? Believe it and fail.

The language, under heavy scrutiny, embodying the whole of the living contemporary world must be our master. How can an intelligent man say to himself that he will take some line, some arbitrary or convenient stanza, and that he is going to use it and make the words fit? He may even succeed but if he does it will be only at the cost of missing his MAJOR opportunity, as Auden obviously does and a whole train of copyists in his train. The major imperative is to make the line fit the language, not the language the line, and to discover there the new structural integer, completely new, forged under the hammering of contemporary necessity to make a more comprehensive and significant structure. Then and only then may what the poem "says" be brought to meet the line as neatly as you please.

Metaphor, all the pretty glass balls, all the thrilling details of writing verse must, today, be subjugated to this prime necessity of studying, of hearing the language for what must come out of it: the structure of ideas which will permit us to proceed among enlightenments.

This imperative modern complex of understanding in a writer which very few realize, very few are patient enough to adhere to, while they see the graceful successes of their period gamboling on the green, is clearly known to Rosenberg. He uses the right words, conscientiously, consciously, and following a sensual application to "nature." He is not abashed by the harshness of the words' meanings or by their cranky or lumpy contours. He takes them by necessity, by contemporary necessity and uses them—allows himself to be molded by their real angles and bulges. Whether he uses the words objectively *enough*, clean *enough* from the horrors of "mood," from sentiment or even sentimentality, I shall not attempt to say. But he does use them at times in the composition of a poem as if they were worthy to be used, without prejudice—the things that *must* be used to make poems.

Anything we want to say and know enough to say might be made from our living language if we knew how to use it. At least Rosenberg knows how to begin to use the language, how to attack the problem, how to make the words do what they must do to enter an expressive modern patter. His broken line, I begin to think, is the most a poet can do with the exigencies which bedevil him today. I have thought something more regular could be accomplished but lacking the genius, it is not yet to be done. By pushing too hard we fall back where we came from into metrical sterility. Our modern line is not satisfactory to me—but it is best, I think, not to beat our brains too much in the search for a completely satisfactory finality, summarizing the day. Get the words down in some kind of honest use—the rest will have to wait. We do not as yet understand all the implications.

I don't know whether or not Rosenberg has chosen the right subjects for his attacks. Of course that's entirely his own business so long as he adheres to the strict imperatives, the learned (rarely learned) necessities of his art today. He knows enough of Stein, he has read Pound and others—and he has absorbed a few of the necessary moves. He is equipped, I think, to go as far as his contemporary realizations of what life is today permits. I'd like to see him try some more organized composition using what in this book he shows he has invented and absorbed. He may have the makings, we are all studying ourselves to see what is in us, we are all conscious of the new necessity to organize our gains. Rosenberg has an opportunity to go ahead because he is not a sinner, by a cleanly approach he has remained clean at least.

This book is made up mostly of early work. I find it a little tiresome, it seems to me a little too much a language study (a bad thing to say here). Many of the poems do not come off, they are not exciting enough, not differentiated enough one from the other, they seem all drawn after one model. This is, of course, an exaggeration but it is the feeling I get from the book. Here's a man I respect. I am not satisfied with him, probably because he exhibits too many of the incompletions I see in myself. Perhaps he will be the one to come out of the present stage of his writing to a fuller realization of his cues. If by a statement of this sort I have helped to clarify his mind, if I have been able to be of assistance to him in realizing what is to be done next, this stress will not have been wasted. We all owe one another everything we are to be; it is a sign of lazy intolerance, between poet and poet, artist and artist, that we do not advance faster.

An Extraordinary Sensitivity

Louis Zukofsky's 55 Poems

Poetry, 1942

BECAUSE A man lives obscurely it does not mean that his work is good, but if he does good work in the arts—or perhaps I had better say, superlative work—it is more than likely he will remain in obscurity. There is a kind of monkhood in excellence, it does not become the street. I wonder, even, if superlative traits of the mind and spirit do not rightly detest popularity. The painstaking excellences in Zukofsky's poems are beyond any school and "meaning." They are just good, just excellent work and because of their precise excellence, that gives a fineness of texture to the writing. I think they are invalidated for general appreciation. What to do about that I do not know.

The poems are uneven. They try a difficult approach to the reader's attention, a very difficult approach, so that there are many factors involved in their failure—even though their successes are of a superlative quality when achieved. Such a poem, for instance, as "10" of the *29 Poems (1923–1931)* is a success. Both the writer and the reader cannot vary a hairline from the purpose. But we are all variable, in mood, in ability—morning and evening make us different men—very seldom are we at a peak of interest in anything, let alone poetry and difficult poetry at that.

In general the poems are arranged chronologically begin-

Review of Louis Zukofsky, *55 Poems* (Prarie City, Ill.: Decker Press, 1941); in *Poetry*, 60, 6 (Sept. 1942): 338–40. Yale, Za/ Williams/286, has a draft of four typed pages with handwritten corrections by both Zukofsky and Williams.

ning with student days and student excellences, an ear for
excellences and for supreme excellences only. There's a
hard start. Zukofsky picked up the rare felicities of all he
had displayed to him by his teachers, the essences of his
Chaucer caught in a phrase, a sort of poetic chemistry, an
almost too fine perception, but not without an overall
strength that proved itself qualified to make the selection.
This was brought together in his "Poem beginning 'The.' "
This is about all he saved from that period. It stays together
and is still effective.

Then he begins with lyrics. These are accompaniments to
thoughts, to recreate them again from the page—if possible.
Just sufficient (put down) to point and pick up—not to clog
or interfere with the movement—like the baton of a con-
ductor that does not play any notes but points and picks up
the sounds it does not make (the sounds made by other
instruments).

Related to books, to reading, to study—to other books
back of them: To other thoughts in other books—a con-
tinuity. A transference from classic images to present-day
vision, comparable only when old thought is put in present-
day (dress) objects, giving them life—again—by continuity
with life as it has been in the past.

The skill of brevity requires deep feeling—or it is jargon.
See clearly and feel, a hint (pointedly) is enough, more
would be too much.

This is a dangerous sort of writing, for if it doesn't click,
if it doesn't do the magic and arouse the reader or doesn't
find one who is sensitive enough, trained enough and ready
enough to place himself exactly in tune with it to appreciate
its just observations and careful statements of fact—or if, in
writing it, the poet isn't instructed by deep enough feeling
(as sometimes happens here) it becomes a mere gathering
and reaching. Explicit (as contrasted with this) writing at
least always makes sense. Here unless the sense is instructed
the writing makes too often no sense.

But explicit writing is so very often as it were a runner

fastened to a cart and this, when it succeeds, is so much a runner free, that the method is wholly justified. But, as I say, it is difficult for the writer and the reader, and always dangerous, for to bore by an unsolvable obscurity is the worst of all writing. And when sense, even if ploddingly, cannot solve a sentence because of an over-absence of its parts—the fault cannot be said to lie with the reader. But to fly, we require a certain lightness—and wings. Among these poems (at their best) we have them. It is a loss that they are not in all the anthologies. They will be.

In Praise of Marriage

Kenneth Rexroth's The Phoenix and the Tortoise

The Quarterly Review of Literature, 1945

LET ME try to be subtle, I'm not very good at being subtle, let me try to make a division—between a poem and its content, between poetry and mysticism in this case: two things with no essential association, sometimes joined together.

I know nothing of mysticism, Christian or other—but I am passionately addicted to the cult of poetry and I do not like to see the two mixed. This is as good a place as any, this book of Rexroth's, over which to attempt a separation. I'm going to try to take out the poetry, appraise it as best I can and leave the mysticism, as far as I can, intact.

But first let me say that this is one of the most completely realized arguments I have encountered in a book of verse in my time. I don't know another book of poems in our language that presents such a compact whole, a completely developed treatment of a serious theme or that gives, at the conclusion, so full a satisfaction as *The Phoenix and the Tortoise*. It is emotionally adult and fully displays, in its steps, a theme worthy of the treatment it receives—without cynicism and without that offensive latter-day intellectualism which abuts finally among the sands of thought rather than upon thought itself rekindled.

This, I take it, is a poem in praise of marriage, a marriage between man and woman, here on earth, in the world as

---

Review of Kenneth Rexroth, *The Phoenix and the Tortoise* (Norfolk, Conn.: New Directions, 1944); in *The Quarterly Review of Literature*, New Haven, 2, 2 (1945): 145–49. Yale, Za/ Williams/121–23 contains drafts.

surely as chemistry is in the world, a poem singularly free from the hopelessness, the welching which is the *fin-de-siècle* polish of our prevailing philosophic clout-heads as Seligman and Ernst used to draw them—twenty years ago.

Whatever his mysticism may amount to, even in that, by the way he handles it, I am ready to say that Rexroth is an upturn from that nadir. The thought of earthly marriage gains a new dignity as well as a refreshment of its mystery from his treatment—a welding with the mind at its best, a seriousness, that leaves at the conclusion of the reading, a taste of honey in the mouth, an effect of something well done—in spite of a certain lack in the poetic means, as I hope to be able to make clear presently.

Rexroth, so I am told, is a mountain climber of no mean distinction who will go up a rock-face unlikely to be attempted by most professionals. He climbs apparently out of some mystic purpose—as another might become a Trappist monk and the connection with poetry is perhaps the same—a mystical assertion. Perhaps this explains a passage in the long opening poem upon, "Whymper, coming down the Matterhorn / After the mountain had collected / Its terrible, casual fee, / The blackmail of an imbecile beauty":

> When, lo! a mighty arch
> And beneath it a huge cross of light
> Appeared, rising above Lyskamm
> High into the sky. . . .

> and appalled,
> We watched with amazement the gradual
> Development of two vast crosses
> One on either side   . . .

How he means us to take that is more than I can say.

To start at the beginning, the long opening poem is a factual account of a night spent on some wild, unpeopled

place near the sea at the foot of mountains—apparently in
winter. It is a narrative in barest outline peopled by the
flights of thoughts of the man, the poet, who lies in a sleep-
ing bag the night through beside his wife watching moon-
rise, the stars and finally the coming of day while she sleeps.
This has been a pact between them, something to which
they looked forward and have planned. Just after dawn he
leaves her and climbs to a snowy plain returning only at the
close of the poem.

It is the battle of the individual for autonomy—volun-
tarily surrendered in marriage; frees him in some mystical
way. But I make no claim for my interpretation, I am
merely guessing.

My concern as I said at the beginning is with the poetry.
Much can be said against this *Phoenix and Tortoise* of Rex-
roth's as a poetic achievement—I am taking poetry as an
absolute for my criterion. But, examining it, even in the
title, an interesting insistence upon exact language—and a
certain perversity, exhibit themselves illustrating this quality
of the poet's mind.

It must not be forgot that *The Phoenix and the Turtle* is
another similar title used previously by another poet—upon
what I take to be about the same theme. But, of course,
"turtle" in that case means dove. But Rexroth specifically
means what he says, "tortoise" and no bird.

I say it's odd, this interplay between two languages in the
title, the English and the American—and hard to tell just
how far Rexroth wanted to carry the analogy. For if mar-
riage is not the theme of both poems at least death is the
counter-theme and "chastitie" or as Rexroth might put it,
"parsimony," its echo.

Concerning the poetry one might object to everything in
the book on the basis that Rexroth has learned nothing from
the concept of verbalism—purloined by Gertrude Stein and
capitalized by Joyce but really the genius of a generation,
the concept of words as things. The Word, in short. But is
not this the sole present-day claim to an authentic religious
approach to meaning, to mysticism in the arts? It must make

all other approaches, especially through antiquated dogma, all but laughable.

But to Rexroth words have absolute meanings synonymous with the context of ideas, which he accepts. Dangerous ground. Rather, for the poet words come first and the ideas are caught, perhaps, among them. The poet invents his nets and catches the birds and butterflies of philosophy. It does not go the other way.

Thus it is inevitable that Rexroth should have wished to be the modern Juvenal but finding that too onerous a task should end his book, in the third part, on the classic modes of Martial to whom the thought was everything and verse the instrument—among much the same debris we see them floundering in today.

The book is cast in three parts, the first, the theme poem, rather long, somewhat too loaded with "proofs" than seems quite necessary, carries one on for all that by its very seriousness—and the resources employed, which are impressive. Everything that the human mind has conceived of physical fact concerning the universe and upon which thought has dwelt from the amoeba to Kirkegaard and more, seem here to have been touched upon—but this is no catalogue but a mind-filling argument—that runs through Jeans and Eddington over the tips of the Sierras for its accomplishment with a persistence that is startling when we find ourselves athletic enough to follow. In the end a curious intoxication takes hold of the reader—or at least took hold of me, a giddiness which did, after all, carry me fascinated through this long approach. After that the book was easy. The battle for autonomy lost, I take it, in the immensities of space, the poet returns to his wife who emerges, as he appears on the rocks above, nude from the surf where she has been bathing. I shall come back to this.

Then follow the shorter and most beautiful poems making up the body of the book of which I shall say nothing more. Finally there are the brief translations and imitations from the Greek and Latin anthologies which make up the book's third part and form the conclusion. I am always fascinated by translation directly into our language from the older classics, they seem to gain something to my ears by having avoided all intervening contacts. Some of these are of that order and most welcome. The inventions in the classic manner, too, have their place.

The classic strength of the position, the intellectual address toward marriage, taken in the theme poem permits the particularization of the shorter poems of the second part as well as the hilarious pulverization in the brief pieces at the end. As if to say, this strength is so sure you may pound it to atoms, split it, shred it, grind it and it will still be the same. And this is true. Man is godlike only in marriage, deny it who will. The Phoenix rises not only from its ashes but from its fragmentations also, diamond like. As Rexroth presents it his theme is incontrovertible. By virtue of which appears—

> The free laughter and the ivory feet
> Treading the grapes—the tousled hair—
> The dark juice rising between the thighs
> Of the laughing, falling girl, spreading
> Through the dark pubic hair, over
> The laughing belly.

I used the word serious a moment ago. There should be a new definition of seriousness or a reaffirmation of seriousness relating to the art of poetry today. It is such a badly understood term. This is a serious poem otherwise it could not bear such criticism as I am attempting to apply to it. Primarily it is serious in thought. That which is serious takes into account ALL that has been learned since classic times and bases its performance on that, NOT on what has been dragged up bodily from the past to howl down the present. The only thing we can take bodily from the past is the seriousness of the past, the refusal to lie, the refusal to accept anything that had not been tested by the BEST brains of the time. Seriousness today must be tested or retested on PRESENT knowledge.

It means, and Rexroth has it, daring, it means immaculate honesty of thought, it means uncommon reading. After all we've got to read or at least, if we're a Mozart, we've got to know. Rexroth may *go* to his mountains, mount them at dawn on skiis but he doesn't STAY there. He drags his mountain around for the argument's sake with him by a strap over his shoulders. That is to say his interest isn't mountains but knowledge—too much so for the verbalism his poem seems to hunger for but—we can't have everything at once I suppose.

Oh well, there's no writing about genius but genius and in lieu of genius, to weld it to speech, what one has to say had better be valued by a kind of logic. Rexroth has that in abundance.

But it is the seriousness of his thought and measured words that hold up what would otherwise have got far too close to bathos for comfort. At the conclusion of the first long opening section when he reappears on the rock and sees his wife among the breakers: that's a hard thing to have made acceptable. One can easily imagine the effect in most hands.

Such a strained Wagnerian effect could not possibly be accepted unless it *were* serious, unless the argument approaching it were sound and brought the mind inevitably to that conclusion. A poem is serious when everything in it, whatever is attempted, comes out without us having to make excuses for it—either on the score of the mind, the heart or the art itself of poetry. When we can say Yes, that is so, then the poet has lifted himself by the muscles of his mind from banality and proves it on the page by the fact of the writing—the test then is reversed upon us, to prove ourselves as able. This he succeeds in doing.

But I find little if any verbal invention in Rexroth—there is no inventive flash, no wedding figure of verbal design. The wedding he speaks of is not *in* the words, his words merely carry it about. Nothing of the Phoenix is in them, rather in the logic. There's a marriage which Rexroth does not contract but he does for all that use a new language.

> This Matrimony called Holy,
> This is the lens of intention,
> Focusing liability
> From world to person, from passion
> To action: and conversely,
> The source of potential in fact.
> The individual—the world—
> On the bookshelves there is only
> Paper soiled by history.

This is his whole poetic means. He goes on—

> The space of night is infinite,
> The blackness and emptiness
> Crossed only by thin bright fences
> Of logic.

Well, there it is, a book full of learning, full of skills, full of reading—where an adult mind may browse today for a long time without blushing either for the writer or himself. It is strong meat and drink written in a verse which is clear as water, a simple facile style that should enhance a reader's pleasure by an easy access to the meaning even though there is little intoxication in its devices.

I must make myself clearly understood: It is a delightful, unaffected verse that by the fact rises actually at times to the marriage; i.e., poetry, which I have described but not often enough. It is a verse free from the clichés of the old poetic "mill," that must give any modern brain the creeps— a verse that does succeed in bringing the ancient anthologists near us, into the next chair, at table, in the garden where we sit, talk and walk about as they.

With this success of a "new" language the rest may remain as mystical as you please as far as I'm concerned.

Parker Tyler's The Granite Butterfly

Accent, 1946

IT IS interesting to me to attempt to recover my reasons for saying, as I did after I had read Parker Tyler's poem in nine cantos, *The Granite Butterfly*, that it is the best poem written by an American since *The Waste Land*—certainly by far the best long poem of our day. Perhaps I had better have said, the first long poem by an American that has managed to emerge since the sweet blight of *The Waste Land*. Few poems since that catastrophe have reattained the vigorous insight into what was being attempted here up to that day. Tyler somehow, by a very devious route, has come about to resail that old and very promising course. So I believe. To me his poem is an event of major significance.

The possibility of a poem's being written in America, a major poem taking its context from direct experience, has been strongly forwarded by Tyler's poem. It is an impulse to write well resumed here. A resumption of the will to write, to recover from the materials their innate relatedness—with respect to the mind at the full, the alert, instructed mind that thus begins once more to clothe itself in suitable manner here.

To be a poem a writing must have two movements, from outside inward and from inside out. The movement must be generated from the nature of the material and the material must take its structure from the emotion, the quality of the

---

Review of Parker Tyler, *The Granite Butterfly* (Berkeley: Bern Porter, 1945); in *Accent*, Urbana, Ill., 6, 3 (Spring 1946): 203–06. Buffalo C37 has three drafts.

driving person behind it. Successfully it must be as whole as a horse leaping a ditch—and much the same, the horse, by the way, has always been associated with the poem.

To try then to discover why I think Parker Tyler's poem is important—to rediscover the reasons for my instinctive liking for the work—it is a whole: it moves like a horse or like any living thing of swiftness and weight, it is all of itself. The verse takes its élan from the material and the material has the same resiliency, solidity of thought, as the pliant lines.

The verse is as immediate, as intelligent as the very unencumbered thought: nothing is imitating anything except *within* the poem where everything imitates everything else—it moves together to go from here to there. And it does go. You do not have the feeling of intrusive meanings pushed on the sense by a hangover of form. You do not have an irrationality of form tearing down the sense. It is inventive, spontaneously adjusted part to part, and gives that feeling of resiliency because it is all one animal. All one poem newly made, deftly formed part to part. I do not think Tyler hesitated one moment in writing it. It is an end result of honesty and instruction—at its best.

This is something not easy to get. It comes of the blossoming of an environment. We are all too prone to distrust our instinctive judgments and belittle our pleasures. We do not believe that *we* shall ever do anything good. And we shan't—unless we are able and instructed. Unless we practice, unless we see many varieties, English, Russian, French, Balinese, Argentine. We've got to be in a position to have observed everything. But once we have established our consciousness and exercised our talents, the time must come when we too shall attempt to take off—in our own right—and fly.

And when we do, every part of our equipment as well as the courage and intelligence behind our venture must be interrelated in the machine, the poem which signalizes our success.

This is one of the few recent poems that attempt to fly of their own resources, interrelated to be a functional whole— of any first-rate quality of thought.

Do I exaggerate? Perhaps. But not in my major thesis that this is the *kind* of thing we must do to succeed. And that this is a new courage and a new success—for this succeeds in being pleasurable. Little verse is pleasurable.

To come down to a final definitive statement—I know of no poet in America (or elsewhere at the moment) who has composed into a poem evidence of a mind as untrammeled by the hish-hash of conventional beliefs, as alert and informed as Parker Tyler shows in this poem. Come at it as he may have done, by what devious courses, either by heredity or by accident—all these things mean nothing at all—he has arrived at a status of adulthood as a modern being. All others, at the moment, seem maimed to me beside him: most sound as if they were not above the newspaper level. It isn't, mind you, the intelligence alone; it is the ripened awareness of the tentative putting forth of new leaves in the world, the man. This is the first pleasure in the poem. It is not "special pleading" as all second-rate art is, it is enlightening, nourishing. A poem must nourish the whole man. First by the comprehensive, the responsiveness in the new and the newly opened, behind it. Couple this quality of mind, of the man (in a poem) to the second awareness, the awareness of the newly won in technical elaboration, the escape from the tawdriness of the dead line and trope to an unfettered freedom of metrical resources, couple these two and you have the *makings* at least of a great poem. It doesn't matter so much what is specifically "said" in the poem, it is what is really expressed *overall* in the poem as a single thing, a single enlightenment in the very fibre of the poem, the poem itself, that is the only and full meaning. The mind and the skill, the enlightened mind that has discovered the waking moment of the world which it inhabits and the ability to give new clothes, new voice to that morning of the world—the poem itself. That is what this poem of Tyler means to me,

that is why I admire it. That it has dull moments, condi-
tioned by certain special qualities of the poet's mind and
consequent skills, is of no importance. It has defects but it is
for all that "right." It walks, it jumps, it snorts and . . . it
is the animal moving.

An analysis of the poem might go something like this:
Well, here's a study for you. I suppose it's synecdochic,
metonymic—logical? But neither metaphoric nor ironic
surely—the reduction of a predicament, an intellectual pre-
dicament, to terms not easy to nail down.

Well, to begin again, what does it dramatize?—for it ap-
pears to be a dramatization, emotive, a dramatic poem—with
a hero, a possible hero (the Granite Butterfly), a hero of
specific qualities sufficiently important to the poet to present
as a major work.

Personally I don't give a damn who. I take little pleasure
in ideas unless they are translated to me through the emo-
tions—which take their place. So here we are back again
where we started.

Well, emotion is what I'm seeking—let the rest go. What
sort of emotion is to be discovered here?

It's an icy sort of consternation, a stony sort of butter-
fly—not necessarily a paradoxical situation if you consider
that rock is as transient a chemical as flesh is, as a wing is: a
butterfly wing. We live in an age when matter generally is
known to be just force frozen, if Einstein knows what he is
talking about.

So we have the figure of a stone butterfly (even before
we read the poem)—the most fragile identified with the
most naturally enduring (certain metals, crystals are more
enduring than granite though granite is more massive in the
world): there's your metonymy, your reduction.

Well, but the emotion: that's emotion at its peak, its tragic
peak—the granite butterfly. Now fracture that into the in-
terrelated parts of a poetic composition and you'll have your
answer. Every poet (poem?) partakes of the whole and *rep-
resents* (synecdoche) the whole and the whole is no more,
cannot be more, than its parts.

The poem, if it is emotion, is to move us—or it isn't a work of art. Move us to what?

We are moved to feel, we are moved to feel shame at our own clothes, at the food we put in our mouths to live (why?), at all the snug little warmths we pack about our fearful carcasses (and therefore souls: transubstantiation) against the horrible cold of the world and its ideas that inhabit it and us.

Shall we accept this attack upon our defeat and our self-protectiveness? With pleasure? Is the poem that good? That humble?

No, I don't think it is humble. That would be my first objection. It is destructive to the pettiness of our moods—but it is not reassuring. Not in the faintest degree reassuring.

If it's read—and is a work of art—then it is to be read with pleasure (the pyramid is the test: bottom to top). What pleasure? A pleasure of self-abasement before the granite butterfly.

Are we all not just that? We believe in our persistence, everything we do proclaims this—that we do anything proclaims it. We are, at our imagined best, important—important enough to write.

All right, the granite butterfly is man—or rather, art, i.e., Man. It is that artist, man, untorn by the expanding universe. Or is it? It is, definitely, so intended: synecdochic.

But is it good writing? Its affection of the distortions of the present writing mood is not always to its advantage. Compare the much more complete contours of Pound's early cantos—the much richer texture of his lines. Would Tyler agree to this? Certainly. This is a moderner verse—void, almost entirely void of metaphor (its absence recently so well pointed out as a feature of modern poetry by Taupin, see *The Quarterly Review of Literature:* Fall 1945 issue). This verse of Tyler's is much more lithe, much leaner than anything Pound ever did. Its sheer metaphor is nowhere near the color of Pound's passages. But this is correct, as it should be.

This verse is much more modern than Pound.

The artist sets forth from his mother's womb—a Gene-
sis—without much light. That's the modern of it, rather its
antithesis "blind." Listening to the "black music." The iden-
tity of the sexes—"all one cloud." Good. Very modern
(Athenian!) but well used here.

In this part great pleasure of the reading (pp. 10 to 11).

Yes, "interlude of the blood." I take back what I said
about no humility. There is even humbleness: "Desire to tell
everything." Well, go ahead. *It is only time that moves.*
Not the stranded butterfly. No motion there?

The humility of the confession, that is not a confession,
but the image of a confession that moves us *in the writing*
even though it does not take place: which it should not do.
I enjoy the writing beginning, "No. Each wrinkle of in-
spiration," etc.

The "landscape" in the next part is well placed. Good un-
emotional (faked) landscape too. Landscape for itself (I
hope). Hobbema? Not much color. Distance. This whole
scheme synecdochic? I avoid another term of commoner
descent—a very happy scene: the past, childhood? Is all this
before the catastrophe? Confessional. Fine stuff.

I don't get the Negro "Oedipus" though (at this point).
Son to whom? To kill what father, marry what mother?
This comes out later.

With the next section, "Portrait," the artist comes into his
own: he recognizes himself as himself. But is this Shake-
speare or himself he is drawing? Or both? (Compare with
the ensuing description Shakespeare's drawing of the stal-
lion in *Venus and Adonis*.) The following detailed descrip-
tion of a man is special stuff, not so good. The interest
slumps—stopped, luckily, just at the point of indifference.
Not suggestive of Leonardo, Masaccio (?) as it would seem
to pretend—the frescoes of the Sistine Chapel. Not "in-
formed" enough.

The whole of the "Metamorphosis" is excellent—of the
best. It is this sort of writing that clinches the matter for me.

The somewhat obscure image of the pyramids juxtaposed,

peak to peak, is very interesting when we oppose the two
incidents of the rape of the white woman by the Negro who
has beaten up her lover—or husband?—and the rise of the
serfs who take over the Count, Alexei Escutonoff, and his
wife.

This juxtaposition of two lurid stories is a very interesting
literary feat: very artificial, very real at the same time and—
the two pyramids—a trope that might be described as alle-
gorical overlay. But at the same time—it lets in the light.

This is worth studying for the light it throws on Tyler's
mind. It is a poetical device, a literary strategy by which
he snares the reader's attention, the vulgar reader one might
say, and by the accuracy, the honesty, of the comparisons
manages so that he is able to "say" many things in his poem
that could not be said otherwise.

It may be that the last scene is too violent—that Tyler has
forgotten himself and turned the poem into a tricky melo-
drama. I don't believe this. I think it is deliberate, that it
belongs to the poem, and, in fact, lets the granite butterfly
flutter its wings very excitingly.

The Genius of France

André Breton's Young Cherry Trees Secured Against Hares

View, 1946

ANDRÉ BRETON in his verse (which is himself, that is to say, anybody) displays all the conventional virtues of French poetry: the Racine of the drama, the Baudelaire of strict quatrains—expanded to a false looseness. This is not true, there is no looseness in Breton's work, it is all calculated, the tight plot precedes all composition, a coralization microscopic in detail of its vastness. I was tempted to say its limitlessness—but refrained for good reasons.

As with Catholicism and Sovietism everything is planned in Surrealism of which Breton gives here, in his new book of poems, such a balanced display. (All this is contrary to the spirit of the Constitution of the United States.) Complete freedom of enterprise is unknown there. That is why they exported The Statue of Liberty to New York harbor and kept only an insignificant replica for the Seine. A closed system.

That is definitely the enormous virtue of the French and their despair. Breton is well acquainted with all this and for that reason (secretly) has been willing to accept all the imposters from America and elsewhere into the confraternity of Surrealism. All but one whose name need not be mentioned since everybody knows it.

Thus it is with Breton's simple and crystal-clear verse:

Review of André Breton, *Young Cherry Trees Secured Against Hares,* trans. Edouard Roditi (New York: View Editions, 1946); in *View,* 7, 1 (Fall 1946): 43–47. The manuscript and one draft are Yale Za/Williams/284–85.

Everybody knows beforehand everything that will be said. It is completely without invention in the American sense— this is its greatest achievement. Everything Breton will say we know is completely predictable and is thus reassuring to schoolmistresses and the young who need the support of the master.

How is it that from France whence we have come to expect nothing but disastrous uncertainties we get this crystal-clear writer? I say it is because of convention, the great convention of French thought, from Descartes to the present day. And before Descartes and on into the timeless future. WE CAN EXPECT NOTHING NEW FROM FRANCE IN THE WORLD ANY MORE. This Breton recognizes and proves in his revolutionary work, this is what he is saying over and over, this makes him a leader of modern—What shall I say? perception? thought? accomplishment.

No.

Nothing of this! All that is antithetical to Surrealism. It is for this that renegades who succeed are expelled from the group. It is for this that *emigrés* are retained as brothers. BECAUSE THEY ARE TRAITORS.

Traitors to what? TO FRANCE!

Just as Picasso the Spaniard has destroyed Paris, made it a mews of the world so that no Frenchman can any longer paint—but must yield his strength to American women (as they did until recently to others)—so Breton must covertly uphold the conventions of the great past of his native country.

But it must be done sub rosa. It must be done without letting the others discover how quietly flows the great river of his genius beneath the false soil of the fields and skies he paints in his poems with the brushes used by miniaturists in making their copies of the portraits of Napoleon by David. It makes one think of La Place Henri IV in Paris today.

Oh but this is difficult and onerous work. A man must labor under strange constraints to accomplish it. One could see Breton in New York for the past four years walking the

streets or sitting drinking with his cronies at the Mont D'Or
on E. 48th Street but never, never could one see beneath
that pudgy surface the true son of France sleeping far from
the dull gazes of the casual passerby.

Thence emerges this magnificent and quieting book:
Young Cherry Trees Secured Against Hares. What title
could be more subtle or more revealing? We see the fea-
tures of the author disclosed (through an aperture in the
dust jacket) as those of Liberty surrounded by the other-
wise familiar characters of Bartholdi's famous statue. Is this
pawkiness an attempt to attract the pennies of the casual
reader? Of course!

I say the gesture is courageous and TRUE. It is France
redivivus. It is André Breton with absolute seriousness pre-
scribing the history, the literature and the thought of France,
the calculator, the crystalizer of reason in the world—for
the ease of our tormented spirits. It is a flight from abstrac-
tion to common sense. What is liberty? André Breton.
Could anything be more necessitous? (The book is for sale).
Or refreshing?

I say that by this self-limitation (which solely permits the
excess of design familiar to us today) this classic coldness of
line, this lack of invention among the physical materials of
the poem, THIS COMPLETE EXCLUSION OF THE
PERCEPTIONS UPON WHICH THE BEST OF OUR
OWN POETRY IS FOUNDED, in this restraint, of French
literature generally, we see perhaps the only possible MODE
by which such extremes of thought as the world faces today
may be disciplined.

American poetry which seeks to smash the line apart, to
model it after an expanding universe, to admit to its forms
the same character of natural forms—is warned by Breton
(in this book) that such an attack is futile and cannot suc-
ceed. Opposite our iconoclastic adventures he displays for
us the cold outlines of a classic past—disguised, to be sure,
made modern by a reapplication of terms to new mechanisms
but in reality the continuing great conservatism of French

thought—which no one but he who in himself personifies that pure lineage can fully know.

Look at the titles of his poems: "Sunflower." "Freedom of Love." "Fata Morgana." "War." "To the Wind." "The Vertebral Sphinx." What more usual or prosaic? Simple as green beans. Pure classicism. Oh we do not realize what France means to the world! Especially to this world whose end we think we see—and see nothing clear—nothing but change without reference to THINGS, of which the world is made. Until we learn through such as Breton how to apply our senses anew.

Shapiro Is All Right

Karl Shapiro's Essay on Rime

The Kenyon Review, 1946

SUPPOSE ALL women were delightful, the ugly, the short, the fat, the intellectual, the stupid, even the old—and making a virtue of their qualities, each for each, made themselves available to men, some man, any man—without greed. What a world it could be—for women! In the same figure take all the forms of rime. Take for instance the fat: If she were not too self-conscious, did not regret that she were not lissome and quick afoot but gave herself, full-belly, to the sport! What a game it would make! All would then be, in the best sense, beautiful—entertaining to the mind as to the eye but especially to that part of a man which we call so mistakenly the intellect. It is rather the whole man, the man himself, alert. He would be analyzed by their deportment and enriched in the very libraries of his conscience. He would be free, freed to the full completion of his desires.

Shapiro speaks lovingly of his "rime," which he defines here and there in his poem—variously, as it should (not) be defined. It is the whole body of the management of words to the formal purposes of expression. We express ourselves there (men) as we might on the whole body of the various female could we ever gain access to her (which we cannot and never shall). Do we have to feel inferior or thwarted because of that? Of course not. We do the best we can—as much as the females of our souls permit. Which isn't much,

---

Review of Karl Shapiro, *Essay on Rime* (New York: Reynal and Hitchcock, 1945); in *The Kenyon Review*, 8, 1 (Winter 1946): 123–26; and reprinted in *Selected Essays.*

generally. Each man writes as he is able under the circumstances under which he exists.

The trouble with this exercise of Shapiro's is that it is so damned easy to read, so interesting, such a pleasure. One can sympathize with a man sitting down in a "camp" somewhere, bored stiff by removal from his usual environment and playing (*in vacuo*, so to speak) with the problems he must some day face in practical work. He doesn't solve much, he doesn't expect to solve much, he wants only to clarify, to make a definite distinction between the parts of the great body that presents itself to him for his enjoyment. He attacks it bravely. She lies back and smiles—not with any intent to intimidate. She is very definitely sure of herself and—friendly. Whether she will be stirred to passion by his attack is a question. But he is young and that's a lot.

Well, you don't get far with women by quoting Eliot to them. Maybe the Sacred Hind means something to them—and wistfulness is dear to the female heart but I don't believe it beyond a certain point. She gets tired of being tickled merely.

However, we're talking of the art of writing well in a modern world and women haven't much to do with that, I guess. Not directly. America is still too crude for that. I don't think any place is much better. Not France. Not England—so far as I know. And not Russia. Of course it's ridiculous to think of any land, as a land, in this respect. Women are as various (and as rare) as men.

What Shapiro does point out however is that—

> No conception
> Too far removed from literal position
> Can keep its body.

I imagine that will put a quietus on the "abstractionists" so far as writing (with words) is concerned. It's all right to make Maltese crosses of poems and use words as pigments—but, well. . . . Women want men to come to the point. Writing, too, is like that. At least I think that is what

Shapiro means, relative to the prosody. If so I agree with him.

I admire his respect for Milton (*pace* Winters) especially with reference to the amazing transition Milton effects between the dialogue and the chorus in *Samson*. But I am especially interested in the view he takes of Milton the craftsman, to whom he calls strongest attention—though I must say it would have been better if he had a little stressed the necessity Milton was under in achieving his effects to distort the language in ways we may not descend to. He however ignores, as what craftsman must not, the mere subject of Milton's major poem. Lesser critics do not get beyond that.

Shapiro intimates the *formal* importance of Whitman—another thing nobody notices. Nobody notices enough, that is.

Oh, well, I've only read halfway through his poem as yet. I think it is illuminating in its summations of the field, the large expanse of what we must approach to be masterful.

I came at the book with positive aversion. What the hell! But he has won me. I think Shapiro may [do] very well—at least I permit him to go on writing. He isn't a liar, he isn't an ape, he isn't just sad over the state of the world and the stars, he doesn't even bother to concern himself with humanity, or economics, or sociology or any other trio.

He's almost painfully interested in writing as it has been, masterfully, in the world and as it may be (under changed and changing conditions) in the world again. He keeps on the subject. And that's rare. More power to him. I hope he finds her rarest treasures—I am not jealous.

Beginning toward the last thousand lines I find—

> But grammar
> Like prosody is a methodical afterthought,
> A winter flower of language.

There are many such successful aphorisms among the 2,000 lines, not the worst part of the poem—good summations of fumbled concepts we all play at remembering.

Then he goes off on A. It may be a personal matter with him but I don't know one man writing in America today who ever reads A. or so much as thinks of him or his work when writing. I may be uninformed, I merely mention what to me is a commonplace. Vazakas once went to see A. at Swarthmore and found him a nice boy, still, and very kind—but I didn't discover that he came away with any broader impression—and with the next sentence we were talking of other matters. This infatuation I think reveals Shapiro's faulty objective in some of his work. A. seems frankly to be desperately fumbling with a complicated apparatus—to find, to find—could it possibly be something not discoverable here? That would really be too bad.

We haven't half enough translations. How can Shapiro say historians will discover we've had too many? I am sure Ezra Pound will be known principally for his translations, the most exquisite in our language. Of bad translations, yes, we've had too many—and of translations of bad poetry, popular at the moment, far, far too many. Rilke and Rimbaud *ad nauseam*. Why don't we read *them* at least in the originals? Every translation I have ever read of either painfully stinks.

Yop. "And less verse of the mind."

I can't agree on Hart Crane. He had got to the end of his method, it never was more than an excrescence—no matter what the man himself may have been. He had written it right and left, front and back, up and down and round in a circle both ways, criss cross and at varying speeds. He couldn't do it any longer. He was on his way back from Mexico to—work. And couldn't work. He was returning to create and had finished creating. Peggy [Guggenheim] said that in the last three hours he beat on her cabin door—after being deceived and thrashed. He didn't know where to turn—that was the end of it.

That he had the guts to go over the rail in his pyjamas, unable to sleep or even rest, was, to me (though what do I know—more than another?) a failure to find anywhere *in*

his "rime" an outlet. He had tried in Mexico merely to
write—to write anything. He couldn't.

Yes, love might have saved him—but if one is to bathe to
satiation in others' blood for love's sake . . . ?

Belief would be marvelous if it were not belief but scien-
tific certainty. But you can't go back and believe what you
know to be false and no belief has ever existed without holes
in stones that emit smoke—to this day. Belief must always
for us today signify nothing but the incomplete, the not yet
realized, the hypothetical. The unknown.

Where then will you find the only true belief in our day?
Only in science. That is the realm of the incomplete, the
convinced hypothesis—the frightening embodiment of mys-
teries, of transmutations from force to body and from body
to—nothingness. Light.

The anthropomorphic imaginatives that baffle us by their
absence today had better look to Joyce if they want a pope
and endless time.

Anyone who has seen 2,000 infants born as I have and
pulled them one way or another into the world must know
that man, as such, is doomed to disappear in not too many
thousand years. He just can't go on. No woman will stand
for it. Why should she?

We'll have to look to something else. Who are we any-
how? Just man? What the hell's that? Rime is more.

Introduction to Byron Vazakas' Transfigured Night

1946

Invent Create Achieve—Henry James

BYRON VAZAKAS is that important phenomenon among writers, an inventor. There are few inventors in the arts. He has been led, more by irritation, I think, than by anything else, to an investigation of the poetic line, to attack the problem of measure, of which the conventional line is such a very bad approximation—the line in which the worst clichés of the art of poetry lie anchored—to see if something more could not be done with it than the past permitted.

The result has been arresting, though unspectacular. I doubt that even he yet fully realizes what he has accomplished. It's too simple a device.

Now you don't get inventions without insistences of some sort to induce them: bad lights, awkward weights, long distances to controvert; and where the mind is concerned, as in the arts, the situation is no different. Inventions come in usually at the anodic opening or the cathodic closing; they are likely to be an inaugural or a culmination. In this case it was an inaugural related to a nascent culture—which it

---

This Introduction to Byron Vazakas, *Transfigured Night* (New York: The Macmillan Co., 1946) first appeared as a prepublication review in *The Quarterly Review of Literature*, 2, 4 (1946): 346–49. Buffalo C38 contains two drafts. Yale Za/Williams/128 contains one draft, and Za/Williams/246a contains the manuscript. In *QRL* the epigraph from Henry James is in quotation marks and the source is footnoted as "The Madonna of the Future."

would be presumptuous to call American—pressing for expression here.

I am speaking of writers, particularly poets. We have had our Henry James and those—who can be bunched without naming them—who ran away from the United States to English rather than to England for their opportunities, like James, sensing no break here. When they did so, they left behind something which has had to rescue itself as best it could without them.

In America, that pliant land, an undisciplined new language has been striving for several generations, without those valiants, to assert itself formally. It has lacked invention to give it the means. We have had no basic revelations in the language itself to guide us, something to equate the psychologic differences between England and America as two dissident cultures opposed one to the other, though having, to be sure, much in common. New ways of splitting the language into component units suitable for our new verse requirements have been signally neglected here. The brilliance abroad has been too overwhelming!

For my part, I have always felt that this un-American lack of initiative has been blanketed upon us largely by the colonial attitude of our universities and their flagrantly outdated English departments. In any case, Vazakas is not a university man.

Walt Whitman did make a beginning toward a formal organization of the American tongue, but it is something for which he is given no credit, since no one thinks of his devices upon the page as of formal significance. His misfortune is that he came in on the destructive phase. And while he broke down staid usages, he found nothing to take their place, merely scattered himself broadcast. That was his form, but it ended there. . . . These poems pick up the thread where Whitman dropped it, and make a positive step toward what must next be brought into view. Comprising a first book, they are remarkable enough to warrant the highest praise I can give.

Vazakas is still a young man. He writes as he breathes, and means to make good poems, as good as he can make them. I don't say he is the wonder of the world. I merely say that of the forty or fifty poems by him I've seen in manuscript, the latest show a formal development which I think is very important. This, for me, is his history.

That isn't all, of course. Aside from that particular thing, there's a basic language of poets which he well employs, a metaphoric residuum which is the same the world over, pre-formal. Vazakas is at home there also, effortlessly, "as effort-less as heaven."

We see our world in the best of these poems, as in all good poetry, as part of ourselves transposed from a world that has no concern for us, and before which we stand em-barrassed, as before the newspapers. Merely by his passing, the poet will give it a shape and make it habitable, "I lounge half-heartedly across the room / disturbing the dust that is not yet me. . . ." And it is where he *is* that he accomplishes this feat.

How foolish to seek new worlds, sometimes, when we must know that any world warmed by the arts will surpass the very Elysian Fields if the imagination reaches its end there. No world can exist for more than the consuming of a match or the eating of an apple without a poet to breathe into it an immortality.

It's good to know that such a man as Vazakas is walking among us, and intends to go on doing so. I like the lack of choice and the complacency with which he takes it for granted that merely by being where he happens to be he transforms the place to his desire.

He is gentle-vitriolic, kind-inhuman, forgiving-obdurate, a poet whose urbanity is inviolate. He seems more the artist, the poet in the full sense of a transformer by work of the imagination, than anyone I know. Nor is this to be a poet's poet; this is to work at his trade; he's a good hard worker at his job. A railroad coach, a doctor's office, the flumes of a skyscraper, the convalescent's eye, "the faculty of yesterday

to remember and disturb," anything, everything is his con-
cern. It doesn't matter what or where, so long as a formal
emphasis can be imposed upon it.

Vazakas doesn't *select* his material. What is there to select?
It *is*. Like the newspaper that takes things as it finds them—
mutilated and deformed, but drops what it finds as it was,
unchanged in all its deformity and mutilation—the poet,
challenging the event, recreates it as of whence it sprang
from among men and women, and makes a new world of
it . . . *Night transfigured;* this is Vazakas.

It is in the *manner* of the writing, the method of his treat-
ment of the subject, that the poet reveals his purpose to
transform it.

Not having to search for his material, disdaining to search
for it, Vazakas hasn't had "to go anywhere." There he is . . .
anywhere, therefore *here,* for his effects. And being here, he
sees here; and hears here. And what does he hear? Our
language.

What I wish to point out is that it was his habits, his
good habits as a poet, which brought Vazakas to his dis-
covery. The typography looks something like a toy cannon,
a long top sticking out to the left, over a base of three
shorter ones:

> This is not the classic torso
>   pompous with its death, but
>   the obscene disorder of the
>   dying who cannot accept . . .

But what to call it? It isn't a line. Nor is it a stanza, for a
stanza is made up of a series of lines, and this has none. It
isn't prose because it is so definitely a measure. I put it aside
at first as just another of those things.

What an unimaginable pleasure it would be to read or to
hear lines that remain unpredictable, hold the ear in suspense,
conceal all the elements of surprise to the end, and yet re-
main orderly, retain a perfect order, a meter to reassure us.

This combination of order *with* discovery, with exploration and revelation, the vigor of sensual stimulation, is of the essence of art. It brings relief. Nothing but invention, formal invention using always a new sensual facet for its recordings, can bring that relief . . . and pleasure.

I should say, and have long said, that we need a basic invention to break the dominance of the trite, tight line which convention has bequeathed us generally for the writing of poetry today. Not that we haven't tried. Not some pulling and padding, some skimping and stretching, which is no real break, an expedient no sooner mastered than discarded dejectedly, but something that will, in our case, get the last of English out of our nostrils . . . a downright creation.

What we have wanted is a *line* that will allow us room in which to develop the opportunities of a new language, a line loose as Whitman's, but *measured* as his was not.

The thing to notice about this more or less accidental discovery of Vazakas, is that it has a very definite regularity resembling, however vaguely, a musical bar. A bar, definitely, since it is not related to grammar, but to *time*, as Vazakas uses it. The clause, the sentence, and the paragraph are ignored, and the progression goes over into the next bar as much as the musical necessity requires . . . a sequence of musical bars arranged vertically on the page, and capable of infinite modulation.

> In the outer office, the wind moans by
>   steel window-sash, echoing the terror
>   of my being here. No other hand
>   constructed this; no brain conceived
> So monstrous a detachment . . .

Certainly a large part of my pleasure in reading the poems in the later part of this book comes from the escape from trite forms. More and more, I am convinced that Vazakas has hit upon a delightful as well as a basically worthwhile expedient in the contour of these later poems; good for the poet as well as for the reader, a release to the ear and to the mind.

. . . I mean not the horse, but the rider. One takes the beast bareback, like an Indian, and doesn't post at every step: one, two, one, two, but goes with the animal as the animal goes; and yet remains a man. Ancient horses do not seem to have had the stature of those of today; even the Tartar horses were small. I wonder if the gait of the horse didn't affect the line in those days. Maybe the railroad begat Walt Whitman, and our present day autos ourselves, Vazakas among us.

What has Vazakas actually accomplished? This: He has completely done away with the poetic line as we know it, a clean sweep, not a vestige of it left. This is far beyond Whitman's looseness. And what neither Whitman nor anyone else envisioned—the poetic line annihilated—Vazakas has invented: a workable expedient to replace it. He has found a *measure* based not upon convention, but upon music for his reliance, a measure that is inviolable to the old attack. He abandoned an eye habit with all its stale catch, threw all that aside for pure ear.

Furthermore, by returning to music, whence poetry came, by going over from *all* the unconscious checks which the old line and its various empty combinations imposed, by going over from these to an auditory measure, Vazakas has at the same time made a transit from English, for us an hieratic language, to our own spoken tongue, freeing that to its own melodies. He brushed aside everything that might impede its music, caught by the music, caught by the music alone. As a starter, this is enough for any man.

A New Line Is a New Measure

Louis Zukofsky's Anew

The New Quarterly of Poetry, 1947–48

At *least* (and that's the place to begin) Zukofsky has the intention of singing *anew* when almost all poets otherwise have forgotten the objective. *Singing.* Singing *anew:* in that order. I don't hear any blasting out of hymns, granted, but I do hear at least an intention, basic and right, and rare and intelligent and homely and passionate and subdued.

This poetry is lyric in a way we have hardly sensed at all for a century. It is invention of a kind that music cannot and need not copy. But like music it is capable of being adult— to the day of its creation. It is capable of going *with* invention in music which almost all modern verse is definitely NOT capable of doing. Almost all modern verse is metrically sterile. It is sensitiveness to metrical invention that makes this verse arresting.

But poetry has other allegiances than that. Poetry has to satisfy before all else the word. It is the words that have primary place in a line and in a poem, which is an arrangement, an invention of lines, if possible, anew. I know no work in rime today that has such clean, such well-used words in it as these, minutely adjusted to be what they are intended to be in each particular line and to be nothing else.

The poems in this book are the fruit of an evolving, a patient unfolding of many developments in courtesy, in intellectual honesty, in plain ability to survive and write. They

Review of Louis Zukofsky, *Anew* (Prairie City, Ill.: Decker Press, 1946); in *The New Quarterly of Poetry*, New York, 2, 2 (Winter 1947–48): 8–16. Buffalo C41 has six drafts.

depend on love, love between individuals who don't lie to each other, or try to fake anything. They come of alertness to the gradual unfolding of ideas which may be called modern, they are so old.

This book is brilliant through an overall consciousness of its own warmth, its own despairs, its own indifferences to anything but its own excellence in the writing. It is happy, happy of a welcoming warmth. That is one of its subtlest and most obvious successes—its serenity in love. For by knowing how to write Zukofsky has found it possible again to express love. You cannot express anything unless you invent how to express it. A poem is not a Freudian "escape" (what childishness!) but an adult release to knowledge, in the most practical, engineering manner.

These poems do, very definitely, have to do with the structure of the line, the poetic line, in complete consciousness—no accident. The line is the meat, and not, not what it says.

In this poetry the line has been reaffirmed in its perfection. *Not* because other lines were imperfect. They were not. *But because this line (identical) is wholly different from what they were formerly and is still perfect, because it does not exclude what the old perfect line excluded, metrically.*

This is devastating! It smashes the whole world into virtues the sense refuses to perceive.

Is it inconceivable that in a single line, in a single poem the world can be shattered to bits? And that it will not realize it for a hundred years—while schools go on teaching anachronistic sterilities thereafter for generations—resentfully, with perfect organization—and the young will grow up bewildered and blunder into so called marriages and mass murders? While the "cure"—oh, the cure.

It may be inconceivable that in a single poem the world can be set right, but it is the truth. Nothing does happen, except in the minds of a few; but it is drastic, what sometimes happens in the minds of a few.

Good taste, that's the thing; and not by exclusion, in the

vulgar way, but by an inclusion that puts its grace upon common objects, that raises the common to grace. That's what a poem is, here. Objects. Things. Benefited. Beneficed.

To the mind, well adjusted to the requirements of its day—adjusted to an understanding of daily happenings in the terms that have become prevalent and necessary in the various mental and physical activities which comprise an age—certain works of expression (the arts) are acceptable and others are not.

Nowadays almost all that passes for poetry is not the result of a fruition but a stasis. A lovely stasis, a pleasant stasis. But a stasis. The wall is there. We may ignore the wall and cast about for supernatural alternatives, but as long as we live we shall not get past the wall in dreams. Poems are the effects of engineering skills in poets. It takes more than thinking backward or thinking at all to write a poem. It's got to be written precisely in one particular manner at any one particular moment in the world's experience to be a poem in that day.

Everything else is wadding, beautiful wadding. Wadding is swell couches where lovely creatures recline, male and female, for their own reasons. But it isn't writing.

These lyrics of Zukofsky's are adult, a development and an accomplishment in that which implies the writing of a poem that is acceptable to a modern mind.

How? As an iron post can destroy a car. As time can destroy (or right) a stone: by setting up a standard to which any concept or series of concepts must adapt themselves, if they can. This makes imperative an entire series of readjustments, destroys the former inadequate standards. Or brings them into a new accuracy. Or else!

Or else what?

In other words you don't grasp the meaning of destroy.

The university would still stand and function, wouldn't it?

But a university, a university is a matter of knowledge. Why do you suppose the establishments hate the modern? And all bridge-tenders are old? The line, if it be "the New,"

stands. There it is. What are they going to do, ignore it?
Then they are no longer "the university" but something less.
They have been destroyed. What do you suppose makes all
the stinks about us? The dead.

Now we're really going. Almost. It's almost time to have
what has been impossible heretofore, to have a journal. To
have an organ to implement the drive ahead. Everything of
moment in the writing of that value which emerges as poems
and has no other escape has been dammed out of existence
by the establishment, which substitute death for life; by
philosophy, by "learning," by the furious critics. Only a
trickle has come out under the dam now and then. At once
they rush out the emergency squads to plug the leak, the
leak! in their fixed order, in their power over the water.

What I would say is that this is the first clear, the first
adequate reason that we, among ourselves, have ever had for
an accounting, and with it a ledger, a periodical with a firm
enough purpose to support a possible greatness. All purposes
to make a magazine heretofore have been vague, partial, tan-
gential, there has been no comprehensive, penetrant enough
promise of development to last more than a few issues. And
so the issues have died, or become a fashion or achieved
what other pleasant destiny.

But a revolution in the line, maintained by first-rate work,
gives a chance for vast revisions that potentially penetrate
the very bases of knowledge and open up fields that might
be exploited for a century. It is the key, the true key that
will really turn a lock, the toughest lock there is. The poetic
line can be the key opening a *way* to learning, the hidden
implement which could, once learned and supported by
great *work*, poems, make knowledge work—though it lies in
a stasis now. It is blocked by rigid misconceptions of what
the poetic line is, the old a grill as before a prison window,
the new, the grill gone.

These poems are only a nick, a crevice letting in the
light—but it is *the light!* From that tiny aperture appears,
willy-nilly, the dread against which many have immured

themselves. Were there more poems to add to these, a journal might wash out the whole valley—spreading terror.

Discoveries are the lifeblood of the arts as of the sciences, of love, of anything you may name. They may be techniques in miniature, adroitnesses, of mood and method—but every once in a while a major discovery (usually prepared by generations of daring and obscure work) emerges. In that case it is not easily exhausted but goes on fertilizing the imagination for generations, always expanding, disclosing new phases of its basic enlightenment.

A revolution in the poetic line might be such a basic discovery, such a disclosure of new techniques, and may very well prove fertile for generations. And very possibly, to my mind certainly, the slight seeming poems in this book are of that order, fertile, prolific in possibilities. These poems do not exhaust the regions of the imagination which might be opened to expeditions. They graze it; they are by that generous. They represent a great discovery, not a little one but a vast expanse.

I can hear the sound again of possible music, something not heard for years. I am tired of the trivial measures of clever verse, the intellectual non-music, and the imitative that is *only* the imitative; as if we, *we* could revive the songs of the Elizabethans. Their music is our staleness. We know it was once fresh but never for us can it ever be that, never be the freshness of that day. And the more "authentic" it is conceived to be, the hollower it becomes.

Without invention nothing can go on. With a fleck of the bright future a whole can again be imagined and the music picks up again. I hear a new music of verse stretching out into the future.

Henry V is one of the great experiences in the history of motion pictures. It is not, to be sure, the greatest: the creation of new dramatic poetry is more important than the recreation of the old.

TIME, April 8, 1946—*p.* 58, *col.* 3.

This is true enough as far as it goes and knows how to go but there is no hint given as to the necessity for a new form *before* a *new* poetry of any sort can be written; no hint as to the necessity first to *destroy* the old. *When I say destroy I cannot naturally refer to what exists but only to that which does not exist, the imitation.*

Applying this to the present case, to lyric poetry rather than dramatic poetry, we find that the new is made up of several phases clustered about one key phase, that is, one great phase upon or about which there are several minor but essential newnesses: as upon a wave there are roughnesses of smaller ripples which the big wave carries.

In Zukofsky's work there are many small excellences, clustered about the main one of a new understanding of the line structure, which is the great novelty bearing the others.

First, the spareness of the language; the language in general is related to the sounds of speech. (Remember that in a poem the sound is primary to the word; the line is made up of sounds that add to the word, which in the aggregate is the poem. That's why in some modern poems a word is split in half at the end of a line, to emphasize the primacy of the sound.) (NOTE: I did *not* say the sound is more important than the meaning.)

The language here is a speech pared to its essentials, to the salient pertinences of speech. There are elisions but the natural *order* of speech is maintained, a contemporary speech which does not lean on the conventions of past usage and so discovers an order of its own which the poet seeks to fit into a pattern.

This is the first essential, to *discover* a new metrical pattern among the speech characters of the day which will be comparable to but not derived from the characters of past speech. *For each speech must have somewhere in it that quality corresponding to the potential greatness of the environment which engendered it.* The poet feels about for that distinguishing character.

Therefore and by that process the lines in these poems—

followed, as it may be, awkwardly and with difficulty, for a half inch at a time, but correctly—get a tactile quality of the words, without which there is nothing.

This, to the point, is lyric poetry, love poetry. It is brief. And modern love is so often so tawdry precisely because it has no expression—save one. Physical. But if it had, today, any poems that *could* cluster about its silent head, their language would be unaffected, fast, to the point.

"I have never done this before, neither before nor after I was married—until now. But I am not cold, am I? I'm not cold." "You waited for a major crisis in your life." What expression is *there* of love? It is modern speech. It is to the point. It implies poems. *Those poems will express confidence in the language, not a past language with past usages but a present language.*

One works *in* the language for such relief.

Much older verse intruded too much upon our passion and tended to make it seem artificial: therefore we thought the verse artificial—it did not suit our mood. All love poetry close enough to be tolerated must, today, be reticent in order to penetrate.

What are you gonna do? Deny love? Divorces fill only the newspapers. We're not journalists. The whole range of passionate speech is at least brought into view by these poems.

They don't try to SAY anything where nothing can be said. They seek to *embody* love in the words. To make love. Can there be no words for that in our language?

I find it not wholly true that "each line constitutes a word," as Mallarmé is said to have said. It is more or less true, but only if one accepts stated forms of poems as valid, such as the sonnet or a similar form. If that be the accepted form, then it is necessary to break that up into lines as the essential integers to escape the necessity of thinking of the sonnet as a *meaning* only. Mallarmé had to get away from the "beautiful sonnet," that lovely "thought," the sententious statement, the too tender appeal. He had to think of the sonnet, since he adopted the sonnet and did not or could not go further; he had to think of the sonnet as a structure, as a sentient composition. It was logical for him to speak of the "lines" as words. It was a good step.

But once having taken the next step, once having got away from all accepted and fixed forms as such, it was no longer necessary to think of "lines" as new integers, rather as themselves the opportunities for structural inventions, fluent.

The next step was and is to think of the totally NEW poem in which the lines take their new place as every other part is new, related to a basic invention greater than any heretofore fixed conceit.

By an extension of the line more feeling is let into a poem than in the older inadequate line. But wait a minute: free verse was a means to an end. There is actually no "free verse." All verse is measure. We may not be able to measure it, we may not know how but, finally, it is measured.

Then a new line is a new measure.

It is a more inclusive measure, not perhaps emotionally, that is however possible, but more inclusively of the general spectacle of the world. And it lets more in, very specially, of the *present* spectacle of the world. It lets in the moods of our present life, which thus is presented (in a poem) as real to us. Not a diminution from the Attic or the Renaissance or Elizabethan England but to us, today as real, trenchant, to the point and inclusive of the whole world of our feeling and our minds.

We appreciate the real and ourselves as real only by the arts, only by invention, only by a new line, a new measure. In this poem is a new measure and for that reason it is important. For that reason it is great.

How can such a little thing as expanding a measure do all that? Can you think of any way to escape such an implication? It's got to do all that if we are to live and feel and be in our own location as we are, and know that the earth and the universe are ours.

Minute as a new measure may seem in a relatively obscure poem, if the enlightenment is there it is the business of the critic to proclaim it fiercely with every bit of discernment and power that is in him, with every snatching together of energy he has.

In this book, the one poem that embodies all that the rest of them tentatively effect is No. 42. The others in my opinion approach that, but that achieves what they all attempt. In this poem, all Zukofsky's art, that is to say, his life, has fruited.

Read this poem and look at the lines, see what they include, see how they bend to the gales implied but do *not* break, rather expand physically before the pressures and the speeds of thought. There lies the new. And the release. And the happiness:

No. 42

You three:—my wife,
   And the one, whom like Dante,
   I call the chief of my friends,

And the one who still writes to me—
   This morning we are in the mess of history,
   That low crime, and like the devil in the book of *Job*

Having come back from going to and fro in the earth
   I will give the world all my hushed sources
   In this poem, (maybe the world wanted them)

I will be so frank everyone
   Will be sure I am hiding—a maniac—
   And no one will speak to me.*

---

* Williams' review concludes by quoting the remaining twenty-five stanzas of this poem.

Comment on Basil Bunting's "The Complaint of the Morpethshire Farmer"

Four Pages, 1948

ON BASIL BUNTING's poem in *Four Pages:* (1) Read, as I was told to do recently, Crabbe's "Village." (2) Two summers ago at Wilmington, Vermont, I was told of the impossibility of getting anyone to gather sap for sugar or to do any farm work at any price, for the most part. Why? $5,000,000 worth of real estate, farm land, had been bought up by wealth during the preceding year. And why, again? Top executives of the usual corporations have to show a loss on their income. What better vehicle than a farm? And with what disastrous effect on local farm labor, since the more they pay (the owners) the more loss they can show. Thus if they produce maple sugar at $2 a pint, minimum, it means nothing but benefit to them though it is disaster to everyone in the neighborhood, except, of course the farm-laborer who grabs for the pennies while his own land runs down. Such artificial manipulation of prices, as our present income tax laws permit and even foster, tends inevitably toward such abuses.

Williams' comment in *Four Pages*, Galveston, Texas, 8 (Aug. 1948): 3, is about Bunting's poem in *Four Pages*, 5 (May 1948): 3. The poem can also be found in Bunting's *Collected Poems* (London: Fulcrum Press, 1968). Ezra Pound is the one who told Williams to read Crabbe.

Poetry with an Impressive Human Speech

David Ignatow's Poems

The New York Times Book Review, 1948

THESE POEMS, the best of them, ought to be printed on pulp and offered at Woolworth's, a dime a copy. They'd sell, too. For these are poems for the millions, in the cities and out of them, those who would read, and read poems too, poems such as these, if only they could get to them: manna in the wilderness. There is a widespread demand for good poems, poems about ourselves—that we can understand.

But here the work can be respected by those who know what good writing means and yet it touches and illuminates the humblest lives about us—without that offensive patronage which uses humanity for the effects of art. When I first picked up the book I paged through it lightly in the usual way, but soon came to a poem that attracted me, "To a Friend Who Has Moved to the East Side." It starts:

What did you expect you were getting?

That's enough, in a short review, to give the effect of my meaning. There's the language and there's the straight look that goes with it. From that point on I read with interest. But the Fifth Section convinced me that I was dealing with a first-rate poet. Here you will find five poems, the accumulated work of Mr. Ignatow's thirty-four years at the craft, whose tragic force, economy of language and plastic sense

---

Review of David Ignatow, *Poems* (Prairie City, Ill.: Decker Press, 1948); in *The New York Times Book Review*, 53 (Nov. 21, 1948): 50.

governing the words begin to shape up into something impressive. I was deeply moved.

Slowly the plastic of our language becomes more and more apparent to us as we dare more and more to depart from English. That it is a painful process of recognition is forced on us every day—the schools, except for an individual teacher here and there, are wary of this plasticity. So that not from the schools but from such a man as Mr. Ignatow, to whom language is like his skin, must we look for those innovations which will set us upon our feet in our writing. Even the word "innovation" is dangerous. But it is the new, the unnamable new, in such a humble sense as that set forth in these poems, on which we must rely if ever we are to lift our heads in the art: our language, of a plastic all its own. Such things go to the root.

Mr. Ignatow writes of what he knows. Therefore most of the poems come from the New York City "underworld." There's no slang. Slang is mere escapism. But this is almost an odor, foul with love. Such poems as those in the Fifth Section would be understood by a North Dakota farmer's wife in January and cheer her against the snow. Yet they are New York. But they happen to be poems.

This is not the place to speak about what constitutes a modern poem. It isn't, at least, imitative in metrical pattern. Mr. Ignatow, in the best of the work, gives a new sense of a low, melodious humming.

Diamonds in Blue Clay

Peter Viereck's Strike Through the Mask

The New York Times Book Review, 1950

EVERY MAN, I suppose, has his genius; Peter Viereck, in spite of himself, has his. To bring it to final perfection—even on the gallows or under the curse of Congress, if need be—is the objective a poet must keep, pruning himself always toward that end, keeping it constantly in mind.

In such a context Mr. Viereck is a very young poet. The genius, or shall we say talent, is there, though badly in need of pruning.

I should like to preach to Mr. Viereck: Morals are a matter of the art, the way the words are joined, whether the government of the words could not be usefully transposed, say, to the U.S. Senate chamber toward a solvency of ideas there.

Gertrude Stein was a moralist and never better than when she wrote—*and, and, and, and,* etc.

Is that obscure?

And, has many meanings and many shades of meaning. When it is used three or four times in a row it has, each time, a different meaning dependent on the order of its use. That is what is meant when we speak of the art, words placed according to their separate meanings; that is what is meant, when it is well done, to have a moral sense. We do not fall into the strings, we play the piano.

Is that clear?

Review of Peter Viereck, *Strike Through the Mask* (New York: Scribners, 1950); in *The New York Times Book Review,* 55, 11 (March 12, 1950): 14.

No. Of course not. But I assure you it is not quite all limited to esthetics. Do not try so to limit it. That's all I ask: that that be observed by someone and taken to heart. The future of literature or writing or of the use of words in the poem toward a poem depends on that. On that alone.

Taking up Mr. Viereck's book: It's a small one. But a poet can show himself in one or two poems as well as in twenty— no matter how great an urge there may be toward the pro-lix. One poem properly addressed toward the difficulties can shatter the world. It's a question of the adjustment of words. Diamonds lie hid in tons of blue clay.

Mr. Viereck's talent rises like a lovely bird from a cow-pasture, in the purest sense lyrical, sensitive, distinguished in feeling. But why the man has to bother in this small book with much of the other stuff is more than I can say. He even devotes a prose essay to it, filling the last six or eight pages with something which is, as far as I can see, a complete waste of time.

I wish, instead, he had given us more short pieces as delightful and rewarding as "Serenade," and "Counter-Serenade," "She Invokes the Autumn Instant," etc.

Letter to the Editor, Richard Rubenstein

Gryphon, 1950

DEAR RUBENSTEIN:

We must believe and force it to be true that the poem IS stronger than stupidity. We're doing all right generally speaking with the poem around here recently, it's encouraging—such work as you print in your *Gryphon*. But we've got to do it better, and harder and there must be more of it and it has to be more insistent. That it IS the answer to "the stupidities," that it will actually eat out the heart of the political dogmata and build a world to supplant.

We don't believe that basic principle hard enough. The poet is the practical maker. He is shat on, spit on for one only reason: they are afraid of him. The cravens know that he alone has the answer to their cowardices. He has them nailed as a snake nails a bird. They're afraid of him. And so they do everything in their power not only to defeat him but, worse than that, to defeat him in his own mind.

The stupid poet calls himself an "esthete." That means he has withdrawn, withdrawn in other words. Just that. He ain't playing for keeps any more. He's beyond that. I'll say he is! But he's got to stay in, right up to the hilt and give it his whole back and thighs if he's going to be effective. I'm speaking in images, plainly, but only because I've been reduced to that by circumstances.

The poem to be able to survive in the face of the enemy has to reduce itself to "seeds" to stay with him, to keep on

---

Letter published in *Gryphon*, San Francisco, 2 (Fall 1950): 32.

his flesh, like a louse if it comes to that. But never to cease the attack. The real attack, the practical attack which has as its object destruction, to destroy those who try to make the poem seem ineffective.

I want to insist again that the poem is not ineffective. It is working pretty well in our schools. The effects of the poem can be seen in the newspaper accounts of the grotesqueries taking place in the Senate of the United States. A mind accustomed to the poem as it is gradually being understood can never be quite as deceived by the testimony of the scurrilous liars who beset us as they could have been had we not the poem to test them against.

I want to rub it in. This is a practical fight taking place largely in the circumambient atmosphere of our lives. We are at a disadvantage before the organized degenerates who govern us. They try to defame us by decrying our strengths. The poem is a dangerous and subtle instrument which is one of our very best methods of attack. Keep hammering.

WILLIAM CARLOS WILLIAMS.

Mid-Century American Poets

Edited by John Ciardi

Not previously published, 1950

ANYTHING I'M going to say about the poems that make up this book will be comparatively unfair as it is not my purpose to treat them individually, much as I might like to, but to look at them as parts of a coherent whole to be touched on or not as my theme requires.

This is a book of verse and prose by fifteen mature, for the most part, American writers: two women and thirteen men. The prose in each case serves as explanatory statement to the verse which follows; an attempt on the part of each writer to make clear what he is at. The result is a treatise that should be of the greatest interest to the curious reader who has begun to wonder what all this pother about modern verse signifies.

It is a book that can, surprisingly, be taken as a whole (are we developing an American style?) to permit a study of a segment of our growing competence. There are not many books of modern verse as diverse that are yet a whole. I salute the discretion and the taste of the anthologist, John Ciardi, who made it. It is as a book for study that I wish to present it.

Previously unpublished review of *Mid-Century American Poets*, ed. John Ciardi (New York: Twayne, 1950). The anthology includes poems and statements by Richard Wilbur, Peter Viereck, Muriel Rukeyser, Theodore Roethke, Karl Shapiro, Winfield Townley Scott, John Frederick Nims, E. L. Mayo, Robert Lowell, Randall Jarrell, John Holmes, Richard Eberhart, John Ciardi, Elizabeth Bishop and Delmore Schwartz. The text is Za/Williams/159 in the Yale collection, five typed pages with pencil corrections; Za/Williams/158 contains two other drafts.

Listen to this from the prose preamble to the section given
over to E. L. Mayo:

> What I have said in this matter, I now realize, is quite
> in accord with Shapiro's contention (in his *Essay On
> Rime*) that authentic novelties in rhythm and meter in
> poetry are captured in prose before they are isolated in
> verse. My only proviso . . . that the more direct and
> natural route for idiomatic and rhythmic innovations to
> take would be from *speech* to verse . . . that the speech
> rhythms of twenty years ago were not the same as they
> are now.

It is interesting to note upon this point not so much what
Mayo has written but Elizabeth Bishop's "Songs For a Col-
ored Singer."

I don't think this book should be taken as covering a wide
section of the field but that is one of the defects of its quali-
ties. You can't call it *The Complete Poet* because its scope
is limited, designedly, to the work of certain writers who
do not themselves cover the field. There are reaches which
no one in the book touches—just as in Aristotle's *Poetics*,
due to the accidents of time to be sure, there is nothing
about dithyrambic verse. But that granted, this might well
be taken as a text for the student even the better so for its
limitations; Karl Shapiro's demonstration of the stages in the
development of one of his best short poems usefully extends
this concept.

Everything here is temperate, not too experimental (not
half enough in my opinion) but not, I am grateful to be able
to say, regressive. There is very little that escapes the domi-
nance of the iamb, usually the iambic pentameter, other than
in Theodore Roethke's daring offshoots. There is, however,
a fine variety in such lines as—

> Midnight the year's last day the last
> high hour the verge where the dancers comet

If you want rhyme, there is Robert Lowell. I am always astonished at Lowell's rhyming, the finest I know. It is like Inca stonework though it rather makes me think also of a tiger behind bars, a sort of Merry Mount in reverse. But such lines do go with the fierceness of the man's self-restraints. Rhyme, when it is used should be full and four-square in our language, not mis-set. If we are going to rhyme, I'd say to my ideal pupil, let's rhyme this way.

The finest ear in the book, to my thinking, is that of John Holmes. You'll go far before encountering anything today as silken in texture as the opening lines of the poem "Herself"—

Herself listening to herself, having no name,
She walked in an airy April sun, clothes close on her

I mention this designedly as, for myself, I'd like to omit the word "sun." But the poem is a beauty.

Such things and much more to be discovered in the book lead me to believe that, perhaps, we may be leading off in the arts, if it will be permitted, against a recourse to war as the only answer to our present dilemmas of mind and spirit. That we may be approaching a discovery and even a mastery of the means of expression that may bring us, against the machinations of the subtle convention mongers, peace.

Some things in the book are of indifferent worth or at times downright bad: sloppy rhymes, inversions of phrase, distortions otherwise of the natural sequences of speech, fixed habits of versification that bring a line up flush against the wainscoting—for what reason? We still get the baneful sonnet which says always the same thing, quite beyond control. But with Papa Shapiro present and his poetics in the background much of this can be overlooked—not however in teaching.

I admire Randall Jarrell but his acerbity seems too often to be a matter more of nerves than conviction.

But the most teasing verse in the book to one of my susceptibility, verse to be read over and over in order to lay hands upon something that wants to escape (in the construction) and yet we would hold it as if against its will, is contained in the poems of John Holmes.

I could read Holmes over a dozen times and still find a musical felicity among the words to surprise me; he has an ear for the juxtaposition of sounds that is satisfying as daylight. I've never read anything else of his, I speak only from what occurs in this book and so may err in judgment but what I see here, I like.

Pure Imagism is a dead mode but the lesson it taught, to quit filling in a set of dead lines with philosophic or other chatter and calling that a poem, was never better illustrated than in what is shown here of the work of Winfield Scott. His attack makes clear what is meant by fixing the eye on the object first, accurate placing of the object to make it stand up in its private conditions. If his effects are not profound and I do not say they are not, they are as profound as the conditions warrant—and may discover profundities unsuspected until we learn to open our own eyes as he has opened his to the local scene. His work is indispensable to this assemblage. His "Green Moray" is an arresting poem.

In a poem as in any writing the backbone of it is to have something to say, to say it and to quit. You don't stop to fill in a pattern. The movement of the thought appears in the movement of the structural make-up. Today it is less a matter of ritual than ever, there is no use in following an established sequence of lines or groups of lines thinking they will put the content over somehow, as in the past. They will not.

Today the invention displayed in the structure displays at the same time the content. An ear, a mind, a wit and a desire to extend the art—coupled with the power to do it, is all that is needed.

Discharge Note

Afterword to Merrill Moore's Case-Record from a Sonnetorium

1951

YES, THE sonnet *was* sick! By sheer persistence Merrill Moore has saved his life, made him a useful citizen. I don't think he would even LIKE to go back to his happy past if he could. That is a triumph of therapy: to have the patient not even WANT to be young again but to wake up to what there is left to him, without regrets.

That's where the disease lay. Regrets. Nostalgia for the past. By attacking that virus in the very SPLEEN where it lay hid, pulling it out into the light (through examination of the BLOOD smear) and applying the radium of his enlightened thought, Moore has CURED him! O modern triumph!

That the malignancy will certainly in the end destroy him is not the question: he may and no doubt will long outlast many of his contemporaries. Young as they are, with blood counts showing hemoglobin of 95% to 105% and normal differentials, they may succumb to war, to wine or to women and all the ills of exhaustion to which they subject us. But he, mellowed and secure, will continue to years that they shall never see.

So, I salute Merrill Moore, Master Poet and Physician. He has devoted his life doubly in this occasion to the service of a distinguished patient. Modest though he has been, display-

---

Published at the end of *Case-Record from a Sonnetorium* (New York: Twayne Publishers, 1951), p. [63]. The title page says: "*Cartoons* by Edward St. John Gorey / *Illustrated with Poems* by Merrill Moore / *Consultants:* Louis Untermeyer, *Esq.* / *Professor* John Crowe Ransom / Henry W. Wells, *Ph.D.* / William Carlos Williams, *M.D.*"

ing the abnegation of the true servitor of mankind, Moore has taken a noted invalid, full of years, one who has served well—and given him a new life

It is wonderful to see the old boy hale again.

Verse with a Jolt to It

Kenneth Rexroth's Beyond the Mountains

The New York Times Book Review, 1951

IF YOU call Shakespeare's *Pericles* a poem, it has to stand up against a certain set of values; if you call it a play, that's something else again. It might be a good play but a bad poem or the reverse. I shall not try to evaluate these four plays of Kenneth Rexroth other than as verse, for they are destined, I feel sure, to be read rather than acted. What a pity! They and other plays in modern verse should be acted out before they can be judged as drama. There is no stage for it. There is NO stage in America suitable for it.

At the start I plead that the problem of writing dramatic verse for the contemporary stage is complicated for me almost beyond solution. When the scene is cast in a day the intimacies of whose speech are unknowable to us, the difficulties are increased though the practice is reputable and so we must accept it. Then place the action in ancient Greece where at a remote period the theatre reached a zenith never since equaled for sustained tragic effect and where are you? You're up against Racine and the dignity of the French twelve-syllable line. There is Shakespeare, of course, but that's something else again: an Elizabethan robustness of language and metaphor cannot today be imitated without a condescension on the part of the hearer, which is fatal.

The four plays, "Phaedra," "Iphegenia," "Hermaios," and

Review of Kenneth Rexroth, *Beyond the Mountains* (New York: New Directions, 1951) in *The New York Times Book Review*, 56, 4 (Jan. 28, 1951): 5.

"Berenike" are grouped under a general heading, *Beyond the Mountains*. Based on classical Greek myths, they have the theatrical form of the folk dance, with dialogue as verse. This dialogue offers a solution to the problem I presented above—read as verse, it is superb. Rexroth, happily, has eschewed the iambic pentameter throughout. What can be done with our speech in the situations he chooses to present is excellently done; his Phaedra, for instance, is no Frenchwoman. The line is savage and brief.

For Rexroth is one of the leading craftsmen of the day. There is in him no compromise with the decayed line of past experience. His work is cleanly straightforward. The reek of polluted Shakespeare just isn't in it, or him. I don't know any Greek, but I can imagine that a Greek, if he knew our language as we ought to but don't, would like the athletic freshness of these words; he'd like their elementary candor, the complete absence here of the sexual lamb chop, French fries and petit pois (frozen from a can).

As verse, reading them through, the plays are a delight to me for the very flow of the words themselves. The pith is there, don't mistake me, and there with a jolt to it (in the very line, I want to make it clear) that goes well below the surface. But the way of the writing itself is the primary attraction. It palls, at times, I acknowledge it, but that is the defect of the method. It does not falsify. It is a feat of no mean proportions to raise the colloquial tone to lines of tragic significance.

There are bound to be errors from an excess of devotion to a necessary method, we can't know everything at once; even after the ten years of work Rexroth has given these plays there are spots I do not admire (as if that were always necessary).

I have a curious feeling about the work as a whole that, though it is not acknowledged in the text, we have been given a sort of "Essay on Man": spring, summer, fall and winter. Rexroth might smile at this, but near the beginning Iphegenia and Achilles surely swim in warm waters while in the "Berenike" ice is creeping in from all sides. The tale, as it stands, is of the final blotting out of the Hellenic remnants. And so for all of us soon perhaps.

Sex? It is all sex. I once knew a metal worker who would pick up a red-hot horseshoe between his bare thumb and fingers without injury. But you've got to know how, to do that. An elementary passion, such as that which moves these characters, if it is integral in the play of the words, which it brilliantly is, affects these words violently; it doesn't lie over them like slime. Why else do you suppose men read the sports pages?

I add to that that I have never been so moved by a play in verse in my time.

Letter to Robert Creeley

Origin, 1951

March 3, 1950

DEAR CREELEY:

My own (moral) program can be chiefly stated. I send it for what it may be worth to you: To write badly is an offence to the state since the government can never be more than the government of the words.

If the language is distorted crime flourishes. It is well that in the unobstructed arts (because they can at favorable times escape the perversions which flourish elsewhere) a means is at least presented to the mind where a man can go on living.

For there is in each age a specific criterion which is the objective for the artist in that age. Not to attack that objective is morally reprehensible—as evil as it is awkward to excuse.

Bad art is then that which does not serve in the continual service of cleansing the language of all fixations upon dead, stinking dead, usages of the past. Sanitation and hygiene or sanitation that we may have hygienic writing.

W. C. W.

Letter published in *Origin*, Dorchester, Mass., 1, 1 (Spring 1951): 34.

In a Mood of Tragedy

Robert Lowell's The Mills of the Kavanaughs

The New York Times Book Review, 1951

IN HIS new book Robert Lowell gives us six first-rate poems of which we may well be proud. As usual he has taken the rhyme-track for his effects. We shall now have rhyme again for a while, rhymes completely missing the incentive. The rhymes are necessary to Mr. Lowell. He must, to his mind, appear to surmount them.

An unwonted sense of tragedy coupled with a formal fixation of the line, together constitute the outstanding character of the title poem. It is as though, could he break through, he might surmount the disaster.

When he does, when he does under stress of emotion break through the monotony of the line, it never goes far, it is as though he had at last wakened to breathe freely again, you can feel the lines breathing, the poem rouses as though from a trance. Certainly Mr. Lowell gets his effects with admirable economy of means.

In this title poem, a dramatic narrative played out in a Maine village, Mr. Lowell appears to be restrained by the lines; he appears to *want* to break them. And when the break comes, tentatively, it is toward some happy recollection, the tragedy intervening when this is snatched away and the lines close in once more—as does the story: the woman playing solitaire in the garden by her husband's flag-draped

---

Review of Robert Lowell, *The Mills of the Kavanaughs* (New York: Harcourt, Brace, 1951); in *The New York Times Book Review*, 56, 6 (April 22, 1951): 6; reprinted in *Selected Essays*. Yale, Za/Williams/160–64, has five drafts plus the finished manuscript.

grave. She dreams of the past, of the Abnaki Indians, the aborigines, and of how, lying prone in bed beside her husband, she was ravished in a dream.

Of the remaining five poems, "Her Dead Brother" is most succinct in the tragic mood that governs them all, while the lyric, "The Fat Man in the Mirror" (after Werfel) lifts the mood to what playfulness there is—as much as the mode permits: a tragic realization of time lost, peopled by "this pursey terror" that is "not I." The man is torn between a wish and a discipline. It is a violently sensual and innocent ego that without achievement (the poem) must end in nothing but despair.

Is the poet New England—or what otherwise is his heresy (of love possessed only in dreams) that so bedevils him? At the precise moment of enjoyment she hears "My husband's Packard crunching up the drive." It is the poet's struggle to ride over the tragedy to a successful assertion—or is it his failure?—that gives the work its undoubted force.

Shall I say I prefer a poet of broader range of feeling? Is it when the restraints of the rhyme make the man restless and he drives through, elbows the restrictions out of the way that he becomes distinguished or when he fails?

It is to assert love, not to win it that the poem exists. If the poet is defeated it is then that he most triumphs, love is most proclaimed! the Abnakis are justified, their land repossessed in dreams. Kavanaugh, waking his wife from her passionate embraces, attempts to strangle her, that she, like Persephone, may die to be queen. He doesn't kill her, the tragedy lying elsewhere.

The tragedy is that the loss is poignantly felt, come what may: dream, sisterhood, sainthood—the violence in "Falling Asleep Over the Aeneid"; "Mother Maria Theresa"; "David and Bathsheba in the Public Garden," excellent work. What can one wish more?

Letter to Lawrence Hart and the Activists

Poetry, 1951

DEAR HART:

Here are some notes that may be of use to you and the Activists. In regard to what you're doing with imagery association, they might be relevant:

"Gongora (Luis de Gongora y Argote, 1561–1627) was the same sort of young man Ben Jonson was in London at about the same time. Gongora played around in Cordoba, gave the gals a time, kidded the cops, drank, raised hell generally. He was a gifted student, but didn't take that sort of stuff too seriously—except to know it cold.

"He didn't know it, but, without thinking he was letting the classroom get him he pretty well fell into line (you gotta make good with them guys if you want to get yourself a name) and wrote 'beautifully' in the accepted manner—only better than anyone else. Hell, you couldn't write *worse* than them guys and get away with it.

"But, having lived around the city pretty loosely for a time, a thought seems to have struck him. It's all right to live one way and write classic stuff but suppose I chucked the classic and write the way I really see the world. What would that do? Let's try it out.

"He saw certain things in impossible juxtapositions, to hell with how other guys see it, this is the way I see it. This belongs next to that. I don't give a damn what the 'masters' say. I don't care a whoop in hell what they want me to see

---

Letter published in *Poetry*, 78, 2 (May 1951): 107–08.

and to write. I'm going to write it my way, and that's going
to be my metaphor.

"The academy boys didn't like it. The man's too violent,
too extreme. We'll acknowlege, they said, that if you want
to force the image there may be some remote justification
for a belief—

"God damn it, that's exactly what I do want to do,
FORCE the image to conform itself to the way I want to
have it shape up—in Lorca's world Gongora wrote the only
poems that he, Lorca, could finally admire.

"How can anybody expect to UNDERSTAND a poem
by Gongora the first time he reads it? How can he EX-
PECT to understand his metaphors. There's a life enclosed
there. How can HE expect to understand such things. Here
is a superb craftsman. All he knows he has enclosed in these
capsules of penetration and feeling and knowledge. And if
you think you can trip through his work as though you
were brushing mud off your trousers . . . nuts to you.

"Lorca's lecture at Salamanca, reported (translated) in the
Quarterly Review of Literature last year, is one of the high
marks of scholarship touching the poem that I know. Every-
one should read it and have it to heart if he knows what the
young would understand by the poem."

Why don't the Activists try a few translations of Gon-
gora? In any case, more power to you.

WILLIAM CARLOS WILLIAMS

A Note on Macleod's Pure as Nowhere

The Golden Goose, 1952

IT'S LIKE harmonics in playing the violin, you do not press down on the strings but just touch them. When no word has its full meaning in the context you have to look for overtones to get a meaning: a risky business but (sometimes) the essence of poetry. At least it had better be the essence of poetry or it is lost.

I hate, of late, to speak vaguely; there isn't time for it. But I've got to speak that way having read the poems. In a sense it's Baudelaire when he reminds you of Hart Crane. The moral values are the concern of the poem. Norman is a moralist gone "wrong," gone poet—but really gone.

"The loveless landscape of innocence" is a good line. I wish there were more such coherent lines—"The myth will be Godiva's frozen nipple. No good or courage can unhorse." That is to say, Godiva's nipple being frozen, it doesn't matter what happens or can happen.

Comment on a selection of nine poems by Norman Macleod that appear in the same issue of *The Golden Goose*, Columbus, Ohio, 3, 4 (May 1952): 172. The Macleod poems are all taken from *Pure as Nowhere* (Columbus, Ohio: Golden Goose Press, 1952). The entire issue is devoted to Macleod; it also contains Williams' "A Poem for Norman Macleod," an excerpt from Macleod's autobiography, "Generation of Anger" (otherwise unpublished), criticism and memoirs by Alfred Kreymborg, William Kolodney, William Mead, Vivienne Koch, a poem by Stanley Rosen, and a Selected Bibliography. A 1950 letter from Williams to Macleod concerning *Pure as Nowhere*, was published by *The Golden Goose* in 1954 and is reprinted in this volume, p. 212.

Thus it is a poetry of despair—that makes of that despair what can be made of despair, something above despair, a poem. And such a poem cannot be coherent—it can only be a harmonic, a connotation never a denotation . . . in a sterile, stiff sort of rhythmical arrangement that is like a poem that suffers rigor mortis. A dead form. The lovely nipple of Godiva is frozen.

It looks as if this is the best poetry Norman has ever written, it scrapes the rock bottom—properly the ghost of the hot boys who set out for the Klondike trail.

The book has a uniformity, a unanimity of feeling. As I said it reminds me of the desperate seriousness of Baudelaire: a regard for stilted rhyme (form).

The pleasure in it, where the poetry rises to triumphant assertion will be only for the few. But it's there. It brings tears to the eyes.

Kenneth Lawrence Beaudoin

Inferno, 1952

KENNETH L. BEAUDOIN is a small, plumpish, roseate man—no longer in his first youth—with a will of iron; perhaps not so much of iron but of some natural bent or twirl or twist that after persistent trial we find to be ineradicable. It has to do with the new in the poetic line. This is curious because you'd think rather the opposite from the man's history.

He comes from an old family that was first heard of in the New World in Canada in the early seventeenth century, about the time of Elder Brewster and that crowd. From there his people, being French, moved to Louisiana. Their old loyalties were retained. The present generation is from Memphis, Tennessee, but not the South of Civil War fixations but an older, much older South that comes from an older break: that between the old and the new world.

It is an old family. It is an American family. It is a family also that is singularly homogeneous in its conscious history. It dates back over longer spans than we usually recognize. It embraces the New World and has continued to the seventh or eighth generation to embrace the New World in all its history, riding over all minor defaulting, to the person of its present living representative, the unswerving Kenneth Beaudoin.

It is important then, the present generation being a poet, in a family who knew themselves to be a family before there was a schism to mold it other than that between the Old World and the New, it is important to know to what this

---

Essay published in *Inferno*, San Francisco, Nos. 6–7 ([May–July] 1952): 67–73.

man is loyal. For to know that is to surmise or catch a
glimpse of that upon which we must build to survive.

This is something in itself to which to pay attention—I
mean the long-range make-up of the man's mind. I know it's
dangerous to argue that way because he may not have been
able through lack of talent to make the most of it. But it
would be something noteworthy were the poet whom I
celebrate even half the man he is. But as it happens the drive
which has attracted my attention has produced work of dis-
tinction marked always by a comprehensive breadth of
understanding of the objective in mind: a worldwide obliga-
tion to face up to new requirements broader, deeper than
anything that has governed the ankylosed line of the past—
at no matter what cost.

Sometimes Beaudoin in his eagerness to praise, in his devo-
tion to the new, having cast about desperately for a focus
for his attention, has overreached himself and I must caution
him against that. There ain't that many good poets in the
world at any one time. But his average is high.

Beaudoin knows that the structure of his poem is the crux
of the situation: if the poem has not changed in structure,
in its revealing structure, nothing has changed. You can be
smooth as you please, as profound as your knowledge or
your wit may desire—but unless your wit and your profun-
dity are shown in the changed, the revealing, structural
changes in the make-up of your lines you might just as well
have gone bathing in the sea of a holiday for all the good
that will come of it.

The small magazines of Japan (and there is at least one),
of Germany, England, France or Brazil—unless they SOME-
WHERE reveal the entering wedge, the change will
amount to nothing.

There is only the one thing that counts and that must be
defined and supported. Beaudoin has heard of it, he practices
its disciplines—he has not (nobody has) defined it or much
refined it but he is one of the "hounds of spring" that have
taken the "trace" into their nostrils—and his persistence, and
self-effacing devotion to the hunt marks him for its own.
He is a man of that distinction. Such men must be honored.

We have not many here so persistent and so self-effacing.

He has not published a book of his own—that is, a formal book. He has, instead, continued to publish his papercovered booklets for the past ten or fifteen years, where he could. He has fought for the work of other young and unknown poets. He has, after their deaths, published their reliques— some of them noteworthy.

Such has been the republication, with a note, of the poems of James Franklin Lewis. Again he has called attention to the lyrics of John Kingston Fineran, poems of considerable merit which he has felt the obligation to see not lost.

This publication posthumously and presumably at his own expense of the work of men for whom he felt some respect is typical not only of him but of the kind of concern he has for the poem: you must not let any flake of it die unattended. It is like an old-fashioned Christian, we must testify to the faith, to the good life that the man has made important. "These men lived the lives of poets, to the full; we cannot let them die for it is important that men live that way. It is important and I will take it upon myself to proclaim it." And he does. He goes out of his way to have us remember.

Is it worth while? Is it? This fellow John Kingston Fineran, now dead in his youth, leaves this behind him:

For All The Dead

Here is the tomb of one who was good.
May earth lie light, and men remember.
Here is the tomb of one who was evil.
Here is no evil. Here is a tomb.

And for texture take this of another poet whom Beaudoin has stooped to raise up, John Franklin Lewis, also dead, but a poet—it is important that he was a poet:

Snarled Nightbrush

Threads of darkness blowing hither out of the east
Mass in tangles, catch in branches, smother with skeins
Skeins of skeins, heaped, massed, condensed, interdistributed

Hay clotted the blue halo of the sky.
Whence the shattered sun admits her metal fragments,
Randomly clear, through the brushpile mesh of silk.

Unquestionably Beaudoin felt the texture of those lines,
whatever else he felt, and was determined at whatever cost
to see it that for that reason and for no other necessary rea-
son, to have them live so far as it lay in his power to make
them live and be read. He has dedicated himself, consecrated
himself to the living use of the poem and to that he is
wholly, impersonally, devoted.

His latest drive is to see to it that a book, a modern col-
lection of poems by certain living younger poets of whom
he approves, finds a publisher. Doggedly he will go about
seeking a publisher until he finds him. This is not a plea for
those men—but I am willing to go along with Beaudoin and
to say that his single, unswerving drive will be to see to it
that the purity of the language will be the same, but along
with that the inevitability of change in the new mode be
served.

He writes me:

March 31, 1952

My dear Dr. Williams,

This is the largest part of the manuscript. . . . I think it
is a book which should be published inexpensively on
something less than vellum, and with a paper back which
can be sold to people at a price they can afford; by people
I mean just anybody in any drug store anywhere; and I
think L—is essentially a very poor business man if he fails
to recognize this audience which is there. . . . I will send
on the other poems as they arrive, and I will look toward
hearing from you about the poems, what you think of
them . . . any time you get a moment or two to con-
sider them.

He says specifically of his own work, which is included
in the series, his "credo":

Poetry in America today is somehow so like poetry in

England in the fifteenth century. It is poetry in a time when a language is being jelled—formed. English coming out of Norman and Middle English in the one case and American emerging out of Virginia accent and Texas accent and Mid-western accent and Boston accent and Brooklynese and just English English in our case. It is a time when the language is not a single common accent or idiom, but five languages—seven languages—accents—idioms. I find myself writing in what is a patois which borrows from all of them.

The stuff of poetry has not changed too much, of course—it is human stuff, lovers' talk; words growing out of the one still hour of a noisy night; words growing out of April and earth habits. It is the voice of a thousand cockatoos, the snarl of caged tigers; the footfall of elephants; the sound of trees growing. It is the sound of the orifice opening revealing the inside man. It does not matter whether it comes out of the mountains or out of the plains; it is the rarified, distilled voice of this total afternoon.

The work of the man himself is marked by this mood of priestly dedication—and remember, the ancestry was contemporary with that of Ann Bradstreet but WITHOUT an addiction to her iambic models. There *were* poems before her straight-sided modes. His first ancestors were from France.

He is no Puritan. He is even no Evangelist, he does not go about to save the soul either by direct exhortation or by devious modes to adjure us to come to some overwhelming decision after which we shall issue new bathed in light. There is nothing of that in his work. But for persistence, for meticulous devotion to his dedicated task to keep writing on the new path, to have it wherever you come across it on the page fresh with the light of the new day, uncompromising in its formal criteria, he is hard to beat.

There is no equivocation, he is unswerving, he knows the front is as wide as the day, he knows when the sun comes up you can no more contain it than you can contain the fullness and the richness of the new poem which shall take in the wealth of all our lives once it shall have been born. Every breath that refers to it is welcome to him, it comes from the very ground under his feet.

Two Letters to Robert Lawrence Beum

The Golden Goose, 1952

January 5, 1950

THE WHOLE first half of our century, as it relates to verse in "the new language," that is to say *our* language, is a history of the transition from the standard prosody as described by Saintsbury and many another—by precept and example, the prosody of stress, to a prosody of the measurement of time. This is a full dress return to the Greek.

That the prosody of our day will not be the prosody of Homer or Theocritus in detail must be as obvious as that our language is not theirs in basic character—quite apart from its melodious nature. But that we MUST adopt their prosody in principle is quite as obvious when we consider that the job of metrics is to reflect, even to represent, a psychology coming to be as subtle as theirs—to sound, to imagery, as compared with the brutalities of even such a representative of the Middle Ages as Dante.

No one has the guts to dream of a possible metric that will blossom out of the past as a flower blossoms out of a stick of wood. Our age is rich, not poor. It is rich in its inheritances for the mind, for the spirit. It isn't bare. That is why I have battled T. S. Eliot from the first. *There's* another. At the risk of making a fool of myself I have insisted that he has never known what the deepest knowledge of the

---

These extracts from the two letters were selected and edited by Richard Wirtz Emerson, the editor of *The Golden Goose*, Sausalito, 4, 5 (Oct. 1952): 29–32.

198

world offers. It is NOT what he thinks it is; he has vitiated
the good and emphasized the stereotype and the dead, the
therefore dead. . . .

We are NOT poverty stricken in the area of the New
Language, that is, the area of literature which is all we
should speak of. We are the richest in opportunity and,
strangely enough, in accomplishment, in the making of
poems, the richest area on earth. But we must know what
our riches are and we must be single-minded and industrious
in pushing our advantage. . . .

January 9, 1950

Enclosed you'll find a poor bit of theoretic writing, some-
thing I almost never attempt—but I found it necessary to
make the attempt in view of your questions. With good will
you may get something out of it—for basically it says what
has to be said. The only thing is, I despise the form and find
myself no good in it. Don't take it too rigidly. . . .

A democracy of feeling and understanding is tacit in all
I would attempt. (Again, the theory I try to present to
you.) But whether it would ever penetrate consciously to
the masses I very much doubt. But that it would have the
same excellences that the masses—in the sense of a general
group of men (Americans)—would have is the very essence
of what I say.

STRUCTURALLY it would be organized as the masses at their
most democratic excellence should be. In exactly the same
way that Rimbaud's excellence is ultimately an excellence
which would apply as well to government as to the me-
chanics of the poem. It is a *relative*, flexible excellence.

Whitman knew nothing of structure. He hit out blindly
toward what he thought was an excellence of structure. In
Paterson IV that will come up—but as he grew older he
went gaga, thinking a lot of loose talk meant democracy. A
broad spread.

It is our business to build the good, whatever is loose, flex-

ible in what Whitman SAYS into the machine, into the line
in ways he did not envisage.

All this is so much blah—except as we relate it to the
poem.

The appreciation is not structure. . . .

The poem (let's not talk of "poetry") the poem must lift
the consciousness of a culture, a group, from the level, the
basest levels, the levels of the newspaper, to the subtlest
levels of consciousness. It can do this only by organizing the
materials with relation to more complex viewpoints than a
newspaper can afford to deal with—by *structure* in short.

*[Following is the commentary mentioned in the first para-
graph of letter of January 9, 1950.]*

All monistic theories, as they apply to art, are absurd in
our day. This is especially true of a theory of arrest, the
fixed notion of English prosody, highlighted by sixteenth-
century prenotion, unrelated to social, economic and politi-
cal variants, as the standard or even a standard of measure-
ment for us now.

A work of art is a mechanism at its best, applicable to all
the complex human relationships of its day as a means of
making them workable—under the given conditions. That
is to say the factors that make physics, government, eco-
nomics workable or should make them workable should also
be discoverable in the highest pieces of painting, poetry and
music in that day. The mechanism should be interchange-
able. Only thus can we speak of a work as "good" or "bad."
That is the measure. A "good" poem is good as it might be
successfully used in the organization of an entire social, po-
litical economic of its day—or reorganization.

Thus Mozart died at thirty-four poverty-stricken because
the organization of his music had so far surpassed the po-
litical-sociological abilities of those who had the money to
support him that they became dissatisfied with him, suspi-
cious and so let him starve. It must be noted here that the

excellence of his music, its "goodness," was related not to the superficial powers of his day, the aristocracy, but to a deeper reality of the times themselves—an area where government and the preliminary studies of abstract science were tending to break down the past.

The Russians are today trying to turn this relationship of the arts to all other human experience about by trying to fix the work of art in an orbit as an adjunct to the political machinery. The relationship between art and politics, since they require a relationship, is thus right in a way. But they have perverted it in fact by limiting the freedom—in the piece of music, in the poem, that it may not surpass the plodding political picture, may not, in fact, correct the political fixity which has always been its function to save from absurdity when it decays. For the arts do not risk as much the physical organization of a people when danger threatens; their freedom is the saving grace which a society should use for its escape.

To our present day, no sixteenth-century fixation is applicable. We need and we must have a more responsive, a more socially responsive art. The art must rest solidly on the social base of its time—which cannot be fixed as all monistic adjuncts must necessarily be in basic structure.

And it is of the basic structure of verse that we are speaking. But responsive *in its nature* to multiple stimuli, since that is the essence of democracy—which all theory must approach if true freedom, the life blood of art, is to be approached and rescued.

The "foot" is the key to the line. The passage of time (not stress) is the proper (democratic) key to the foot (approaching Athens)—and music.

Music may yet lead the way—though music has its own problems.

Think of "English" and "American" as one language among us to be called the "old" and the "new" language.

On Measure—Statement for Cid Corman

Origin, 1954

VERSE—we'd better not speak of poetry lest we become confused—verse has always been associated in men's minds with "measure," i.e., with mathematics. In scanning any piece of verse, you "count" the syllables. Let's not speak either of rhythm, an aimless sort of thing without precise meaning of any sort. But measure implies something that can be measured. Today verse has lost all measure.

Our lives also have lost all that in the past we had to measure them by, except outmoded standards that are meaningless to us. In the same way our verses, of which our poems are made, are left without any metrical construction of which you can speak, any recognizable, any new measure by which they can be pulled together. We get sonnets, etc., but no one alive today, or half alive, seems to see anything incongruous in that. They cannot see that poems cannot any longer be made following a Euclidian measure, "beautiful" as this may make them. The very grounds for our beliefs have altered. We do not live that way any more; nothing in our lives, at bottom, is ordered according to that measure; our social concepts, our schools, our very religious ideas, certainly our understanding of mathematics are greatly altered. Were we called upon to go back to what we believed in the past we should be lost. Only the construction of our

---

Essay published in *Origin*, Dorchester, Mass.; 1, 12 (Spring 1954): 194–99; reprinted in *Selected Essays* without Williams' letter of "10/3/53." Yale Za/Williams/226–27 contains two drafts. *Origin* was edited by Cid Corman.

poems, and at best the construction of a poem must engage the tips of our intellectual awareness, is left shamefully to the past.

A relative order is operative elsewhere in our lives. Even the divorce laws recognize that. Are we so stupid that we can't see that the same things apply to the construction of modern verse, to an art which hopes to engage the attention of a modern world? If men do not find in the verse they are called on to read a construction that interests them or that they believe in, they will not read your verses and I, for one, do not blame them. What will they find out there that is worth bothering about? So, I understand, the young men of my generation are going back to Pope. Let them. They want to be read at least with some understanding of what they are saying and Pope is at least understandable; a good master. They have been besides scared by all the wild experimentation that preceded them so that now they want to play it safe and to conform.

They have valid reasons for what they are doing—of course not all of them are doing it but the English with a man such as Christopher Fry prominent among them, lead the pack. Dylan Thomas is thrashing around somewhere in the wings but he is Welsh and acknowledges no rule—he cannot be of much help to us. Return as they may to the classics for their models it will not solve anything for them. They will still, later, have to tackle the fundamental problems which concern verse of a new construction to conform with our age. Their brothers in the chemical laboratory, from among whom their most acute readers will come if they know what is good for them, must be met on a footing that will not be retrograde but equal to their own. Though they may recognize this theoretically there is no one who dares overstep the conventional mark.

It's not only a question of daring, no one has instructed them differently. Most poems I see today are concerned with what they are *saying*, how profound they have been given to be. So true is this that those who write them have

forgotten to make poems at all of them. Thank God we're
not musicians, with our lack of structural invention we'd be
ashamed to look ourselves in the face otherwise. There is
nothing interesting in the construction of our poems, noth-
ing that can jog the ear out of its boredom. I for one can't
read them. There is nothing in their metrical construction to
attract me, so I fall back on e.e.cummings and the disguised
conventions that he presents which are at least amusing—as
amusing as "Doctor Foster went to Gloucester, in a shower
of rain." Donald Ogden Nash is also amusing, but not amus-
ing enough.

The thing is that "free verse" since Whitman's time has
led us astray. He was taken up, as were the leaders of the
French Revolution before him with the abstract idea of free-
dom. It slopped over into all their thinking. But it was an
idea lethal to all order, particularly to that order which has
to do with the poem. Whitman was right in breaking our
bounds but, having no valid restraints to hold him, went
wild. He didn't know any better. At the last he resorted to
a loose sort of language with no discipline about it of any
sort and we have copied its worst feature, just that.

The corrective to that is forgetting Whitman, for instinc-
tively he was on the right track, to find a new discipline.
Invention is the mother of art. We must invent new modes
to take the place of those which are worn out. For want of
this we have gone back to worn-out modes with our tongues
hanging out and our mouths drooling after "beauty" which
is not even in the same category under which we are seeking
it. Whitman, great as he was in his instinctive drive, was
also the cause of our going astray. I among the rest have
much to answer for. No verse can be free, it must be gov-
erned by some measure, but not by the old measure. There
Whitman was right but there, at the same time, his leader-
ship failed him. The time was not ready for it. We have to
return to some measure but a measure consonant with our
time and not a mode so rotten that it stinks.

We have no measure by which to guide ourselves except
a purely intuitive one which we feel but do not name. I am

not speaking of verse which has long since been frozen into a rigid mold signifying its death, but of verse which shows that it has been touched with some dissatisfaction with its present state. It is all over the page at the mere whim of the man who has composed it. This will not do. Certainly an art which implies a discipline as the poem does, a rule, a measure, will not tolerate it. There is no measure to guide us, no recognizable measure.

Relativity gives us the cue. So, again, mathematics comes to the rescue of the arts. Measure, an ancient word in poetry, something we have almost forgotten in its literal significance as something measured, becomes related again with the poetic. We have today to do with the poetic, as always, but a *relatively* stable foot not a rigid one. That is all the difference. It is that which must become the object of our search. Only by coming to that realization shall we escape the power of these magnificent verses of the past which we have always marvelled over and still be able to enjoy them. We live in a new world, pregnant with tremendous possibility for enlightenment but sometimes, being old, I despair of it. For the poem which has always led the way to the other arts as to life, being explicit, the only art which is explicit, has lately been left to fall into decay.

Without measure we are lost. But we have lost even the ability to count. Actually we are not as bad as that. Instinctively we have continued to count as always but it has become not a conscious process and being unconscious has descended to a low level of the invention. There are a few exceptions but there is no one among us who is consciously aware of what he is doing. I have accordingly made a few experiments which will appear in a new book shortly. What I want to emphasize is that I do not consider anything I have put down there as final. There will be other experiments but all will be directed toward the discovery of a new measure, I repeat, a new measure by which may be ordered our poems as well as our lives.

September 23, 1953

10/3/53

Dear Cid:

Before I lapse into complete mindlessness which I some-
times fear let us continue our argument. Let me try, in a
word, to state as clearly as I am able what I propose about
ordering the measure of our poems, which is very simple,
and give you a chance more specifically to agree or dissent.

But first as to the reader of good intention I agree entirely
that my mention of him was irrelevant. I apologize. This is
on the plane on which we are attacking a purely technical
matter. It has implications which may ultimately concern
the general reader; a man who is today writing seriously
should not be concerned with that.

I propose that you publish my original "statement" to-
gether with your reply, which I enclose since you may not
have kept a carbon, together with this letter and whatever
you wish to add. Thus, as far as I am concerned, the matter
will be closed. There may remain there additional points
you make in your reply to my original "statement," but
these will have to go by the board.

Speaking of the poem of mine which you quote, "The
Act," I must tell you that I did not count the syllables that
make it up but trusted entirely to my ear. But what is all
our concern about anyway but granted that the best of what
the best of us write comes to us by way of the ear, is there
a valid reason why it should not be studied and understood?
Thus we discover the new which has occurred instinctively
in ourselves and pave the way for our advances. I'll never
give up my poetic past or cease to search it for clues as to a
further advance.

I'll never allow the mere mechanics of a given passage to
dictate the manner of my future procedures and if I seem
to have implied that by what I have said heretofore I retract
it.

The thing now comes down to what I mean by a relative measure. Maybe the beginnings of it or the realization of its necessity first came about in Manley's [Gerard Manley Hopkins] celebrated "sprung" meter, but that was too constipated for general use. Let it pass. A restudy of the Greek tragedies may reveal something pertinent in the handling of the "phrase" as a unit of measure, but I am not competent to handle that. I'm glad you brought it up. It is a valuable suggestion toward getting at what we want.

What we want is a measurable unit which we don't have to follow literally, but satisfies our minds that it is valid. A relative stability, something that can be variously counted even when it puzzles us to count it, even when it jumps out of the count, is what we must have. And that is what I mean by "consonant" with our age, because our age is governed by just such a measure—and must accommodate itself to it.

That doesn't mean that it is ungoverned. It merely means that we have not yet discovered a measure that governs it. We don't need to refuse the instinctive, because on the contrary it is in the instinctive that we must look for an advancement of our knowledge. But knowledge for the freedom it will give us remains our objective.

More specifically (employing knowledge), the foot, since we have to use some sort of technical term to be understood, not necessarily to let it govern our actions, the foot must be understood in a modern world as variable. That is no reason, nor should it be, for employing the term "free verse," which is a misnomer: no verse can be free, but must always be governed. It must be measurable and in measure. And the measure must not be the measure of the sonnet which relates to a measure which we have outgrown.

Such a foot, which the Greeks may have known since they knew everything! may consist of one syllable or even a caesura or a dozen, depending on the ear of the writer and his ability to keep the measure going. He will not, being a poet, presumably a gifted poet, allow his meter to get out of control. That is the only thing that will control him. And that, my dear Cid, will depend on his conception of the maximum ability to follow him. His concern for his reader is a generous concern, much like a father's love for a son, teaching him to know the very best that the older man may transmit to one he loves. He will make it easy to grasp, as far as he can do so, without relinquishing his privilege to outdistance the young man whenever the occasion should arise.

As far as I know that is all I have to say. The subtleties are in the hands of others. Certainly if we can discover a measure suitable to our time and use it intelligently and with daring, instead of falling back on outmoded forms which belie our meaning, we can at least respect ourselves and, I feel sure, the world will learn from us how to live.

Come again. I am still not too old to learn.

Your friend,

BILL

Dylan Thomas

The Yale Literary Magazine, 1954

STRANGE TO SAY I remember Dylan Thomas better as a prose writer than a poet. His *Portrait of The Artist as a Young Dog* and the short accounts and stories written at that time made a great impression on me. I was not then familiar with his poetry. I see in retrospect a view of an English sea resort inhabited by real enough young women and men who lived in boarding houses of the cheaper sort and there carried on their reckless lives. There were views of the sea itself and of a carnival spirit that led to violence and in the end to an amnesiac sequence where the author was left going up and downstairs in pursuit of a girl whom he never found. It is an impression of Dylan Thomas which has colored all that I have learned of him subsequently.

There is another view of him that I have kept when he spoke of himself as a half-grown boy perpetually in trouble over stolen fruit, trespasses beyond walls and troubles of every sort.

The poem must have been, as it is for such young men, an escape. Being a Welshman it had to take the form primarily of a song, which for any man limits it to his youth. But if a man can sing and Dylan Thomas could that with distinction, what else matters? Not old age, Dylan Thomas appeared never to think of old age and need not have thought of it. It is as if he always meant to escape it, and

---

Essay in *The Yale Literary Magazine*, 122, 2, Dylan Thomas Issue (Nov. 1954): 21–22; in *Selected Essays*. The manuscript is Yale Za/Williams/73.

now without any loss to his lasting fame he has done just that.

Reading over his collected poems I have thought of what chances he had to enhance his fame by thinking again and perhaps more profoundly of what he had in mind. But what can be more profound than song? The only thing that can be asked is whether a man is content with it. It is not a drawing room atmosphere that produced the tragedy of King Lear. Wasn't Lear himself a Welshman? But was Dylan Thomas capable of developing the profound attitudes of a Lear? If he was and his scholarship gave evidence of it, he might have gone on to write a verse tragedy—though the times are all against it.

Politer verse, more in the English style, appears to have been impossible for Thomas, it's a constitutional matter, in which a man has no choice. At least I don't think it was a choice that was open to him. Thomas was a lyric poet and, I think, a great one. Such memorable poems as "Over Sir John's Hill" and, even more to be emphasized, "On his Birthday," are far and away beyond the reach of any contemporary English or American poet. Not only in the contrapuntal metaphors which he uses, the fugue-like overlay of his language does he excel, but he is outstanding in the way he packs the thought in among the words. For it is not all sound and image, but the ability to think is there also with a flaming conviction that clinches each point as the images mount. The clarity of his thought is not obscured by his images but rather emphasized.

The wind does "whack" as the hawk which is "on fire" hangs still in the sky. This devotional poem which in its packed metaphors shows a man happy in his fate though soon to die shows Dylan Thomas in a triumphant mood, exultant. What else can a man say or be? He carries the image through to a definite conclusion and as a lyric poet at his best does show the sparks of light which convinces us that he means what he says. He includes the whole world in his benisons.

The second poem, "Poem on his Birthday," is demonic, you have to chortle with glee at some of the figures. But it is the way the metaphors are identified with the meaning to emphasize it and to universalize and dignify it that is the proof of the poet's ability. You may not like such poems but prefer a more reasoned mode but this is impassioned poetry, you might call it drunken poetry, it smacks of the divine—as Dylan Thomas does also.

The analytic spirit that might have made him backtrack and reconsider, building a rational system of thought and technique was not his. He had passion and a heart which carried him where he wanted to go, but it cannot be said that he did not choose what he wanted.

Letter to Norman Macleod

The Golden Goose, 1954

November 29, [1950]

DEAR NORM:

Put me down for *Pure As Nowhere* when it appears. Glad to hear you're writing. You've always been tough for me, there's an irrational quality I can't fathom, jumps the track somewhere. I'm speaking of the poems, but on the other hand I want to read you.

Yeah, I know, there's an irrational quality in everything that's probably its major element, to the good (?) I don't know. All I know is that it represents defeat, the terrific denial of all I desire. I want to dive between women's legs, others want to shoot for their brothers' ass-holes or with rifle in hand to slaughter them.

But the horrible thing is that we've been led astray somewhere recently. Badly astray. Nobody minds dying but for God's sake not for sheer wrongheadedness, for stupidity. Make a poem out of that. Maybe you've got the key after all.

Maybe it'll happen tomorrow, the war will be on and, for the moment, we'll feel virtuous, quieted by a singleness of purpose to save our skins. It may very well be the end of us all. I can't help saying it. And doesn't it always come just when people generally are about to join into some sort of

---

Letter in *The Golden Goose*, Sausalito, Calif., 7 (April 1954): 130.

general shout of enlightenment. It isn't any particular cult.

Glad to have heard from you. I'll see that you get my recently published poems in another week or so. I finished *Paterson* before my swing around the country—I've been on a swing around the country lecturing at Washington U., Reed College, U. of Oregon and at U.C.L.A. Came home via New Orleans. Took Floss along.

Glad you've got your magnificently beautiful boy. And you've got a mother for him too that's really there if I know anything.

Letter to Srinivas Rayaprol

East and West, 1956

May 29, 1951

DEAR SEENA:

This period of adjustment must be a tough time for you. I had no idea that in India itself you would find such prejudices as you describe. I see by that that problems we think of as local are not so but are merely part of the world's inheritance. That at least gives us a release, makes us feel that we have something in common with the rest of the world, makes us feel less isolated. It permits us, perhaps, to smile a little. We are by that to some small extent liberated.

But India is such a vast and confused land (from what you say) that it makes our problems here sound childish by comparison. I know what you mean when you speak of wanting to go to Brazil. It may be a solution. Keep your eyes and your ears open. It might work out and Cosgriff might be the person to arrange it for you. I know at least one person there who might help, he is an American writer, Bob Brown, pretty old by now but a good friend.

It's two months now since I went to the hospital. I am not practising my profession but remain at home writing during the mornings, as much as I can, sleeping after lunch, answering letters, reading and occasionally going out in the

Letter in *East and West*, Secunderabad, India, 1, 1 (Spring 1956): 45–47.

evening to see a friend. It is not the life I am used to. My head is much of the time dull, lifeless not fit for any serious thought. But there are moments when I feel fully alert. I live for such moments. At such times I pick at my type-writer and have managed to do some original work.

I have had to work for my autobiography was not quite finished when I was hit in the head. I have been able to do the last fifty pages of that so that it went to the printer a week ago. I shall see the galley proofs in another two weeks and expect to have the finished book in my hands by September. I will send you one. I did not in the end include any letters, the book grew to be large enough without that.

On June 18 I have to appear on the platform of a theatre at Harvard where I am to read a "fifteen minute" poem at the Phi Beta Kappa ceremonies, an annual celebration to which this year I was invited to be the guest poet (badly said but you will get the gist of it I am sure). I have slaved at that poem for weeks. Now it has been roughly blocked out and I want from now on until the 18 of June to polish it. I'll try to remember to send you a copy of that too. Remind me to do so after the middle of June.

My problem is to make up my mind whether or not to return to the practice of medicine or to devote the rest of my life to writing. Frankly I don't know what to do. For this summer at least I shall loaf along letting my mind drift. I am not going to worry either way. We'll take short trips to visit friends here and there, swim in the ocean now and then, read, write at a novel which I am under contract to deliver to Random House next year—and think and wait for the bomb! Maybe that will solve everything. I am curious to see how much I will improve physically after this accident. Maybe I'm really going to be alert again and fit to work hard. Maybe not, for the moment it will just be a matter of doing as little running around as possible, keeping up with my various simple obligations and letting the breezes blow. Florence is my right hand man who helps me in everything. I would be lost without her.

You speak of your mother. It makes me think of mine.

Not that they can be like each other, they probably are not, or that they can have been like each other (since mine is dead) but my attitude towards my own mother must be very much like your attitude to yours. It was a hopeless feeling, what could I do? But I felt that I should have done more and yet, spiritually, I could do nothing, she was too far away from me. My only feeling was an inexpressible admiration coupled with an anger at not doing more which I could not afford without turning my life into a slavery. I would have been enslaved by her if she had had her will. I fought her because I was forced to fight her to preserve myself. If I had given in she would have swallowed me. She was full of genius that had no outlet, it must have been a great torment to her. We fought. She gave up so much for me that I resented it. I did not want her to so immolate herself; she ruined herself for her sons—but she did it in such a way that I was furious at her. She seemed to ask for punishment, to enjoy it. I have inherited so much of it, a thing I despise, that when I catch myself at that trick I blame her. Well, she's gone now, at ninety-two years of age. My father died at an age three years younger than I am now. He seems a young man to me. It is hard to believe.

You are young, remember it. Not that I mean that you should merely sit back and allow yourself to grow old without resistance, I don't mean that. But get hold of a theory of procedure, a remote objective and work at it relentlessly. It will make the years attractive to you, draw you on, always alive, always referring your isolated observations to a plan which as time passes will grow to have recognizable proportions, something you can identify as yourself, tangible— what other can we have than to look at ourselves in this way as we go.

Give my greetings to your mother and father and tell them that I join them, in some minor degree, in wishing their son a contented mind and the opportunity for such work as he desires.

Affectionately yours,

BILL

The Speed of Poetry

James Schevill's The Right to Greet

The Western Review, 1956

A NEW BOOK of poems has just been placed on my desk, James Schevill's *The Right to Greet*. I never heard of him before. I'm surprised because here is a young man who is far advanced in his ability to write.

He knows for instance that the essence of a modern poem is speed at the greatest acceleration that we have ever known. The sensory image has to be squeezed up into a ball and tossed about with blinding speed. His metaphors are fresh and arresting. They take in objects from our daily lives and by comparing them to the eternities of sky and sea bring us up with a start. It is always a mark of a poet that he has eyes that are never still and a mind that is constantly searching about for a place to alight.

In Schevill's world we feel this restlessness of the poet. But that is never enough. You must have the power to bring the freshly discovered image home, home to roost in all of its wing and breast, a warmth [of] detail which we are glad to claim for our own.

He also shows some evidence that he has read a book and he does know what to see there and record—the life about

---

First published in *The New York Times Book Review*, 61, 12 (March 18, 1956): 37, where it is titled "Restless Poet," this review of James Schevill, *The Right to Greet* (San Francisco: Bern Porter, 1955), is slightly longer in *The Western Review*, Iowa City, 20, 4 (Summer 1956): 325–26. The second sentence of the *Times* review begins, "They are by a young man who. . . ."; and the third paragraph of the *Times* review does not have "a warmth [of] detail. . . ." after "wing and breast."

changed by the imagination into something remarkable. His titles to the poems show he has a wit which is more than just witty. The way he puts the poem on the page is in all ways intelligent and attractive, shows he has respect for the normal processes of the mind.

In all, this is the work of a self-contained man, young, daring and possessed of much skill in his craft. Very attractive to me.

A Poet Who Cannot Pause

René Char's Hypnos Waking

The New Republic, 1956

THE IMPRESSION I get from the poems and fragments of poems of René Char is that they are parts of something larger, from the same block. There is always a disturbing element about them, a sense of awe which comes over from whatever he writes. A Frenchman and an artist he writes with all the respect of his kind of accuracy of detail. At the same time, were he a painter he would not paint like Picasso but Braque. He has all the attachment to nature, its birds and rivers and in short the whole topography of his native land which he knows and loves passionately. He might have been an Henri Fabre or for that matter a Vercingetorix save that his customary manner appears to be too mild. He is attached to the immediately-before-him, which he would investigate to its last *feeling.*

As far as I can see, and I acknowledge that it may not be far, the abstract as a thing in itself is a man without a body. We know by this time, I hope, that art is not nature, but if we had been alert Aristotle should have taught us that long since. But the relation between nature and art remains still to be laid bare, no amount of random daubing by the painters in pursuit of the psyche in blood-red and black is going to alter the *parti.* The *Melancholy* of Brueghel, the use of

---

Review of René Char, *Hypnos Waking*, trans. Jackson Matthews *et al.* (New York: Random House, 1956); in *The New Republic*, 135, 12 (Sept. 17, 1956): 18. Two of the poems in this book are translations by Williams himself. Yale Za/Williams/204–09 contains six drafts.

gold by Fra Angelico or the works of Hieronymous Bosch are not to be ignored.

We are, the public is, on the whole dull witted. René Char is, a man schooled in a long life of multiple experiences, a man of extraordinary patience and courage both moral and physical; he cannot pause in what he has to do because we are too slow to follow him. The artist is inevitably an innovator, not because he wants to be but because he must. He must, in order to see at all (surrounded as he is by his own garbage), look about him. He does not like garbage even when it is served up to him in the best receptacles, our books and daily papers.

But the artist, the poet, René Char for instance, is not by his nature a contemptuous man. He is a determined man and often possibly a wrongheaded one at times when he has not gone far enough in his craft, but never a blind man. When I myself attempted to translate something that René Char had written in French into English, I had to warn myself, as I always do under such circumstances, that I was using not English at all for my work, but the American idiom. That gave me a certain stylistic advantage; rhythmical! I could approach the French much more confidently than if, we'll say, I were an Oxford don or even an Evelyn Waugh. But could my language be recognized for what it was even by my own countrymen? The French should come over into my language more readily than into German or Russian. Its subtle variations of poetic accent are, I feel, much more congenial to a modern American turn of phrase than, at least, to formal English. But these are gradations more to be spoken of as feelings than facts. Or if you want to enjoy a René Char text, read it in the original.

Is it worth sweating our souls out for? René Char's poems are difficult for an American reader—not because of his French but because the sense of the words themselves is difficult to recognize in any specific poem:

L'Alouette

Extrême brais du ciel et première ardeur du jour,
Elle reste sertie dans l'aurore et chante la terre agitée,
Carrillon maître de son haleine et libre de sa route.

Fascinante, on la tue en l'émerveillant.

—or:

III (of a long suite)

Le poète transforme indifféremment la défaite en vic-
toire, la victoire en défaite, empereur pré-natal seule-
ment soucieux du recueil de l'azure.

Sometimes he catches no more than the tail of an idea as it
were in passing and follows, as in one series of poems in the
Botteghe Oscure, where he well succeeds in developing a
cumulative interest; once he gets the theme he follows it in
example after example with telling effect until gradually it
becomes clear by the sheer persistence of what he has to say.
It is a perfectly legitimate device of the artist and increases
the pleasure of the reader by piling up the emphasis with
variations of detail until the total effect is overwhelming.

We are not used in America to that approach. We are
used, strange to say, to formal work that is more cut and
dried. We, as poets, think too much of ourselves—in other
words we are self-conscious. We think of Milton and Her-
rick, even Shakespeare when we write, as poets who have
written great poems. Shall we not write great poems; we
are addicted as a nation to great sonnet sequences. We can-
not understand the French who are more modest. We can-
not understand René Char who has lived through hell in his
life being reticent. His only concern is the art itself and all
that the art implies; not to be God but leaving that to others,
to be content with another regime where there is not so
much competition.

A Note on Layton

Irving Layton's The Improved Binoculars

WHAT ELSE are you going to say about a man whose work you wholeheartedly admire than that he is a good poet? If you consider yourself a critic of poetry, which I do, all the more reason for speaking with all the force you can command in his support. You would be a fool to do less.

When I first clapped eyes on the poems of Irving Layton, two years ago, I let out a yell of joy. He was bawdy but that wasn't why I gave him my recognition. But for the way he greeted the world he was celebrating, head up, eyes propped wide, his gaze roving round a wide perimeter— which merely happened to see some sights that had never been disclosed to me so nakedly or so well.

In writing of a good new poet for the first time the words come crowding to my mind, jostling together in their eagerness to be put down: He inhabits the medium and is at home in it, passionately; luxurious freedom, as of a huge creature immersed in an ocean that he knows he will never plumb and need never fear to reach the bottom of. This is poetry in which he lives unchecked. And he has eyes and he has power to penetrate wherever its lust leads him to satisfy its hungers. More moral men will fly off from a dish which is his natural food and which he takes with a laugh. May he never grow too delicate to take his fill of it and speak of his joy in it with a full appetite. That he is a man, and therefore must be guarded, he knows also. He laughs from a full belly.

Introduction to Irving Layton, *The Improved Binoculars* (Highlands, N.C.: Jonathan Williams, 1956), pp. [9–10].

Not to be confined by a metaphor—he has been to the university and sat grinning and with moist eyes among his peers. He knows the Puritans and what they do and have done. He knows at least two religious beliefs, and how to practice all ten of them. In fact he knows the colors of the spectrum, and how all the colors are split off from it. If you want him to be true to yellow, he will be true to red; and if green, he will be true to purple or brown or black or the most heavenly blue. He has an unrivaled choice of words; an unusual vocabulary and the ability to use it. As far as deftness in the craft of a poet, I think he can do anything he wants to—except confuse himself with the mere sound of his own mouthings or delicate mincings or weighty sounding apostrophes. He is modest in facing the opinions of others—an enormous and increasingly rare virtue. He even respects Ezra Pound but has no inclination to imitate him. He despises Canada (being a Canadian), and loves and would give his heart for it. He loves women and speaks of it freely. They enjoy him also and double-cross and abandon him—and all this his poems show and speak of in the most meticulous English. He uses as much slang as suits his fancy or his need, and no more. He is not bound by the twentieth century if he does not find its language fitting to his purpose, and defies anyone who would bind him to that use. His structure of the poetic phrase is eclectic; that is to say, he does what he pleases with it, and there he possibly goes wrong. But what difference does it make, if he writes well? He has a quick and dogged wit which does not shun to soil its hands; in other words, he can be downright dirty if the occasion calls for it—as it frequently does in dealing with the nicer present-day wits of the United States. The metaphysicians, men and women who want to abandon a British or American way of talking, he is indifferent to—but the same is common with all present-day poets if they are worthy of the name.

Irving Layton has written profusely, pouring out his verses without check. That is the way to write, correcting one's self in the act of writing, the words, held as it were, in solution, latent, eternally in process of being formed. No constipation here—though the action of writing can be repeated and repeated and repeated in multiple draughts until, by sheer repetition, it finally becomes fluid. But that doesn't appear to be his way.

In short, I believe this poet to be capable, to be capable of anything. He's a backwoodsman with a tremendous power to do anything he wants to with verse. I have seen modern verse written in French and in the local dialects of the United States before which he must stand in awe. Lucky for such writers that he exists, for he will not be idle, but attack with his unsated egotism until he has subdued their challenges. There will, if I am not mistaken, be a battle: Layton against the rest of the world. With his vigor and abilities who shall not say that Canada will not have produced one of the West's most famous poets?

Can't say that it is my practice to read or to quote Blake, but I agree with him and with Layton, *"Praise is the practice of art."*

Howl for Carl Solomon

Allen Ginsberg's Howl and Other Poems

1956

WHEN HE was younger, and I was younger, I used to know Allen Ginsberg, a young poet living in Paterson, New Jersey, where he, son of a well-known poet, had been born and grew up. He was physically slight of build and mentally much disturbed by the life which he had encountered about him during those first years after the first world war as it was exhibited to him in and about New York City. He was always on the point of "going away," where it didn't seem to matter; he disturbed me, I never thought he'd live to grow up and write a book of poems. His ability to survive, travel, and go on writing astonishes me. That he has gone on developing and perfecting his art is no less amazing to me.

Now he turns up fifteen or twenty years later with an arresting poem. Literally he has, from all the evidence, been through hell. On the way he met a man named Carl Solomon with whom he shared among the teeth and excrement of this life something that cannot be described but in the words he has used to describe it. It is a howl of defeat. Not defeat at all for he has gone through defeat as if it were an ordinary experience, a trivial experience. Everyone in this life is defeated but a man, if he be a man, is not defeated.

It is the poet, Allen Ginsberg, who has gone, in his own body, through the horrifying experiences described from life in these pages. The wonder of the thing is not that he has survived but that he, from the very depths, has found a

Introduction to Allen Ginsberg, *Howl and Other Poems* (San Francisco: City Lights Pocket Bookshop, 1956), pp. 7–8.

fellow whom he can love, a love he celebrates without look-
ing aside in these poems. Say what you will, he proves to us,
in spite of the most debasing experiences that life can offer
a man, the spirit of love survives to ennoble our lives if we
have the wit and the courage and the faith—and the art! to
persist.

It is the belief in the art of poetry that has gone hand in
hand with this man into his Golgotha, from that charnel
house, similar in every way, to that of the Jews in the past
war. But this is in our own country, our own fondest pur-
lieus. We are blind and live our blind lives out in blindness.
Poets are damned but they are not blind, they see with the
eyes of the angels. This poet sees through and all around
the horrors he partakes of in the very intimate details of his
poem. He avoids nothing but experiences it to the hilt. He
contains it. Claims it as his own—and, we believe, laughs at
it and has the time and affrontery to love a fellow of his
choice and record that love in a well-made poem.

Hold back the edges of your gowns, Ladies, we are go-
ing through hell.

Charles Olson's Maximus, Book II

Published posthumously, MAPS, 1971 [1956]

FROM MEXICO, "Olson's second book of the 'Maximus Poems' arrived yesterday. At a glance it appears to me much better than the first lot, which seemed to me to need cutting. I have varying feelings about Olson. Sometimes he seems terrific and at others incredibly bad and self-deluded. Have you read this book?" This brilliant critical praise of Olson's poetic worth was sent to me in a letter by a woman whose critical judgment I much admire for her own outstanding critical and poetic achievements. One of the best younger writers of my acquaintance.

I am challenged either to agree or reject this summary of Olson's work. If I agree I should be able to demonstrate on the page what I see of the man's ability or failures. And celebrate him.

The man is full of violent prejudices which could be a good thing in a poet if they are intelligently ordered. Olson's prose passages among his verse are often wrong-

---

Published posthumously in *MAPS*, 4 (1971): 61–65; since the essay was published posthumously I have returned to the manuscript, which is Za/Williams/182 in the Yale collection, and my transcription differs in a few minor respects from the one in *MAPS*. The essay is in fairly rough form: four typed pages with some typed but no handwritten corrections; Williams did not even bother to correct many of the obvious typing errors. No doubt the essay would have been worked on further had it been published during Williams' lifetime. The younger writer Williams quotes at the beginning of the essay is Denise Levertov in a letter to Williams Sept. 26, [1956]; the Levertov letter is also in the Yale collection.

headed, full of jealousies and vicious appraisals of his friends but his poems—if they stem from this—can be assigned no more than his loneliness in the critical field. All modern poets are the same; in fact all poets modern or ancient except among their friends if they are any good must be rejected at the beginning.

Poems are a serious business to the race, no poet can be tolerated who wavers in his devotion to the art or his ability. The public is cruel because it is ignorant, lethargic.

One of Olson's chief faults which he shares with Ezra Pound is his disconnectedness, to the reader his sentences or rhythmic assemblies do not make sense—too much has been omitted. The poet says only the INESSENTIAL DETAILS HAVE BEEN SO. That requires judgment—as in modern painting if you look too close you are likely to miss the whole thing. But at times in my judgment Olson leaves out too much or includes too much of the inessential—which gives the effect that my correspondent mentions in her letter: This second book is much better than the first and when it comes off it is brilliant, breathtaking in fact. What more can be asked of a poet?

For instance: This is a story of the events of a man's experience and the particular events of a man's experience in graphic terms, which all good poems must be, put down economically on the page in an organized manner to give the feeling of an organic whole. You can see by this how difficulties of the task are likely to unhorse the artist and make him appear, when he fails, ridiculous. Olson is faced with a problem to make the words walk about as they have appeared to him on a front concerned with Gloucester and the fishing front around Boston—where he had his first experiences as a young man.

It takes him from there over the whole world or as much of it as he had the cash, with a microscopic income, he was able to achieve. Mexico was one of his principal stamping grounds, Yucatan and the Mayan Indians and the American beginnings—which Cortez despoiled. This is the general background, an essentially American poem with no apologies to China, Russia or the rest of the world or antiquity. Can Olson bring it off?

I think he does, at times. For instance: and his successes are well worth the rest of the whole poetic world, in his opinion because he is not modest which no poet can afford to be irritating as it may be to a reader and it may be that he is right.

The opening of the second section of the present book is wholly admirable:

> I have had to learn the simplest things
> last. Which made for difficulties.
> Even at sea I was slow, to get the hand out, or to cross
> a wet deck.
>   The sea was not, finally, my trade.
> But even my trade, at it, I stood estranged
> from that which was most familiar. Was delayed,
> and not content with the man's argument
> but such postponement
> is now the nature of
> obedience,
>   that we are all late
>   in a slow time,
>   that we grow up many
>   And the single
>   is not easily
>   known

But right here begin the difficulties. Has too much, even here, been elided? That must always be as in all art a question of comparative quickness of wit and mental agility to leap from one sense impression to another.

To go on:

> It could be, the sharpness (the *achiote*)
> I note in others,

makes more sense
than my own distances. The agilities

> they show daily
> who do the world's
> businesses
> and who do nature's
> as I have no sense
> I have done either

> I have made dialogues,
> have discussed ancient texts,   etc. etc.

which is the poet's business.

It goes on: "The Song and Dance of" (showing one of Olson's typical foreshortening devices), "Maximus, to Gloucester," in which occurs—

Letter 14

on John Hawkins / on the puzzle
of the nature of desire / the consequences

in the known world beyond
the terra incognita / on how men do use

their lives

"Maximus, to Gloucester," another letter, No. 15, continued from the first book a continued account on the life of Captain John Smith quoting from poetry which I do not recognize, which I presume to be his for he was an educated man of ideas; no matter; "On First Looking out through Juan de la Cosa's Eyes"; "The Twist"; "Maximus, to Gloucester," "Letter 19 (A Pastoral Letter)"

        relating
        to the care of souls
        it says)

"Maximus, at Tyre and at Boston," including "Letter 22" (out of sequence) with which the book ends.

Reading it is a rewarding, really to me a thrilling experience. Categorically this book is much better than the first by which I was often defeated. My correspondent is quite right in finding it at first glance a poem that attracts the eye and, I am ready to say it, my critical objections, and comes off as a major contribution to the contemporary scene and may possibly go much further.

Jonathan Williams has presented the book in an oversize format with dark covers which gives it great distinction.

Five to the Fifth Power

Charles Bell's Delta Return

The New Republic, 1957

CHARLES BELL, in *Delta Return,* has written a book of poems
reminiscent of the old, classic South—extremely appealing
to me, for some reason, though I am not from the same
country. This might as well be a sonnet sequence, yet it is
not, but regular, a series of five-foot, five-line stanzas, five
of them to a poem, five poems to a bracket, the brackets in
series of five, forming books, let us say, three in all. So it is
a three sided figure (a delta) of fives to the fifth power.
That is form with a vengeance. The meter is iambic, but
sufficiently varied to give no feeling of monotony. The
poems are regularly ordered as everything else in the old
South was, yet sometimes violent under a suave, even ele-
gant surface.

   The virtue of these poems is their inner violence—what
they represent of a man's resentment of what he has to with-
stand of what goes on in the university cities and capitals in
our polite world. An amazing freedom of name-calling, col-
loquial diction and particularly descriptive passages relating
to the very trees and beasts and rivers of his chosen locale
which he has been lovingly familiar with since boyhood
enriches the text of the recital. Once in a while he lapses
into a philosophic and scholarly mood which I personally
could well do without, but when he eases himself into some

Review of Charles G. Bell, *Delta Return* (Bloomington, Indi-
ana: Indiana University Press, 1956); in *The New Republic,*
136, 3 (Jan. 21, 1957): 20. The manuscript is Yale, Za/Williams/
59.

such theme as a boy climbing about the branches of a tree and glimpsing the sky above, few passages in recent verse can give me the feeling of soaring into the unknown I feel then.

Many men from the South remember their mothers with particular poignancy. With infinite gentleness Bell has remembered his own mother, her domestic ways and their relationship to the changing world that surrounded the entire family. In one of the sections, the picture of his mother in an apron, looking out of the window or going out among the trees, has left a vague blur on my memory, something indefinable of the women of the South, which I shall never forget.

The poems themselves are precise, even scholarly. They are rather aristocratic in feeling. What can you expect from a man come out of that background? It shows in Charles Bell's entire concept of what a poem should be, his mastery of the form.

This is a book of poems that strikes a high mark among writers in America. It is a book that will appeal to many readers of orderly habits. Don't be surprised at the vigor of the feelings and gentleness of touch you will find here.

Charles Eaton's The Greenhouse in the Garden

Arizona Quarterly, 1957

A CHARMING and gentle book and a well-written one, a book of poems—whose subtlety of invention, whose proud modesty, whose deft inventive use of formal qualities is gently infinite. Who is this Charles Edward Eaton—*The Greenhouse in the Garden?* He must be some older man whose name I have forgotten, who has lived to learn many tricks of the craft of the poem without succumbing to them. His language is somewhat old-fashioned, his images of gardens and ladies who inhabit and cultivate them is outmoded as Magnolias (?)—well constructed, he is triumphant.

Good breeding in this rowdy age is lost upon us and our children. The poem, in the poem, it lives still in the construction of the phrase. But it cannot be trite, a low-down manner has its uses, the poem thirty and forty years ago was sickeningly saccharine in its acceptances. It is nauseating to recall some of the puddings of Tennyson, no matter how the riders charged.

This Eaton has LEARNED something without bitterness and incorporated it into his art. He has NOT yielded the essentials which to him are necessary, basic—how to eschew inversions of the normal phrase, he has learned that there does exist an American idiom which in American mouths must replace the academic.

His use of a modification of the Alexandrine last line of

Review of Charles Edward Eaton, *The Greenhouse in the Garden* (New York: Twayne Publishers, 1956); in *Arizona Quarterly*, 13, 1 (Spring 1957): 89.

Chapman's sonnet is edifying and effective. Nothing but pleasure comes from such knowledge . . . but what am I talking about? This may be a young man, I may be mistaken in my recollections. *Tant pis.*

Sitting naked at my desk this November morning so the urge to write should, at seventy-three, not escape me, I am amazed that after a night's sleep and its dreams the name Charles Edward Eaton was put down correctly.

"A Woman of Marigolds" was the first poem in the book to get to me after I had got used to the manner of writing, then I went back over the poems to confirm my impression of excellence but without finding an excellence equal to that. The first poem in part two, "The Fox Hunt," is technically the best poem in the book, a lively nostalgic poem reminiscent of the past. Well done. It is worthy to grace many an anthology.

Two New Books by Kenneth Rexroth

In Defense of the Earth
One Hundred Poems from the Chinese

Poetry, 1957

THE TECHNICAL problem of what to do with the modern poetic line has been solved by Kenneth Rexroth by internal combustion! Whether that can be said to be activated by atomic fission or otherwise is immaterial. The line, in Rexroth's opinion, is to be kept intact no matter if it may be true, as the painters have shown, that any part of a poem (or painting) may stand for the poem if it is well made; therefore if anything at all is done with it, keeping it intact, it must give at the seams, it must spread its confinements to make more room for the thought. We have been beaten about the ears by all the loose talk about "free verse" until Rexroth has grown tired of it.

But the problem still remains. If you are intent on getting rid of conventional verse what are you going to accept in its place? It is purely a matter of how you are going to handle the meter. Forget for a moment the meaning of the poems in this book, *In Defense of the Earth*, which is not, I think, a good title, the poet has ignored all formal line divisions save by the use of an axe.

The first ten or fifteen poems trespass perilously close upon sentimentality, they can be passed over at once as of

Review of Kenneth Rexroth, *In Defense of the Earth* (New York: New Directions, 1956) and *One Hundred Poems from the Chinese* (New York: New Directions, 1956); in *Poetry*, 90, 3 (June 1957): 180–90. Yale, Za/Williams/120 and Za/Williams/183, contain the manuscripts, respectively, for the sections on *In Defense of the Earth* and *One Hundred Poems from the Chinese*.

mere personal interest to the poet himself, no matter how deeply experienced, having to do with individuals of his family. With "A Living Pearl," the general interest may be said to begin, the technical and ideational interest that is inherent in the poems (there is not room enough in the pages of *Poetry* to quote the poem in full):

A Living Pearl

At sixteen I came West, riding
Freights on the Chicago, Milwaukee
And St. Paul, the Great Northern,
The Northern Pacific. I got
A job as helper to a man. . . .

Tonight,
Thirty years later, I walk
Out of the deserted miner's
Cabin in Mono Pass, under
The full moon and the few large stars.

And so it goes for about seventy-five lines. It is written as verse, the initial letter of every line is capitalized as in Marlowe or Lope de Vega or Edna St. Vincent Millay. But there the similarity to any verse form with which I am familiar ceases. It is a sequence we are more familiar with in prose: the words are direct, without any circumlocution, no figure of speech is permitted to intervene between the meaning of the words and the sense in which they are to be understood.

There is no inversion of the phrase. The diction is correct to the idiom in which the poet speaks, a language "which cats and dogs can read." But it is a language unfamiliar to the ordinary poetry reader. Poems are just not written in those words.

More serious is the question as to whether or not, since poems are universally thought to be musical, Rexroth has any ear for music. And if so what constitutes his music.

Can the lines be counted—forget for the moment the prosy diction? It may have been put down purposely to subvert any poetic implication in the lines that it is associated with the lies of the ordinary poem in the usual facilely lilting measures. This American author is dedicated to the truth. To hell with tuneful cadences in the manner, let us say, of Robert Burns or T. S. Eliot or Rimbaud at least while the world is being cheated and starved and befouled.

Rexroth is a moralist with his hand at the trigger ready to fire at the turn of a hair. But he's a poet, and a good one, for all that. So as to the music of his lines let us not be too hasty. As a translator of the Chinese lyrics of Tu Fu his ear is finer than that of anyone I have ever encountered. It has been conclusively proved to my ear, at least, that if he does not give himself to our contemporary building of the line he doesn't want to soil himself as all others are doing.

Toward the end of this book of eighty-odd pages, after that fine poem "A Living Pearl," with its unfamiliar turns of phrase, there are some shorter pieces or longer ones broken into shorter subsections (like the one to Dylan Thomas) which are arresting by the directness of their speech: by the way, when I attempt to measure the stresses in one of his typical lines, which are short, I find that there are for the most part three. The pace is uniformly iambic, using a variable foot according to the American idiom.

The poems themselves are the importance. Their moral tone is stressed, except in the translation from the Japanese at the end. The book's seriousness, sting, and satiric punch dominate these pages. A miscellany of bitter stabs masquerading as, and meant to be, nursery rhymes, Mother Goose, a-b-c's and other accounts, scathing denunciations of our society which would have done credit to a Daumier or a Goya: "A Bestiary, For My Daughters Mary and Katharine"; "Murder Poem No. 74321"; "Portrait of the Author as a Young Anarchist"—a grieving memorial to Vanzetti and others; and another, "Thou Shalt Not Kill," a memorial to Dylan Thomas.

The latter half of the book is a diatribe of the most comprehensive virulence. It should be posted in the clubrooms of all universities so that it could never be forgotten. For the poem is the focal point for all activity among the intellectuals of the world from New York, Paris and Helsinki. Rexroth puts down many of their names here—a lunatic fringe it may be:

> They are murdering all the young men.
> For half a century now, every day. . . .

Stephen, Lawrence ("on his gridiron"), Robinson, Masters ("who crouched in/His law office for ruinous decades"), Lola Ridge, Jim Oppenheim, Orrick Johns, Elinor Wylie, Sara Teasdale, George Sterling, Phelps Putnam, Jack Wheelright, Donald Evans, John Gould Fletcher, Edna Millay, Bodenheim ("butchered in stinking/Squalor"), Sol Funaroff, Isidor Schneider, Claude McKay, Countee Cullen, Ezra ("that noisy man"), Carnevali, etc. etc.

He may sometimes be mistaken in his choice of those to remember but that is a mere choice among individuals: his sympathies are amply justified.

> He is dead. . . .
> The bird of Rhiannon.
> He is dead. . . .
>
> You killed him, General,
> Through the proper channels.
> You strangled him, Le Mouton,
> With your *mains étendus*. . . .
>
> The Gulf Stream smells of blood
> As it breaks on the sands of Iona
> And the blue rocks of Canarvon.
> And all the birds of the deep sea rise up
> Over the luxury liners and scream,
> "You killed him! You killed him.

> In your God damned Brooks Brothers suit,
> You son of a bitch."

There is another memorable passage showing the sardonic temper with which the poems have been salted down. This occurs toward the end of the "Mother Goose" (for his daughters), and note that he treats his children with the same respect as though they had been adults at whose throats their murderous weapons are addressed. Addressing his countrymen in general he tells them:

> Hide the white stone
> In the left fist.
> Hide the white stone
> In the right fist.
> I am your secret brother.
> Where is the white stone?
> You've swallowed it.

It may not be welcome in a review of this kind to stress an author's pointed reference to an unlovely fact. But in this case when in the text reference has been made to Martial's satires whose whole mood of violent attack on the corruption of his own age has been invoked by Rexroth in his own revolt and revulsion, nothing could be more appropriate to this than the following anecdote:

> There were two classes of kids, and they
> Had nothing in common: the rich kids
> Who worked as caddies, and the poor kids
> Who snitched golf balls. I belonged to the
> Saving group of exceptionalists
> Who, after dark, and on rainy days,
> Stole out and shit in the golf holes.

Kenneth Rexroth has been an avid reader in universal literature. He is familiar with a variety of foreign languages, ancient and modern. He is familiar with the capitals of

Europe, has read extensively of philosophy and the history of the social sciences. I think, as men go, there is no better read person in America. You should see his library! all his books, and most of his collected magazine articles, filed in orderly fashion for twenty or thirty years back for ready reference.

He is an authority on his subject of modern poetry. As a lecturer he is respected (and feared) throughout the academic world.

The present book, *In Defense of the Earth*, has been dedicated "To Marthe, Mary, Katharine"; his wife and daughters whom he speaks of extensively in the first part.

Kenneth Rexroth has recently translated *One Hundred Poems from the Chinese*, one of the most brilliantly sensitive books of poems in the American idiom it has ever been my good fortune to read.

It must be amazing to the occidental reader, acquainted we'll say with Palgrave's *Golden Treasury*, to realize that the Chinese have a practice and art of the poem, which in subtlety of lyrical candor, far exceeds his own. I am grateful to him. Nothing comparable and as relaxed is to be found I think in the whole of English or American verse, and in French or Spanish verse, so far as I know. So that it constitutes a unique experience to read what has been set down here.

Womanhood has been engraved on our minds in unforgettable terms. Oh, I know that women can be bitches, you don't have to be a homosexual to learn that, but the exact and telling and penetrant realization of a woman's reality, of her lot, has never been better set down. It is tremendously moving, as none of our well-known attempts, say, throughout the Renaissance have ever succeeded in being.

This is a feat of overwhelming importance. It is not a question of a man or woman's excess in experience or suffering, for whatever this amounted to, they have had to do; but that in their mutual love they have been made to bear their fates. What does it matter what a woman and a man in love will do for themselves? Someone will succeed and someone will die. In the poem suddenly we realize that we know that and perceive in a single burst of vision, in a flash that dazzles the reader.

The poet Tu Fu (713–770) was the first, with him it begins. Homer and Sappho with their influence on our poetry had been dead for over a thousand years. The use of the metaphor, pivotal in our own day, had not been discovered by the Chinese in these ancient masterpieces. The metaphor comes as a flash, nascent in the line, which flares when the image is suddenly shifted and we are jolted awake just as when the flint strikes the steel. The same that the Chinese poet seeks more simply when the beauty of his images bursts at one stroke directly upon us.

Dawn over the Mountains

The city is silent;
Sound drains away;
Buildings vanish in the light of dawn;
Cold sunlight comes on the highest peak;
The thick dust of night
Clings to the hills;
The earth opens;
The river boats are vague;
The still sky—
The sound of falling leaves.
A huge doe comes to the garden gate,
Lost from the herd,
Seeking its fellows.

Tu Fu

Where is the poem? without metaphor among these pages so effortlessly put down. Occidental art seems more than a little strained compared to this simplicity. You cannot say there is no art since we are overwhelmed by it. The person of the poet, the poetess, no, the woman herself (when it is a woman), speaks to us . . . in an unknown language, to our very ears, so that we actually weep with her and what she says (while we are not aware of her secret) is that she breathes . . . that she is alive as we are.

Where is it hidden in the words? Our own clumsy poems, the best of them, following the rules of grammar . . . trip themselves up. What is a sonnet of Shakespeare beside this limpidity but a gauche, a devised pretext? and it takes four-teen lines rigidly to come to its conclusion. But with be-wildering simplicity we see the night end, the dawn come in and a wild thing approach a garden. . . . But the com-pression without being crowded, the opposite of being squeezed into a narrow space, a few lines, a universe, from the milky way . . . vividly appears before us.

But where has it been hidden? because it is somewhere among the words to our despair, if we are poets, or pretend to be, it is really a simple miracle, like that of the loaves and the fishes. . . .

Where does the miracle lodge, to have survived so un-affectedly the years, translation to a foreign language and not only a foreign language but a language of fundamentally different aspect from that in which the words were first written? The metaphor is total, it is overall, a total metaphor.

But there are two parts to every metaphor that we have known heretofore: the object and its reference—one of them is missing in these Chinese poems that have survived to us and survived through the years, to themselves also. They have been jealously, lovingly guarded. . . . Where does it exist in the fabric of the poem? so tough that it can outlast copper and steel . . . a poem?

—and really laughs and cries! it is alive.
—It is as frightening as it is good.

And the Chinese as a race have built upon it to survive, the words of Tu Fu, a drunken poet, what I mean is DRUNK!

and a bum, who did not do perhaps one constructive thing
with himself in his life—or a Bodenheim.

I go to a reception and find a room crowded with people
whom I cannot talk with except one, a man (or a woman
perhaps) or one who wearies me with his insistencies. . . .
When a few miraculous lines that keep coming into my
head transport me through space a thousand years into the
past. . . .

"A magic carpet" the ancients called it. It costs nothing,
it's not the least EXPENSIVE!

Look at the object: an unhappy woman, no longer young,
waking in her lonely bed and looking over a moonlit valley,
that is all. Or a man drunk or playing with his grandchildren
who detain him so that he cannot keep an appointment to
visit a friend. . . . And what? A few fragile lines which
have proved indestructible!

Have you ever thought that a cannon blast or that of an
atomic bomb is absolutely powerless beside this?—unless
you extinguish man (and woman), the whole human race.
A smile would supersede it, totally.

> I raise the curtains and go out
> To watch the moon. Leaning on the
> Balcony, I breathe the evening
> Wind from the west, heavy with the
> Odors of decaying Autumn.
> The rose jade of the river
> Blends with the green jade of the void.
> Hidden in the grass a cricket chirps.
> Hidden in the sky storks cry out.
> I turn over and over in
> My heart the memories of
> Other days. Tonight as always
> There is no one to share my thoughts.
>
> *Chu Shu Chen*

or this:

Visitors

I have had asthma for a
Long time. It seems to improve
Here in this house by the river.
It is quiet too. No crowds
Bother me. I am brighter here
And more rested. I am happy here.
When someone calls at my thatched hut
My son brings me my straw hat
And I go out to gather
A handful of fresh vegetables.
It isn't much to offer.
But it is given in friendship.

Tu Fu

These men (a woman among the best of them) were look-ing at direct objects when they were writing, the transition from their pens or brushes is direct to the page. It was a beautiful object (not always a beautiful object, sometimes a horrible one) that they produced. It is incredible that it survived. It must have been treasured as a rare phenomenon by the people to be cared for and reproduced at great pains.

But the original inscriptions, so vividly recording the colors and moods of the scene . . . were invariably put down graphically in the characters (not words), the visual symbols that night and day appeared to the poet. The Chi-nese calligraphy must have contributed vastly to this.

Our own "Imagists" were right to brush aside purely grammatical conformations. What has grammar to do with poetry save to trip up its feet in that mud? It is important to a translator but that is all. But it is important to a trans-lator, as Kenneth Rexroth well knows. But mostly he has to know the construction of his own idiom into which he is rendering his text, when to ignore its more formal configura-tions.

This is where the translations that Kenneth Rexroth has

made are brilliant. His knowledge of the American idiom
has given him complete freedom to make a euphonious ren-
dering of a text which has defied more cultured ears to this
date. It may seem to be undisciplined but it is never out of
the translator's measured control. Mr. Rexroth is a genius in
his own right, inventing a modern language, or following a
vocal tradition which he raises here to great distinction.
Without a new language into which the poems could be
rendered their meaning would have been lost.

Finally, when he comes to the end of introduction, he
says, "So, here are two selections of poetry, one the work of
a couple of years, the other the personal distillate of a life-
time. I hope they meet the somewhat different ends I have
in view. I make no claim for the book as a piece of Oriental
scholarship. Just some poems."

At the very end there are data, notes, ten pages of them,
annotated page for page, on the individual poems. And two
and a half pages of Select Bibliography. The translations into
English began in 1870 with *The Chinese Classics*, James
Legge. Included is a mention of Ezra Pound's *Cathay*, 1915.

In the French there is, dating from 1862, the *Poésies
Chinoises de l'Epoque Thang*, and, among others, that of
Judith Gautier's, 1908, *Livre de Jade*. The German versions
are still those of Klabund.

Introduction to Allen Ginsberg's Empty Mirror

The Black Mountain Review, 1957

THE LINES are superbly all alike. Most people, most critics would call them prose—they have an infinite variety, perfectly regular; they are all alike and yet none is like the other. It is like the monotony of our lives that is made up of the front pages of newspapers and the first (aging) three lines of the *Inferno:*

> In the middle of the journey of our life I (came to)
> myself in a dark wood (where) the
> straight way was lost.

It is all alike, those fated lines telling of the mind of that poet and the front page of the newspaper. Look at them. You will find them the same.

This young Jewish boy, already not so young any more, has recognized something that has escaped most of the modern age, he has found that man is lost in the world of his own head. And that the rhythms of the past have become like an old field long left unplowed and fallen into disuse. In fact they are excavating there for a new industrial plant.

There the new inferno will soon be under construction.

A new sort of line, omitting memories of trees and water-

First published in *The Black Mountain Review*, 7 (Autumn 1957): 238–40 and then reprinted on pp. 5–6 of *Empty Mirror* (New York: Totem Press, 1961), this introduction was written in 1952 when Ginsberg had completed *Empty Mirror;* see my Introduction for an account of Williams' involvement with the evolution of Ginsberg's book.

courses and clouds and pleasant glades—as empty of them
as Dante Alighieri's *Inferno* is empty of them—exists today.
It is measured by the passage of time without accent, mo-
notonous, useless—unless you are drawn as Dante was to
see the truth, undressed, and to sway to a beat that is far
removed from the beat of dancing feet but rather finds in
the shuffling of human beings in all the stages of their day,
the trip to the bathroom, to the stairs of the subway, the
steps of the office or factory routine the mystical measure
of their passions.

It is indeed a human pilgrimage, like Geoffrey Chaucer's;
poets had better be aware of it and speak of it—and speak
of it in plain terms, such as men will recognize. In the mysti-
cal beat of newspapers that no one recognizes, their life is
given back to them in plain terms. Not one recognizes
Dante there fully deployed. It is not recondite but plain.

And when the poet in his writing would scream of the
crowd, like Jeremiah, that their life is beset, what can he
do, in the end, but speak to them in their own language,
that of the daily press?

At the same time, out of his love for them—a poet as
Dante was a poet—he must use his art, as Dante used his
art, to please. He must measure, he must so disguise his lines,
that his style appear prosaic (so that it shall not offend) to
go in a cloud.

With this, if it be possible, the hidden sweetness of the
poem may alone survive and one day rouse the sleeping
world.

There cannot be any facile deception about it. The writ-
ing cannot be made to be "a kind of prose," not prose with
a dirty wash of a stale poem over it. It must not set out, as
poets are taught or have a tendency to do, to deceive, to
sneak over a poetic way of laying down phrases. It must be
prose but prose among whose words the terror of their
truth has been discovered.

Here the terror of the scene has been laid bare in subtle
measures, the pages are warm with it. The scene they invoke
is terrifying more so than Dante's pages, the poem is not
suspect, the craft is flawless.

Introduction to Eli Siegel's Hot Afternoons Have Been in Montana

1957

November 3, 1951

MY DEAR MARTHA BAIRD:

I cannot adequately thank you for first writing me and then sending me the copies of Eli Siegel's poems. I am thrilled: your communications could not have come at a better time. I can't tell you how important Siegel's work is in the light of my present understanding of the modern poem. He belongs in the very first rank of our living artists. That he has not been placed there by our critics (what good are they?) is the inevitable result of their colonialism, their failure to understand the significance, the compulsions, broadened base upon which prosody rests in the modern world and our opportunity and obligations when we concern ourselves with it.

We are not up to Siegel, even yet. The basic criteria have not been laid bare. It's a long hard road to travel with only

---

A 1951 letter from Williams to Siegel's wife, Martha Baird, appears on pp. xv–xviii of Eli Siegel's *Hot Afternoons Have Been in Montana* (New York: Definition Press, 1957). The letter had already been published in *Poetry Public*, 4, 4 (Oct.–Dec. 1956): 1–3; excerpts had still earlier appeared in a letter to the editor by Nat Herz, *Poetry*, 80, 5 (August 1952): 303–06. The letter has also been reprinted in Eli Siegel, *Williams' Poetry Talked About . . . 1952* (New York: Society for Aesthetic Realism, 1964) and in *The Williams–Siegel Documentary*, ed. Martha Baird and Ellen Reiss (New York: Definition Press, 1970).

starvation fare for us on the way. Almost everyone wants
to run back to the old practices. You can't blame him. He
wants assurance, security, the approval that comes to him
from established practices. He wants to be united with his
fellows. He wants the "beautiful," that is to say . . . the
past. It is a very simple and very powerful urge. It puts the
hardest burdens on the pioneer who while recognizing
the virtues and glories of the past sees its restricting and
malevolent fixations. Siegel knows this in his own person.
He must be tough and supremely gifted.

The thing that particularly interests me, after a lifetime
of pondering the matter, is the technical implication. To me
it's black and white: either a man has quit or gone forward.
And if he's gone forward he's headed straight into disrepute.
People aren't up to it. And of those who are for you almost
no one knows why. It's all right to speak of aesthetic realism
and you've done good work to get behind a man such as
Siegel. But it goes deeper than that—or until I understand
you better I have to assume it. But Siegel isn't for me an
aesthete or not primarily an aesthete; he's an intensely prac-
tical professional writer who has outstripped the world of
his time in several very important respects. Technical re-
spects.

I have to presume that he knows absolutely what he is
doing and why he is doing it. I think he does. That doesn't
explain, quite, how he happened to hit on the just qualities
of his style in the first place—a lot of talk and verification
would have to be spilled over that before we'd know each
other there. But he did hit a major chord and from the first,
with his major poem "Hot Afternoons" etc. Only today do I
realize how important that poem is in the history of our
development as a cultural entity—a place which is con-
tinually threatened and which we may never attain unless
we develop the position which HE has secured for us. I say
definitely that that single poem, out of a thousand others
written in the past quarter century, secures our place in the
cultural world.

I make such a statement only after a lifetime of thought and experience, I make it deliberately. How Siegel got himself, undamaged by the past, to that position is a puzzle to me. But all genius presents unsolvable puzzles as to their origin. In any case he did, unspoiled; got to an absolutely unspoiled point of practice which no one (not even himself perhaps) was able adequately to grasp. On that rock and only on that rock can we in our cultural pattern build. And being the darlings of our era, the ones who must break with the past (as Toynbee recognizes—though some of us saw it before him) we are obliged to follow what Siegel instinctively set down. We are compelled to pursue his lead. Everything we most are compelled to do is in that one poem.

The immediate effect is of surprise, as with everything truly new, technical surprise. There is nothing, not even an odor of Elizabethan English (on which *all* our training is founded. How he escaped THAT is beyond me.). As I read his pieces I am never prepared for what will come next, either the timing or the imagery. I simply do not know what he's going to say next or how he's going to say it.

This is powerful evidence of a new track. The mind that made that mark is a different mind from ours. It is following different incentives. The eyes back of it are new eyes. They are seeing something different from ours. The evidence is technical but it comes out at the non-technical level as either great pleasure to the beholder, a deeper taking of the breath, a feeling of cleanliness, which is the sign of the truly new. The other side of the picture is the extreme resentment that a fixed, sclerotic mind feels confronting this new. It shows itself by the violent opposition Siegel received from the "authorities" whom I shall not dignify by naming and after that by neglect, an inevitable neglect due not to resentment but by the sheer inability of the general mind to grasp what has taken place.

Even a person such as myself, who has been searching for a solid footing, feeling about in the mud of the times for it while the rain and the hail of opinion batters about my head—even I was not up to a full or any realization of what the *Narr*, the "fool," Siegel had done. But at last I am just beginning to know, to know firmly what the present-day mind is seeking. I finally have caught a glimmer of the basic place which we, today, must occupy. And I have realized our place, in this cultural field, which is inevitably to be ours, to fill or to fail. We're only hanging on by our teeth and fingernails now, or even, today, losing our grip. I think today we are (temporarily, I hope) slipping back.

For those who are working in the materials, the despised technicians, it's a heartbreaking as it is a difficult and often exasperating battle. That's why I say it's thrilling to have had you redirect my attention to Siegel.

What I can do to be of practical assistance to you in pushing Siegel's work, so monumentally neglected, I don't know. It is incredible that he has not been published. And it is just like a man like that, it seems always to come out that way (he is satisfied with the *inner* warmth and does not need external assurances) not to care, not to have pushed himself forward. Instinctively he knows what his significance is. He can afford to wait. But it is time now to bring him forward and I don't quite know what to do.

I can give a reading of his works and I'd be glad to do so at some favorable opportunity; I can't give much time for I am harassed by the importunities of my life as is everyone else. I have to write whenever I am able and when I turn away from that for even the most laudable purposes I feel as if I were losing my life's very blood, irreparably. There is so much to do and there is so little time.

You say Siegel is alive and working. Greet him for me and tell him of this letter. I congratulate you on the intelligent direction of your work and the heart behind it.

Sincerely yours,

WILLIAM CARLOS WILLIAMS

Tram Combs' Pilgrim's Terrace

1957

TRAM COMBS' poems, whether in this manuscript there amount to 365 of them or not, give me the impression of casual composition for over at least a year's time. They are all short, impressions seized at a moment's observation of a St. Thomas garden, where many of his scenes are laid, with a litter of kittens in a box, hibiscus flowers in bloom and moonlight, or else the sun is fiercely shining or the wind blows.

The poems are intensely observed, you cannot speak of snapshots because it moves. It is amazing how the pictures are filled with life, even the hibiscus on its tall stems sways in the wind. Thank God there is not a trace of rhyme in any of these poems from the beginning to the end. The composition would not permit it. Instead each poem is closely organized with attention to the rhythmic structure so that when you read the book you get the feeling of a very subtle and very varied beat which actually soothes the reader's consciousness to the tune of those magic islands where the poet has made his home.

That is, I think, great art or such art in the making, for Tram Combs is not a finished artist and never pretends to be, but he has in himself the making of a superb artist. Some of the poems, to my ear, go completely blah but I think I know what does that—he grows serious about things that do not merit this seriousness. Worldly things. But when it

---

Foreword to Tram Combs, *Pilgrim's Terrace* (San Germán, Puerto Rico: Editorial La Nueva Salamanca, 1957), pp. 7–8.

comes to that seriousness of line and accent which most engages the artist he, at his best, never fails.

There is a sequence at the beginning of these poems, a whole series of poems about cats with fur of various colors and textures and manners and dispositions which is unsurpassable. An understanding of the moods of a small lizard shows brilliant observation bound to no more than the necessities of the case, the structural necessities of the case, under the artist's direct observation. That power to lose himself, without any moral deviation of any sort, is the mark of the true artist or poet. Combs has it with a feeling for everything that breathes and hides under a leaf to save himself which marks him as something alive and with a pulsing throat.

Overall pulses the metrical nature of the poem that signalizes what the secret nature of the poet wants to communicate to us, not directly, that is forbidden—it would be immodest, even a second-rate artisan knows what that means. Poets in this age have had to burrow deep to survive. It is in the construction of a verse, about an island sunset, that the reader will find what is hidden for him there; not what he thinks he will find but something surprising, amazingly simple and altogether delightful. Reading Tram Combs' poems I was completely taken out of myself, lost in that realm of art which soothed, delighted me.

Technically the meter which has a movement, the cause of this soothing effect, is constructed of a loose assemblage of colloquial diction for the most part which constitutes the American idiom. It is noteworthy how this idiom repels the rhythms of blank verse. The reading of Tram Combs' poems is one of the best correctives to the classroom exercises that our present-day students are subjected to, but it must be kept in mind or you will not be able to accomplish it that the intention of this verse is to be regular, incredible as it may seem. A variable foot is the future and the only way that a writer can accomplish this.

Leif Ericson's Violent Daughter

Winfield Townley Scott's The Dark Sister

The Nation, 1958

THIS BOOK is a figure from the Norse saga's *Long Island Book*, the source of all we know about the discovery of America by Leif Ericson in the year 1000. It is a poem, appropriately enough, detailing in dramatic form all we need to know of the exploits of the wild Freydis, Eric the Red's illegitimate daughter, on a voyage to Vinland from Greenland in the fall of the year following the discovery.

It follows the character, detail after detail, of the two boats containing the crews that Freydis had assembled, more or less against their wills, to accompany her—a feat even in those days for a woman, distinguished as she may have been and tough, the daughter of such a father. Disaster must have been a foregone conclusion but not in the way to be expected. It is a gruesome account.

And it is accurate as far as, after these many years, it can be made to be. Step by step we follow the voyage south along the coast of Greenland to Labrador and still further south to the present New England, the two boats holding close together not to be lost. Freydis keeps strict rule over both ships, though she has been at pains to keep in her own boat a fraudulent numerical ascendancy—as later she had a bloody use for.

Among the young Norwegians she chose a lover but dealt with him as she did with the others when the time came

---

Review of Winfield Townley Scott, *The Dark Sister* (New York: New York University Press, 1958); in *The Nation*, 186, 8 (Feb. 22, 1958): 171.

for a decision. Freydis' character, due in part at least to her father's blood which remained pagan to the end, governed all her actions. But it also gave her courage, big bellied as she was with her lover's child, to face the skrellings, the natives with their bows and arrows, and put them singlehanded to flight.

We should be proud of her as an ancestor, though she left us no progeny and though her memory is a bloody one. If she had not lost her baby and nearly died demented the latter half of the story would not have turned out as it did. Winfield Scott has been accurate to the mood of the story. We forget that we know so little of our past, what ancestors we come from. Individuals, tremendous individuals, governed the lives which descended from them. Women, especially, needed to herd together not to be outcasts. They had to be highborn as was Freydis to ignore the stigma of illegitimacy of birth with which for the length of their lives they had resentfully to bear. Helen's rape by Paris set off the Trojan War, but Freydis had no such mass escape. When she lost her child she, being the woman she was, struck right and left to register her hatred of the world.

Scott has used a long line and diction well-suited to the rough speech of his sailor characters who were under their mistress' domination throughout the voyage. He is easy to read. The book is attractively bound with an illustration of the two characters, the fairfaced and the dark sister, across the cover at the front.

Charles Tomlinson's Seeing Is Believing

Spectrum, 1958

THE ENGLISH will not or at least do not accept one of their best younger poets, Charles Tomlinson, because he writes with many characteristics of an American. Not superficial characteristics but the measured strokes dictated by a new world. That is not cricket to an Englishman, to imitate the Yankees. Have they not been carefully instructed during the past six generations that the course of literary training lies in the direction of France and the classics with the whole tradition Beowulf through Chaucer to T. S. Eliot to guide them? Now comes a disturbing note found among the accepted voices of Oxford and Cambridge to join the newer rebels and swell the unholy rout. The worst is that in this young poet Tomlinson, a breach in the technical order of the measure, the sacred construction of the poetic phrase, is sanctioned, and everyone knows that once that has occurred the whole dike against barbary, a finger through it, must collapse.

So the present-day brood of British critics appear to think. It is not an overt rebellion. Tomlinson is a very modest man. He is a mere poet going his own way convinced that something has been done to the poetic phrase that is valid. An Englishman, if he is the guardian of his country's scholarship through an enviable tradition, cannot avoid the

---

Review of Charles Tomlinson, *Seeing Is Believing* (New York: McDowell, Obolensky, 1958); in *Spectrum*, 2, 3 (Fall 1958): 189–91. The manuscript is Yale, Za/Williams/215.

issue but with the grim determination of the breed must follow where his betters have led him. If scholarship has led him astray he must re-examine his sources and finding an error correct it.

This, Tomlinson, working alone and quietly in his Gloucestershire stone cottage among the trees and country homes in a world tumbling about his ears out of the day's news, has taken in hand as a poet to interpret to his country-men as he is able. They will, as I say, have nothing of it. But his poems are artificially built. They have much of the natural charm of the Georgians, a pastoral surface. English-men will be certain to like them once they get over their first suspicions and take them gladly to their hearts. Speed the day.

For there is in such a well made and beautiful poem as Tomlinson's "The Atlantic" such a measure as this:

> Launched into an opposing wind, hangs
>   Grappled beneath the onrush,
> And there, lifts, curling in spume,
>   Unlocks, drops from that hold
> Over and shoreward. . . .

—this, containing from the first, for it is the first poem in his new book *Seeing is Believing*, the essential difference between this poet's work and that of all other English poets writing. He has escaped finally from the staid proces-sion of the iambic pentameter—while cleaving to the rules of English composition as taught in the schools about him; has divided his line according to a new measure learned, perhaps, from the new world. It gives a refreshing rustle or seething to the words which bespeak the entrance of a new life.

This is an entrancing book by the sheer sound of it when read aloud. Many modern Americans I know could learn much from its pages in the conduct of their measure which is often without invention of any sort. You can't be a good poet by whipping up a froth over a lady's behavior in bed or out of it—or a man's either. We forget that *this* is the concern of writing, writing—and you can't get it but by originality in the measures, the lines and how they disport themselves.

"Variant on a Scrap of Conversation" has the woody feeling I think a writer must maintain, before he goes into his damned metaphysics. "Northern Spring" is a beauty, no bad habits to be learned there by the student. But "Meditation on John Constable" gives a depth of feeling toward the English which poor Lawrence might have envied without going to his hysterical excesses. You don't have to go to the depressed areas to learn how to WRITE. "On the Hall at Stowey" is a fine poem which should be proclaimed throughout England if it had any chance to be heard above words stemming from St. Louis, U.S.A., an exhausted measure, an influence now fortunately on the wane from the English past which it persists in imitating. This is serious. For the measure of the present and the future is involved: are we monkeys or men?

Contribution to a Symposium on the Beats

Wagner, 1959

KEROUAC STATES that "the Beat Generation is basically a religious movement, essentially a moral movement." As such it has no real connection with the art of poetry—except to deny all the rules of poetic construction—Kerouac himself writes in prose, that is significant. But you will see as in many of the Beat Generation poets a tendency to return to conventional verse forms even to rhyme.

It is a defiance of moral order completely justifiable under present circumstances which dominate the world. It cannot have too much influence on the art of verse construction but while it lasts, and only while it lasts, as a transition stage, it is wholly justifiable—and not to be put aside. It has made a place for itself in our world that is not to be forgotten and so has a sort of importance. We're almost through with it.

The construction of the poem, the prosaic construction of its lines outlasts all moralistic considerations being geared to a modern world of positive values largely yet to be uncovered by the poet writing today. Their practice is some-

---

Comment in *Wagner* [formerly *Nimbus*], Staten Island, N.Y. (Spring 1959): 24–25. Contributors to the Symposium (in order printed): Marianne Moore, Sir Herbert Read, Philip Rahv, Paul Tillich, Marius Bewley, Lord David Cecil, Daisy Aldan, Lionel Trilling, George Barker, Robert Lowell, William Carlos Williams, S. Foster Damon, William Troy, Norman Mailer, Dorothy Van Ghent, E. E. Cummings, and Edmund Wilson. A "Reply" from Gregory Corso, Allen Ginsberg, and Peter Orlofsky follows the "Comments."

times better than any "beatnik" implications and so will have to be tolerated.

But don't be tripped up by what the poem looks like on the page, for instance, Ginsberg's long lines. They mean nothing.

The best piece submitted by the students was George Semsel's "In the Mad Dog Time," beautifully, tolerantly done. It should be preserved in the annals of the art and widely read.

Of the poems separately considered, that by Peter Orlovsky pleases me best. The construction ignored (and that means the English construction of the lines which is excellent) we have a lyrical outburst which is tellingly organized—the "beatniks" have much to learn from him.

Foreword to Ron Loewinsohn's Watermelons

1959

April 8, 1958

DEAR RON LOEWINSOHN:

Now I come to a great pleasure, the acknowledgment of some excellent poems, *saluti!* Nothing of that nature which is postponed is ever lost except due to a neglect on the part of an interested party and I do not want that.

My wife read the poems aloud to me last night. Part of one of them completely won us, "The Stillness of the Poem." The way you slowed down the third line and made it go over to the following line at the end did all that had to be done to me to convince me of your poetic gift. After that nothing will ever convince me that you can fail as a poet.

You have a difficult road to follow, but what poet has any different? And you alone know your fate unless you are turned from your course by events of the day which may discourage you. Technical problems that beset the modern poet, the division of the poem into lines is your own concern. So far you have shown great knowledge or sensitivity let us say for the line.

Your choice of words and images, is sensitive, accurate, fresh, you convince that you are actively searching for a particular effect and putting down only that which you

Letter published as Foreword to Ron Loewinsohn, *Watermelons* (New York: Totem Press, 1959), p. [2].

have accepted, lie as it may upon the page. It's a fastidiousness which only the accomplished artist accomplishes and only at rare intervals. It is that that we in the end recognize. Civilizations which lack that, are damned, they cannot survive even when we have to take to the caves like animals to outlive them.

All your poems are not of the same character but in general their character is high. "La Mer" is ambitious. It is worthy of all your study. Finish it, you will learn a lot in your art by persisting and using your wits to circumvent yourself in keeping a freshness in the attack. "The Sea-Gull" is tops. The modesty and intelligence with which you refrain from touching draws you to the reader who feels that he wants to trust you. "The Occasional Room" is very well done, trust your own instincts. There is lots more that might be said.

Affectionately yours,

WILLIAM CARLOS WILLIAMS

Zukofsky

1959

ONE LACK with Imagism, as a definition of effort, is that it is not definite enough. It is true enough, God knows, to the immediate object it represents but what is that related to the poet's personal and emotional and intellectual meanings? No hint is given or only a vague one at the best. Imagism was the takeoff for Zukofsky's poems, I think; at the beginning he was moved by a number of fairly well-known Imagistic poets and he was physically part of them but to my mind the amalgam was never successful. There was always a part of this poet which would not blend, something kept him off. I for one was baffled by him. I often did not know what he was driving at.

A disturbing element was his relation to music. It wasn't simple. The contrapuntal music of Bach in particular I knew engaged his attention. It was never a simple song as it was, for instance, in my case. Specifically I am referring to his first long poem "The" and what ultimately came out of it the culmination of all his efforts, the present poem ("*A*"). It was sometimes related to another lengthy poem, *The Cantos* of Ezra Pound, but even there the differences are striking, confusing to the reader for the two are far from being the same thing.

It irritated me so that I could not read the works of this poet with anything like complete satisfaction. He was a different bird from me but I was definitely attracted. Some-

---

"A final note" in Zukofsky, "*A*" *1–12* (Kyoto, Japan: Origin Press, 1959), pp. 291–96; reprinted in *Agenda*, London, 3, 6 (Dec. 1964): 1–4. An early draft of six typed pages is at Yale, Za/Williams/140.

thing else had been proposed to my mind. I didn't realize the cause of my irritation, how could I? It was an entirely different kind of person who was being presented. The concentration and the breaks in the language didn't add anything to my ease in the interpretation of the meaning. I didn't realize how close my attention to detail had to be to follow the really very simple language. The care, the meticulous care with which the words were put down, chosen after they had been selectively handled, the English of them stressed with a view to their timbre and effectiveness in the particular passage in which they are used and, furthermore, in a modern speech which has the interest of the American reader at heart: to be as brief as possible, keeping respect for his times to the forefront of the intelligence, to be never long-winded, witty where wit is called for but brief when the sense permits it.

Add to that the music of the phrase, as with a Campion, to be chosen and protected. It is amazing how clean and effective Zukofsky has kept his composition. I was about to use the word "sentence" but I thought better of it, for though Z. like many modern poets truncates the sentence for the sake of speed I don't think he does this to the point of unintelligibility. He uses words in more or less sentence formation if not strictly in formal sentence patterns, in a wider relationship to the composition as musical entity.

It is really a very simple language. After all a poem is a matter of words, the meaning of words. The *meaning*. I was seeking, perhaps, a picture (as an Imagist poet) to relate my poem to: the intellectual meaning of the word, the pure meaning, was lost, we'll say, on me. Zukofsky when he thought of a rose didn't think of the physical limits of the flower but more of what the rose meant to the mind, to the men who conceived of a rose window in twelfth-century France—or at a more remote age, when our language was being formed.

Men were intent on words then—and music; perhaps the monodic theme the words carried, related to the rose which the words spoke of. To speak of a rose shown in a picture by the impressionists would be an irrelevance.

It goes even further back in our memories. The Gregorian chant or its analogue in the world of music the Jewish chant approaches Zukofsky's meaning and the pleasure he means to give us in his poem. No wonder I was baffled. It wouldn't mesh, the sense wouldn't mesh with any interpretation I had ready. Possibly I should have taken the hint from Celia his wife's *Pericles*, an entire Shakespearean play she set to music, phrase by phrase, period by period, which has never been heard but at private performances. To some extent Louis and Celia must be taken as an identity when their lives are weighed. The musician and the poet should be taken as a critical unit in our effort to understand the poet Zukofsky's meaning.

It must not be lost sight of that Zukofsky's first long poem, "The," was written in 1926 two years fresh after he had been taught his profession of English at Columbia among the others whom he respected. That poem, in part conventional blank verse, had lines which were numbered along the left-hand margin like a text to be studied in class. That the young poet had a satiric objective aimed at the whole academic world is not to be denied. It was reprinted in at least one contemporary anthology, an able bit of satire which can still be read with lively interest. But the thing that still arouses my interest is that it is built according to the same model as the later poem, more or less as the poem "*A*." A whole life has intervened during the composition of these two poems.

In the course of the years, Z. has written many shorter poems, lyrics which have become known especially among writers—for the man has never been widely known. I myself have had my own difficulties with these pieces. Intent on the portrayal of the visual image in a poem my perception has been thrown frequently out of gear. I was looking for the wrong things. The poems, whatever else they are, are grammatical units intent on making a meaning *unrelated* to a mere pictorial image.

Furthermore, an obscure music, at least to me obscure,

related to the music of Johann Sebastian Bach, has dominated the poet's mind, beliefs and emotions.

Z. is a Jew who had a devout father not exclusively concerned with the formal minutiae of his religion, a father whom he loved while he found himself unwilling to follow into the details of his ancient religion according, we'll say, to Leviticus. Z. is also a poet, a poet devoted to working out by the intelligence the intricacies of his craft: he is embedded in a matrix of his art and the multiple addictions which govern him, make him, of this time.

I was about to use word "sentences," as I said, in a description of what this poet does with words but I thought better of it, for Z. uses not overt "sentences," he uses words like mordents in more or less sentence formation but not strictly in the formal patterns in wider relationship to the composition as a musical entity.

That can be confusing but once accepted releasing the essential nature of the sequence it releases much of the pleasure of the composition. Take the poem on the cover of the book, "Some Time":

> Little wrists,
> Is your content
> My sight or hold,
> Or your small air
> That lights and trysts?

That is not an Imagistic poem. The author is intent on something else. He represents an image, true enough, but that is not his chief concern, the content, the carefully selected meaning of the poet, what he is burning to say, makes the mere image secondary.

And what is the poet so intent on saying? Something to which his care has always been devoted, the spiritual unity of the world of ideas. The meaning, the *musical* meaning, of the phrase (as with Pound) is paramount—hence their early association as poets. The music of poets varies with the sensitivity of their ears.

Preface to The Roman Sonnets of G. G. Belli

Translated by Harold Norse

1960

GOGOL WANTED to do the job, and D. H. Lawrence, each into his own language but they were written not in the classic language Italian that scholars were familiar with, but the Roman dialect that gave them an intimate tang which was their major charm and which the illustrious names spoken of above could not equal. The idiom that they most affected was a language of the people to whom the sonnets were addressed and for whom they were written. Without a change of heart among scholars they would be rebuffed by such an attitude of mind as was Belli's. The nature of the shocking facts he had to disclose with such ironic candor in such a form as the sonnet, of all forms, so used to being employed for delicate nuances of sound and sense, forbade in their minds cruder employment.

But that is just the point which insists on being made. The times were crude, especially so for the underdog with whom these sonnets deal, but not so crude that they could not see themselves, in their imaginations, in high office. Belli saw it also and he knew how, politely, to bring them down—and up!—to their betters by a knowledge of the language.

It was a perfect situation for exploitation by an idiom which had no classic pretensions, in fact rebelled against all scholarship, yet held its head high. What could be better than an idiom of one of the greatest countries of the world, an idiom that as yet had no official standing, the American? This would be the language to use for the translation, a language comparable to the original Roman dialect.

Preface to Harold Norse, trans. *The Roman Sonnets of G. G. Belli* (Highlands, N.C.: Jonathan Williams, 1960), pp. [5–6].

And what was more appropriate to this purpose than an American conversant with this idiom by long acquaintance with it, from childhood, now living in Rome, an informed poet, a poet living very often a hand to mouth existence for his craft? He knows what Belli had the heart to feel for his fellow Romans of the period in which he lived.

The idiom into which Harold Norse has translated these sonnets was inaccessible to anyone before the present time. American scholars don't know anything as far as the resources of this idiom are concerned, for they have had only the "English" of their upbringing dinned into their ears until they have grown insensitive to everything else about them. It is not only the words which should be noted but the way in which they are spoken which characterizes this idiom. Harold Norse knows this medium, knows moreover its dignity and has a deep love for it, for it is his own.

Not to want to appear cryptic, it is necessary to push the point a little further: these translations are made not into English but into the American idiom in which they appear in the same relationship facing English as the original Roman dialect does to classic Italian. The idiom spoken in America is not taught in our schools, but is the property of men and women who, though they do not know it, use one of the greatest of modern languages, waiting only for a genius of its intrinsic poetry to appear.

The difference between it and the language taught to us in our schools is essentially a prosodic one which we have only as yet recognized by ear. The measure is what we refuse to recognize, the "metre" as Chaucer calls it in his poem in which he speaks of Boethius. It is in the measure of our speech, in its prosody, that our idiom is distinctive. That Harold Norse has as birthright which makes him at home with their translation.

He has succeeded with it in producing felicitous lines when anyone not so equipped must inevitably have failed. We have waited until the present day to have these fascinating and shocking and irreverent sonnets of Belli come to the eyes of the English-speaking world. Sometimes there appears to be a justice in literary history.

Introduction to Mimi Goldberg's The Lover and Other Poems

1961

THE LOVES of Mimi Goldberg! might have been a better title for this slim book of poems—it has taken a certain amount of affrontery to release even this much to a world which can't be said to be clamoring for the expression. Yet there are those who have urged this young woman to put her verses between covers.

Why?

There is a mode of poetic expression which is likely to be lost if it is not used at the present time of the resurgence of the academic, classroom teaching, in many of our most important schools in spite of the more or less popular Beat Generation. But something solid was achieved during the turn of the century and should not be let go quite yet, not at least until we have digested it in our minds enjoying it as best we may. These poems are a segment of this writing.

A conventional approach is not a part of them. There has been much loose talk of the American idiom which has reached this poet through the speech of her intimates. You cannot dismiss it without thought. The poet has devoted herself wholeheartedly, without any thought of any retreat. Here is the closed circle of a woman's domestic life, her children as they grow about her whom her mind enfolds reaching out to them as if it were herself another child in their midst. She shares what she knows with them, a living wonder to her.

Introduction to Mimi Goldberg, *The Lover and Other Poems* (Philadelphia: Kraft Printing Co., 1961), pp. iv–vi. Yale, Za/ Williams/141–42 contains two drafts.

Measure is what we must get to in the modern world which is a domestic affair for a woman; she needs to know distances between her pots and pans if she is going to feed her family aright and not stick her thumb through the pie crust. She has to be a practical woman and a good poet, you can't fool around with foolish ideas in that sort of medium. Leave that to men if they want to be *Till Eulenspiegel* leading ultimately to their own destruction, a woman has to think of her family.

Measure has to be a poet's chief concern especially in the present condition of the world. It is a poet's chief concern with life. If she find measures and not trite ones in this vast field it will occupy her mind, going back and forth if she has a mind, which this woman has, inventing her schemes.

Invention is what this poet succeeds in doing. This makes it difficult for the reader. It consists, for the most part, of variations of the timing of her lines. I insist that this is an important gesture in the stage we have got to in our verse making. It is not flip but related solidly if lightly to the composition of the whole.

The short poems are of approximately sonnet length. A single strophe of a few lines on common subjects not at all plebian, on an insect, flower, or domestic situation concerning the family close to earth or taking a flight into a concern sometimes with the celestial orbs, but not as our physicists have recently done but much more seriously, like a woman. She relates herself back to the heart. Poetic measure is her concern.

An example of what she does with her material is one of her most attractive poems, in which she loses herself completely; it is immediate to a domestic emergency—alarming enough—which she handles with considerable literary skill. It is the entrance of a bee into the private life of the apartment with a sense of alarm to all members who find themselves there this sunny morning. She and her two small sons have lost themselves in the pursuit of the insect. She gives herself completely in this fifth-floor apartment tearing about from one room to another in wild abandon until

this prehistoric gorgon has been captured and at once hu-
manely liberated in a burst of pity at the close of the poem,
its direful sting intact.

The poem is self-conscious but that at the moment is not
its concern. And more than that, for this sex-conscious
young woman cannot content herself with so simple a solu-
tion to her life problems, after Freud. The construction of
the poem itself has to offer her its solution, and if so, intelli-
gence has to be included in any rewording of the words of
the poem itself.

That is why our attractive poet, who is indeed attractive,
concerns herself with difficult problems. The splitting up of
sentences to their component parts concerns her deeply for
her very life's sake. In other words, it has to be taken with
all its idiosyncracies upon it. A woman has to give herself
without question when the mood is upon her. She cannot
question herself, what she is transcribing—and yet if she is
a poet she has to use her eyes not only to see her primary
image but also everything that concerns her, as a woman.

The modern scene is no different than what it has always
been for a woman unless she has been castrated and this one
has so far escaped that.

Robert Lowell's Verse Translation into the American Idiom

The Harvard Advocate, 1962

THAT THEY are not classroom English I take for granted. That they are something more akin to the local American way of speaking, in other words to what we hear every day makes him our fellow, as it made our fellow of the same name crudely our fellow over a hundred years ago. But the present Lowell is not crude, quite the opposite.

A translation into another language involves in the first place a choice of the language into which the translation is to be made. This language is used in this country by Robert Lowell with supreme ability and naturalness until it is acclaimed even in the classroom.

It must be heard to be appreciated. I have seen the enormous difficulties as witnessed by his work sheets in rendering the texts of some of the poems of Baudelaire in getting the precise accent of the words to stand up without a foreign un-American implication. This requires unceasing devotion to the text, and accurate work.

Here is a poet who knows what he is doing, devoted to the best in his language, with courage to go ahead with his own tasks, and a cultured addiction to his native way of speaking. You can't fool such a man because he will make up his own mind. When he hears a word spoken in a certain way he hears it so spoken and that is the end and you can put it into your lexicon as final.

May we have many more in America of the same caliber.

Review of Robert Lowell, *Imitations* (New York: Farrar, Straus and Cudahy, 1961); in *The Harvard Advocate*, 145 (Nov. 1962): 12. Manuscript is in the Yale collection, Za/Williams/211.

Introduction to Ronald Bayes' Dust and Desire

1962

YOUR STYLE in these poems shows that the American idiom as well as the variable foot is your constant concern. The present and the future of the language we speak depends on your generation—the vigor of your attack on the problems with the language is very important to me, it's up to you of the present generation to carry it forward.

You have been inoculated with the authentic virus. I like your poems. . . . I must be forgiven if I show a weakness for "Lydette" which is more lyrical than some of the others; that comes through to me perfectly. I want to test the ear of a poet if I am to accept him and in this poem you reveal a perfect ear. I am grateful. I am conscious of a perfect ear in whatever you write but THE AMERICAN must be strictly adhered to if it is to succeed. You do just that. . . .

I'm proud of you as an artist, your intelligence shows no sign of weakening under the strain the measure puts you under. As craftsmen it would be better if we lived closer together as they did in London or Florence during the sixteenth century for a nearby exchange of ideas but we'll have to do the best we can. . . . Right now with a new language to work on if we are up to it we have at least a chance. Let's see what we can make of it.

Introduction to Ronald Bayes, *Dust and Desire* (Ilfracombe, Devon: A. H. Stockwell, 1962), p. 6, where it is titled "Introduction to the Second Edition: A Note to the Author by William Carlos Williams," dated June 1960.

Index

"A" (Louis Zukofsky), 42–46, 46n, 264–67
"A Bestiary, For My Daughters Mary and Katharine" (Kenneth Rexroth), 238
"About Stones" (Sydney Salt), 83
Accent, 139, 139n
Ackroyd, Peter, 12
Activists, 189–90
After Strange Gods (T.S. Eliot), 12
Agenda, 264n
"A Journey Away" (Carl Rakosi), 44
Aldan, Daisy, 260n
"A Living Pearl" (Kenneth Rexroth), 237, 238
"A Love Poem About Spring" (Sol Funaroff), 95, 96
"American Etiquette" (H. H. Lewis), 73
American Writing: 1941, 111–14
Ammons, A.R., 6
Anew (Louis Zukofsky), 161–69
Angleton, James, 105
An "Objectivists" Anthology, 42–46, 42n
"A Poem for Norman Macleod" (William Carlos Williams), 191n
Aragon, Louis, 68, 78, 80
Aristotle, 178, 219
Arizona Quarterly, 234, 234n
"Asphodel, that Greeny Flower" (William Carlos Williams), 15
Auden, W.H., 13, 26, 69, 78, 112, 113, 115, 125, 126, 127
Autobiography (William Carlos Williams), 25, 215
"A Woman of Marigolds" (Charles Edward Eaton), 235
"A Worker" (Sol Funaroff), 95

Bach, 46, 264, 267
Baird, Martha, 249, 249n
Barker, George, 12, 260n
Barnard, Mary 37 (91)
Barnes, Djuna, 12
Baudelaire, 146, 191, 192, 273
Bayes, Ronald, 274
Beaudouin, Kenneth Lawrence, 193–97
Beat poets, 16, 30, 260–61, 270
Bell, Charles, 232–33
Bell, Marvin, 6
Belli, G. G., 268–69
Bellini, 88
Beowulf, 257

"Berenike" (Kenneth Rexroth), 184, 185
Beum, Robert Lawrence, 198–201
Bewley, Marius, 260n
Beyond the Mountains (Kenneth Rexroth), 183–85, 183n
Bishop, Elizabeth, 111n, 113, 177n, 178
Blackburn, Paul, 5
Blake, 224
Bloom, Harold, 10, 23
Bodenheim, Maxwell, 239, 244
Boone, Daniel, 70, 72
Bosch, 220
Botteghe Oscure (René Char), 221
Bradstreet, Ann, 197
Braque, 219
Breton, André, 146–49
Bridges, Robert, 53
Brown, Evelyn Marjorie, 50
Brown, Robert, 214
Brueghel, 219
Bunting, Basil, 11, 45, 170
Burns, 238
Butts, Mary, 45

Campion, 265
"Capri Parade" (Sydney Salt), 83
Carnevali, Emanuel, 239
Case-Record from a Sonnetorium (Merrill Moore), 181, 181n
Cathay (Ezra Pound), 246
Cecil, David, 260n
Chapman, 235
Char, René, 219–21
Chaucer, 130, 248, 257, 269
Christ, Christianity, 120, 121, 132, 195
"Christopher Columbus" (Sidney Salt), 83–84, 83n
Christopher Columbus and Other Poems (Sydney Salt), 83, 83n
Chu Shu Chen, 244
Ciardi, John, 177, 177n
Collected Early Poems (William Carlos Williams), 5
Collected Later Poems (William Carlos Williams), 23
Collected Poems (Basil Bunting), 170n
Collected Poems (Laura Riding), 97–100, 97n
Collected Poems (William Carlos Williams), 5
Combs, Tram, 253–54
Cooper, Peter, 106

Corbière, 123
Corman, Cid, 37 (91), 202-5, 202n
Corso, Gregory, 260n
Cosgriff, 214
"Counter-Serenade" (Peter Viereck), 174
Crabbe, 170, 170n
Crane, Hart, 8, 90, 153, 191
Creeley, Robert, 5, 6, 37 (91), 186
Cullen, Countee, 239
Cummings, E. E., 8, 96, 204, 260n

Damon, S. Foster, 260n
Dante, 59, 92, 119, 198, 247, 248
Daumier, 238
David, 147
"David and Bathsheba in the Public
    Garden" (Robert Lowell), 188
"Dawn over the Mountains" (Tu Fu), 242
Delta Return (Charles Bell), 232-33, 232n
Descartes, 147
Deutsch, Babette, 111n
Dickey, James, 5, 6, 27
Discrete Series (George Oppen), 55-59, 55n
Dixon, Myra, 50
Donne, 103, 110
Duncan, Robert, 5, 6
Durrell, Lawrence, 12
Dust and Desire (Ronald Bayes), 274, 274n

"Earth Bound" (Ellen Saltonstall), 50
East and West, 214, 214n
Eaton, Charles, 234-35
Eberhart, Richard, 37 (91), 177n
Eckman, Frederick, 5
Eddington, 135
Einstein, 142
El Greco, 88
Eliot, T. S., 8, 11, 12-14, 22, 26, 27, 28,
    29, 45, 57, 71, 106, 112, 126, 151, 198,
    238, 257
Elizabethans, 165, 168, 251
Eluard, 89
Emerson, Richard Wirtz, 198n
Empty Mirror (Allen Ginsberg), 16, 19,
    247-48, 247n
Ernst, 133
Essay on Rime (Karl Shapiro), 150-54,
    150n, 178
Evans, Donald, 239

Faber & Faber, 12
Fabre, Henri, 219
"Falling Asleep Over the Aeneid" (Robert
    Lowell), 188
Fantasy, 2, 115, 115n
"Fata Morgana" (André Breton), 149
Ferlinghetti, Lawrence, 5
55 Poems (Louis Zukofsky), 2, 129-31,
    129n
Fineran, John Kingston, 195
First Will and Testament (Kenneth Patchen),
    103-4, 103n
Fletcher, Frances, 45
Fletcher, John Gould, 239
"For All the Dead" (John Kingston
    Fineran), 195
Ford, Charles Henri, 87-88
formalist poets, 26

Four Pages, 170, 170n
Four Quartets (T.S. Eliot), 13
"Four Saints in Three Acts" (Gertrude
    Stein), 52
Fra Angelico, 220
"Freedom of Love" (André Breton), 149
free verse, 22, 24, 168, 204, 207
Freud, 162, 272
Frost, Robert, 8, 10, 11, 12, 28, 33
Fry, Christopher, 203
Funaroff, Sol, 94-96, 239
"Fundamental Disagreement with Two
    Contemporaries" (Kenneth Rexroth), 43
Furioso, 105, 105n

Gallagher, Elizabeth, 50-53
Gautier, Judith, 246
"Generation of Anger" (Norman Macleod),
    191n
Georgian poets, 258
Gerber, John W., 37 (77)
Gide, 123
Ginsberg, Allen, 6, 11, 12, 15-16, 17, 18,
    19-20, 21, 24, 25, 26, 30-31, 33, 37
    (91), 225-26, 247-48, 260n, 261
Gogol, 268
Goldberg, Mimi, 270-72
Golden Treasury, 241
Gongora, 189-90
Goya, 238
Gray, 68, 80
Greek, Greek poetry, 53, 135, 168, 183-
    84, 198, 207
Greeley, Horace, 66, 67
"Green Moray" (Winfield Scott), 180
Gregorian chant, 266
Gryphon, 175, 175n
Gunn, Thom, 12

Hall, Donald, 11, 12, 14
Hardy, Thomas, 12
Hart, Lawrence, 189
Harvard, 215
H. D., 8, 11
"Her Dead Brother" (Robert Lowell), 188
Here and Now (Denise Levertov), 24
"Hermaios" (Kenneth Rexroth), 183
Herrick, 221
"Herself" (John Holmes), 179
Hitler, 121
Hobbema, 144
Holmes, John, 177n, 179, 180
Homer, 76, 198, 242
Hopkins, Gerard Manley, 207
Horizons of Death (Norman Macleod), 60-
    62, 60n
"Hot Afternoons Have Been in Montana"
    (Eli Siegel), 249-52, 249n
"Howl" (Allen Ginsberg), 16, 30, 33
Howl and Other Poems (Allen Ginsberg),
    225n
Hughes, Ted, 12
Humphries, Rolfe, 111n
Hypnos Waking (René Char), 219-21, 219n

Ignatow, David, 5, 6, 9, 25, 26, 31-32, 37
    (91), 171-72
Imagists, 180, 245, 264, 265, 267

Imitations (Robert Lowell), 273, 273n
In Defense of the Earth (Kenneth Rexroth), 236–41, 236n
Inferno, 193, 193n
Inferno (Dante), 247, 248
"In Sisterly Fashion" (William Carlos Williams), 105n
"In the Mad Dog Time" (George Semsel), 261
"Iphegnia" (Kenneth Rexroth), 183
"It" (Sidney Salt), 84

James, Henry, 155–56
Jarrell, Randall, 109–10, 109n, 111n, 113, 177n, 179
Jeans, 135
Jeremiah, 248
Jews, Jewish religion, 226, 266, 267
Johns, Orrick, 239
Jones, Mary Helen, 50
Jonson, 189
Joyce, James, 8, 11, 12, 81, 134, 154
Juvenal, 135

Kerouac, Jack, 260
King Lear, 210
Kipling, 71
Kirkegaard, 135
Klabund, 246
Koch, Vivienne, 191n
Kolodney, William, 191n
Kreymborg, Alfred, 191n

Lafayette, 29
"L'Alouette" (René Char), 221
"La Mer" (Ron Loewinsohn), 263
"Last Words of My English Grandmother" (William Carlos Williams), 105n
"Late Lyrics" (Charles Henri Ford), 88
Latin poetry, 135
Laughlin, James, 16
Lawrence, D. H., 11, 12, 239, 259, 268
Layton, Irving, 222–24
Le Front Rouge (Louis Aragon), 78
Legge, James, 246
Levertov, Denise, 5, 6, 7, 17, 20, 24, 29–30, 32–33, 37 (91), 227n
Lewis, H. H., 68–82
Lewis, James Franklin, 195
Liberty, 105, 106
Library of Congress, 20
Life Studies (Robert Lowell), 11, 23, 24, 29, 33
Livre de Jade (Judith Gautier), 246
Loewinsohn, Ron, 262–63
Long Island Book, 255
Lope de Vega, 237
Lorca, 89, 190
Lord Weary's Castle (Robert Lowell), 20
"Lost Son" (Theodore Roethke), 18
Lowell, Robert, 6, 8, 10, 13, 15, 20–24, 26, 29, 31, 37 (91), 178n, 179, 187–88, 260n, 273
"Lydette" (Ronald Bayes), 274

Macleod, Norman, 60–62, 65–67, 191–92, 212–13
MacNeice, Louis, 12

Mailer, Norman, 260n
Mallarmé, 167
MAPS, 227, 227n
Marlowe, 237
Martial, 135, 240
Marx, Marxism, 70–72, 74, 95, 96, 105
Masters, Edgar Lee, 239
Matthews, Jackson, 219n
Maximus II (Charles Olson), 2, 227–31
"Maximus, at Tyre and at Boston" (Charles Olson), 231
"Maximus, to Gloucester" (Charles Olson), 230
Mayer, Stanley Dehler, 2
Mayo, E. L., 177n, 178
McAlmon, Robert, 45
McKay, Claude, 239
McQuail, James, 1, 63–64
Mead, William, 191n
"Meditation on John Constable" (Charles Tomlinson), 259
"Me, myself" (Walt Whitman), 92
Metaphysics (Allen Ginsberg), 18
Mid-Century American Poets, 177–80
Midfield Sediments (H. H. Lewis), 70n
Millay, Edna St. Vincent, 237, 239
Miller, Henry, 111n
Milton, 14, 80, 152, 221
Modernism, 8, 13, 15, 17, 26
Modern Language Association, 5
M, One Thousand Autobiographical Sonnets (Merrill Moore), 92n
Moore, Marianne, 8–9, 12, 16, 26, 260n
Moore, Merrill, 21, 92–93, 181–82
Morse, Samuel French, 25
Mosaic, 60, 60n
"Mother Goose" (Kenneth Rexroth), 238
"Mother Maria Theresa" (Robert Lowell), 188
Mozart, 137, 200
Muir, Edwin, 8
"Murder Poem No. 74321" (Kenneth Rexroth), 238

Nabokov, Vladimir, 111n
Nardi, Marcia, 16, 17, 123–24
Nash, Ogden, 204
Nathan, Raymond, 50
New Critics, 6, 20–21, 23, 26
New Directions, 123, 123n
New Masses, 75, 75n, 94, 94n
Nims, John Frederick, 177n
"No. 42" (Louis Zukofsky), 169
Norse, Harold, 268n, 269
"Northern Spring" (Charles Tomlinson), 259

O'Hara, Frank, 6
Olson, Charles, 2, 13, 25, 28, 37 (91), 227–33
One Hundred Poems from the Chinese (Kenneth Rexroth), 241–46, 236n
"On First Looking out through Juan de la Cosa's Eyes" (Charles Olson), 230
"On the Hall at Stowey" (Charles Tomlinson), 259
Oppen, George, 25, 45, 55–59

Oppenheim, Jim, 239
Origin, 186, 186n, 202, 202n
Orlovsky, Peter, 260n, 261
"Over Sir John's Hill" (Dylan Thomas), 210

"Pard and the Grandmother" (James McQuail), 1, 63–64
Patchen, Kenneth, 2, 3, 103–4, 109, 110, 115–22
Paterson (William Carlos Williams), 5, 9, 15, 18, 20, 24–25, 28, 199, 213
Pearson, Norman Holmes, 16
Pemble, W. J., 25
Penn State, 17
Pericles (Shakespeare), 183
Pericles (Celia Zukofsky), 266
"Phaedra" (Kenneth Rexorth), 183–84
Phelps, William Lyon, 51
Picasso, 147, 219
"Pictures in a Mirror" (Evelyn Marjorie Brown), 50
Pilgrim's Terrace (Tram Combs), 253–4, 253n
Plath, Sylvia, 14
Poe, 68, 80
"Poem beginning 'The' " (Louis Zukofsky), 130
"Poem on his Birthday" (Dylan Thomas), 210, 211
Poems (David Ignatow), 171, 171n
Poems (Marcia Nardi), 123n
Poésies Chinoises de l'Epoque Thang, 246
Poetry, 5, 55, 55n, 68, 68n, 75n, 129, 129n, 189, 189n, 236, 236n, 237, 249n
Poetry Public, 249n
Pope, 203
Portrait of the Artist as a Young Dog (Dylan Thomas), 209
"Portrait of the Author as a Young Anarchist" (Kenneth Rexroth), 238
Pound, Ezra, 8, 11–12, 15–16, 22, 25, 27, 28, 29, 33, 45, 55n, 89, 106, 108, 112, 128, 143, 153, 170n, 223, 228, 239, 246, 264, 267
Prince, F. T., 13
"Projective Verse" (Charles Olson), 25
Pure as Nowhere (Norman Macleod), 191–92, 212
Puritans, 8, 28, 197, 223
Putnam, Phelps, 239

Racine, 146, 183
Rahv, Philip, 111n, 260n
Rakosi, Carl, 44
Random House, 16, 215
Raphael, 88
Rayaprol, Srinivas, 214–16
Read, Herbert, 260n
Rebel Poets, 73
Red Renaissance (H. H. Lewis), 68n, 75, 75n
Reed College, 36 (70)
Reisman, Jerry, 45
Rexroth, Kenneth, 6, 43–44, 132–38, 183–85, 236–46
Reznikoff, Charles, 45
Ridge, Lola, 239

Riding, Laura, 97–100
Rilke, 153
Rimbaud, 153, 199, 238
Road to Utterly (H. H. Lewis), 68n, 75n, 76
Robinson, Edwin Arlington, 239
Roditi, Edouard, 146n
Roethke Theodore, 6, 7, 8, 10, 17–18, 20, 26, 37 (91), 177n, 178
Rosen, Stanley, 191n
Rosenberg, Harold, 125–28
Roskolenko, Harry, 101–2
Rubenstein, Richard, 175
Rukeyser, Muriel, 25, 89–91, 177n

Saintsbury, 298
Salt, Sydney, 83–86
Saltonstall, Ellen, 50
Salvation (H. H. Lewis), 68n, 76
Samson (Milton), 152
Sappho, 242
Schevill, James, 1, 217–18
Schneider, Isidor, 239
Schwartz, Delmore, 177n
Scott, Winfield Townley, 177n, 180, 255–56
Scrutiny, 12
Seeing Is Believing (Charles Tomlinson), 257–59, 257n
Selected Essays, William Carlos Williams, 87n, 150n, 187n, 202n
Selected Letters (William Carlos Williams), 105n
Selected Poems (William Carlos Williams), 109n
Seligman, 133
Semsel, George, 261
Sequence on Violence (Harry Roskolenko), 101–2, 101n
"Serenade" (Peter Viereck), 174
Sewanee Review, 20
Shakespeare, 68, 80, 93, 108, 144, 184, 221, 243
Shapiro, Karl, 150–54, 177n, 178, 179
"She Invokes the Autumn Instant" (Peter Viereck), 174
Siegel, Eli, 17, 249–52, 249n
"Snarled Nightbrush" (John Franklin Lewis), 195–96
Snyder, Gary, 6
Solomon, Carl, 225
"Some Time" (Louis Zukofsky), 267
"Song of Myself" (Allen Ginsberg), 27
"Songs For a Colored Singer" (Elizabeth Bishop), 178
Sonnets From New Directions (Merrill Moore), 21, 92, 92n
Sorrentino, Gilbert, 24, 37 (91)
Spectrum, 257, 257n
Spender, Stephen, 12–13, 69, 78
Steffens, Lincoln, 72
Stein, Gertrude, 8, 52, 128, 134, 173
Stephen, 239
Sterling, George, 239
Stevens, Wallace, 8, 10, 12, 25, 28
Strike Through the Mask (Peter Viereck), 173–74, 173n
"Sunflower" (André Breton), 149
Surrealism, 146, 147

Taggard, Genevieve, 105, 106
Tate, Allen, 21, 23–24
Taupin, René, 143
Teasdale, Sara, 239
"10" (Louis Zukofsky), 129
Tennyson, 234
Thanksgiving Before November (Norman Macleod), 65–67, 65n
"The" (Louis Zukofsky), 264, 266
"The Act" (William Carlos Williams), 206
"The Atlantic" (Charles Tomlinson), 258
"The Bellbuoy" (Sol Funaroff), 95
The Black Mountain Review, 247, 247n
"The Book of the Dead" (Muriel Rukeyser), 89
The Cantos (Ezra Pound), 12, 29, 89, 143, 264
The Chinese Classics (James Legge), 246
"The Complaint of the Morpethshire Farmer" (Basil Bunting), 170
The Criterion, 12
"The Cure" (William Carlos Williams), 105n
The Dance of Death (Merrill Moore), 92n
The Dark Sister (Winfield Townley Scott), 255–56, 255n
"The Desert Music" (William Carlos Williams), 15
The Dissolving Fabric (Paul Blackburn), 5
"The Fat Man in the Mirror" (Robert Lowell), 188
"The Fox Hunt" (Charles Edward Eaton), 235
The Garden of Disorder and Other Poems (Charles Henri Ford), 87–88, 87n
The Golden Goose, 190, 190n, 198, 198n, 212, 212n
The Granite Butterfly (Parker Tyler), 17, 139–45, 139n
The Greenhouse in the Garden (Charles Edward Eaton), 234–35, 234n
The Harvard Advocate, 47, 47n, 273, 273n
The Improved Binoculars (Irving Layton), 222n
The Journal of Albion Moonlight (Kenneth Patchen), 2, 115–22, 115n
The Kenyon Review, 20, 150, 150n
The Liberal Weekly, 123
The Literary Workshop, 1, 50, 50n
The Lover and Other Poems (Mimi Goldberg), 270–72, 270n
The Mills of the Kavannaughs (Robert Lowell), 21–23, 187–88, 187n
The Nation, 255, 255n
The New Quarterly of Poetry, 161, 161n
The New Republic, 89, 89n, 111n, 113, 219, 219n, 232, 232n
The New York Times, 7, 50n, 51
The New York Times Book Review, 171, 171n, 173, 173n, 183, 183n, 187, 187n, 217n
The New Yorker, 125n
The Noise that Time Makes (Merrill Moore), 92n
"The Occasional Room" (Ron Loewinsohn), 263
The Open House (Theodore Roethke), 18
"The Park" (Myra Dixon), 50

The Partisan Review, 109, 109n, 110
The Phoenix and the Tortoise (Kenneth Rexroth), 132–38, 132n
The Phoenix and the Turtle (Shakespeare), 134
"The Place, for Yvor Winters" (Kenneth Rexroth), 43–44
The Quarterly Review of Literature, 132, 132n, 143, 155n, 190
The Right to Greet (James Schevill), 1, 217–18
The Roman Sonnets of G. G. Belli, 268–69, 268n
"The Seagull" (Ron Loewinsohn), 263
"The Song and Dance of" (Charles Olson), 230
The Spider and the Clock (Sol Funaroff), 94–96, 94n
"The Stillness of the Poem" (Ron Loewinsohn), 262
The Symposium, 42, 42n
"The Twist" (Charles Olson), 230
"The Vertebral Sphinx" (André Breton), 149
"The Waste Land" (T. S. Eliot), 8
The Western Review, 217, 217n
The Williams-Siegel Documentary, 249n
The Yale Literary Magazine, 209, 209n
Thinking of Russia (H. H. Lewis), 68n, 75–76, 75n
"Thistle in the Desert" (Elizabeth Gallagher), 50–53
Thomas, Dylan, 203, 209–11, 238
"Thou Shalt Not Kill" (Kenneth Rexroth), 238
"Tilden Street" (Mary Helen Jones), 50
Tillich, Paul, 260n
Time, 165
"To a Friend Who Has Moved to the East Side" (David Ignatow), 171
Tomlinson, Charles, 25, 37 (91), 257–59
"To the Wind" (André Breton), 149
"To Walt Whitman" (Raymond Nathan), 50
Toynbee, Arnold, 251
Trance Above the Streets (Harold Rosenberg), 125n
Transfigured Night (Byron Vazakas), 155–60
Trial Balances, 63, 63n
Trilling, Lionel, 260n
Troy, William, 260n
Tu Fu, 238, 242–44, 245
"Two Horses" (Sydney Salt), 83
Tyler, Parker, 17, 139–45

US1 (Muriel Rukeyser), 89–91

Van Ghent, Dorothy, 260n
Van Gogh, 121
"Variant on a Scrap of Conversation" (Charles Tomlinson), 259
Vazakas, Byron, 153, 155–60
Venus and Adonis, 144
Vercingetorix, 219
Viereck, Peter, 173–74, 177n
View, 39, 39n, 146, 146n

"Village" (Crabbe), 170
Villon, 76
"Visitors" (Tu Fu), 245

Wagner, 137
Wagner, 260, 260n
Wallace, Emily, 37 (77), 97n
"War" (André Breton), 149
Warriston, R. B. N., 45
Washington, George, 29
Watermelons (Ron Loewinsohn), 262-63, 262n
Watkins, Vernon, 12
Waugh, Evelyn, 220
Wellsley, Dorothy, 25
Werfel, 188
Whalen, Philip, 36 (70)
Wheelright, Jack, 239
Whitman, Walt, 30, 33, 68, 80, 92, 152, 156, 159, 160, 200, 204
Whittemore, Reed, 105-8, 105n
Wilbur, Richard, 177n
Williams, Charles, 12

Williams, Elena, 215-16
Williams, Florence ("Floss"), 24, 213, 215
Williams' Poetry Talked About . . . 1952 (Eli Siegel), 249n
Williams, William Carlos (works), 5, 9, 15, 18, 20, 23, 24, 25, 27, 29, 45, 105n, 109n, 150n, 199, 202n, 206, 213, 215, 219n
Williams, William George, 216
Wilson, Edmund, 111-14, 111n, 260n
Winters, 152
Woolworth, 76, 171
Wylie, Elinor, 239

Yeats, William Butler, 11, 12, 25
Young Cherry Trees Secured Against Hares (André Breton), 146-49, 146n
"Young Lilting Bough" (Sydney Salt), 83

Zabel, Morton Dauwen, 111n
Zukofsky, Celia, 266
Zukofsky, Louis, 2-3, 6, 11, 15, 25, 37 (91), 42n, 44-45, 46, 129-31, 161-69, 264-67